ARE YOU BEING ROBBED?

ARE YOU BEING ROBBED?

8 ESSENTIAL KEYS

TO RECLAIM YOUR

GOD-GIVEN PURPOSE

ERIC B. EURĒN

Are You Being Robbed?

Trilogy Christian Publishers A Wholly Owned Subsidary of Trinity Broadcasting Network

2442 Michelle Drive Tustin, CA 92780

Trilogy Christian Publishing/TBN and colophon are trademarks of Trinity Broadcasting Network.

Cover design by: Eric B. Eurēn.

Editor: Kiana McKaughan

Visit the author's website to download the free Study Guide at www.areyoubeingrobbed.org

For information about special discounts for bulk purchases, please contact Trilogy Christian Publishing.

Trilogy Disclaimer: The views and content expressed in this book are those of the author and may not necessarily reflect the views and doctrine of Trilogy Christian Publishing or the Trinity Broadcasting Network.

While the author has made every effort to provide accurate telephone numbers and internet addresses at the time of publication, neither the publisher nor the author assumes any responsibility for errors or changes that occur after publication.

Manufactured in the United States of America

10 9 8 7 6 5 4 3 2 1

Library of Congress Cataloging-in-Publication Data is available.

ISBN: 978-1-68556-167-3

E-ISBN: 978-1-68556-168-0

Dedication

I would like to acknowledge the very special people who have made it possible for me to bring this book to fruition.

First, I want to thank my precious wife, Shanee Eurēn, for her constant love, dedication, support, and encouragement, without whom this book would not have been possible. To my mother, Diana, and father, Barry, for raising me in a loving, Christ-centered home, thank you with all my heart. To Amber, the best sister a brother could have. To the rest of my family, thank you for believing in the ministry work I do.

Thank you, Keith McKaughan, for always being there to give me advice and to sharpen my mind. A special thank you to my editor, Kiana McKaughan, for working so hard and making sense of my ramblings. To my spiritual brother and friend in ministry, Derrick Aguiar, for helping me become a better preacher. To Tom and Teryl Sundquist for always covering me in prayer and support. Dear Pastor Wally, thank you for your faithfulness in defense of persecuted Christians around the world and for giving me the opportunity to preach the good news of Jesus Christ. Ken Ventura, for your groundbreaking book *Man vs. Boy?*

I want to acknowledge and give special thanks to my many faithful friends who have supported, encouraged, and prayed for me and for this ministry. Finally, to my church community: here we stand, ready to share the good news of Jesus Christ. God bless you!

In remembrance of two amazing, God-fearing men that influenced my life and are now with the Lord Jesus Christ: my Grandfather, Rev. Bill Hollingsworth, and Dr. Rev. Ted Rose

Table of Contents

Preface

This book has been over ten years in the making, starting in 2007 when I began a three-year transition from architecture into full-time ministry. During this time of transition, I saw firsthand that the majority of people going to church were being robbed of the fullness that God had made available to them. Many had no basic understanding of the promises of God nor of the essential tools He gave His people to claim them. Knowing how to walk grounded in the bedrock of Jesus Christ and in His promises is a necessity for a Christian living in a fallen world. I established Everlasting Ministries in hopes of being able to see Christians equipped to walk in this fullness. I set out on a mission within the church to share the gospel and make disciples. My goal was to tackle head-on the serious epidemic of anemia within the body of Christ. It was during this time that I clearly heard the Lord calling me to write this book, and the name He gave me was, *Are You Being Robbed?* That title became the direction for its contents.

It took seven years of diligent study of Scripture and plenty of prayer and research to prepare for the eight chapters in this book. During this time, I kept the name of the book to myself; when talking to others about it, I used the code name "The Owner's Manual."

After numerous challenges with technology, including losing three years of work to a faulty hard drive and with personal setbacks arising from family trauma, there were many times when I was ready to give up. But whenever I was about to throw in the towel, God was there, encouraging me to continue on. He even used people who had never met me to encourage me. Total strangers would tell me that God wanted me to finish "The Owner's Manual." This was always significant to me because I had only shared that I was writing a book with that code name with three close friends and my mother.

On Christmas of 2016, my wife, who believed in this book, gave me an iPad. This doubled my efficiency, as the computers I had been working with were over ten years old and were bogged down with old programs. So after transferring all my notes and research over from my PC, I started writing. In February 2018, I partnered with my editor, Kiana McKaughan, with the goal of finishing the book in one year. Even with all our hard work, it took two additional years to complete. I am thankful to have this book finished and am looking forward to the blessing it can be to others.

Now, I don't have a corner on the theology market, and I am far from perfect. But in my desire to serve the one who *is* perfect, I have written this book to you from a place of sincere love, with a desire to see you walk in who God made you to be. God's perfect will is the best for our lives, and part of His will is for us not to be robbed. My intention as a pastor is to accurately represent the authority of Scripture with God's grace and guidance and with the Holy Spirit's help.

I am blessed to have many friends who are pastors, a few of which are also mentors to me. Some are from charismatic denominations, like the Assemblies of God and Four Square churches, and others are from more liturgical denominations, such as the Lutheran and Anglican churches. Having been raised in the Assemblies of God and Lutheran churches myself, I have an understanding and respect for just how broad the body of Christ is. Many of my charismatic friends have, at some point in our friendships, thought that I am too conservative concerning doctrine and the gifts of the Holy Spirit, while some of my friends from more traditional churches think that I am too charismatic. I assume these variations in opinion will carry over to whoever reads this book. If you find yourself in one of these categories, I encourage you to take any challenges to your views seriously and not to immediately discard the information. Look deeply into Scripture, take it before the Lord, and make space for the Holy Spirit to do a new work in your life wherever needed. God bless.

Introduction

Then said Jesus to those Jews which believed on him, If ye continue in my word, then are ye my disciples indeed; and ye shall know the truth, and the truth shall make you free.

John 8:31–32

Are you being robbed of the fullness of God's best for your life? There is a thief at work in the world, and being a Christian doesn't make us automatically invincible to his thievery. Living the life of a Christian isn't always easy, but there are many blessings and promises available to us as followers of Jesus Christ. It is our job to walk in those promises by meeting the biblical conditions that will prevent us from being robbed. Unfortunately, many Christians are vulnerable targets of theft when it comes to the fullness of God. Worse, many of these are also unwitting accomplices to the robber's crimes. They can be fooled into robbing others of the blessings and talents God has for them to pour out for the good of everyone.

Here are some questions that you can ask yourself to find out if you are living in the fullness of God's provision and blessings: Is your real identity in Jesus Christ? Do you know your calling? How well do you know God? What is God's perfect will for your life? Do you recognize and clearly hear God's voice? Do you have all the tools for discernment, and are you using them? Are you filled with the Holy Spirit? What is your testimony, and how does it relate to the blood of Jesus Christ's overcoming power?

If you are unsure about some or even all of these, you are not alone. Many Christians struggle to find answers to these basic, foundational questions. In this book, we will examine all eight questions and unveil the keys to living a secure, prosperous Christian life, full of eternal blessings and free from spiritual robbery.

The inherent desire of every human being is to live a full, prosperous, and blessed life. In the beginning, God created Adam and Eve in the garden. Everything for a life full of blessing was freely available there, requiring very little effort on man's part. But everything changed when sin came into the world. The fall of Adam and Eve in the garden unleashed cosmic repercussions because their actions were in direct opposition against God and His best for man. Our desire to possess those things that we were created for still remains deep in our DNA, but we struggle with the dichotomy of this pure desire opposing the fallen nature of our flesh and this world. The war with sin besieges mankind to the point of hopeless submission unless there is intervention from God through the Redeemer, Jesus Christ.

God warns us that the robber is a very real threat, as 1 Peter 5:8 explains: "Be sober, be vigilant; because your adversary the devil, as a roaring lion, walketh about, seeking whom he may devour." Is the robber controlling your life by keeping your thoughts on your afflictions? The call to be sober is a call to be clear-minded and consciously focused on God. The call to be vigilant requires an active awareness at all times. Instructions for overcoming the thief and walking in security from thievery while remaining sober and vigilant are found in the Word of God.

There is an old saying that "the truth hurts," and the truth of the Word of God is sharper than a two-edged sword (Hebrews 4:12). It can hurt, but it is for our benefit. This is why the robber is perpetually launching an all-out assault on truth. The world wants us to believe that there is no such thing as absolute truth and that any truth spoken from the Word of God that hurts or offends others should be banned. The agenda is to relegate truth down to feelings and opinions instead of facts. The thief is at the source of this doctrine; he is behind everything that is in direct opposition to God. The truth will set us free, but the robber wants to keep everyone bound. Do you believe in the absolute truth of the Word of God? If not, then you are in danger of becoming blind to the truth! This book will focus on the Way, the Truth, and the Life (John 14:6) as we explore the key conditional promises to living a full, prosperous, and purposeful life in a fallen world.

Who Is the Robber?

John 10:10 says that the robber is the one who comes "to steal, and to kill, and to destroy." The robber is our adversary, the devil, and his temporary title is "the prince of this world" (John 14:30). Second Corinthians 11:14 tells us that he pretends to be an angel of light, and at one time, he was the most beautiful thing created. He is the head of the realm of evil and is in direct opposition to God in every way. The robber's opposition to God also means that he is against our best interest. By default, the goal of every action he commits against us is death and destruction, and whatever he cannot kill, he will steal.

Scripture tells us that the robber is the source of affliction (2 Corinthians 12:7), that he steals the Word of God that is sown into the hearts of man (Mark 4:15), that he blinds the minds of the unbelieving (2 Corinthians 4:4), and that he hinders the work of missionaries, as he did to Paul (1 Thessalonians 2:18). Just as Jesus Christ sows good seed into the world, the thief, in his opposition toward God, is sowing evil seed:

He answered and said unto them, He that soweth the good seed is the Son of man; The field is the world; the good seed are the children of the kingdom; but the tares are the children of the wicked one; The enemy that sowed them is the devil; the harvest is the end of the world; and the reapers are the angels.

Matthew 13:37–39

17

How Can He Be Stopped?

The great news is that the robber is already defeated, and he is powerless against Christ because of Jesus' finished work on the cross. Colossians describes what He has done for us and against the robber:

> *And you, being dead in your sins and the uncircumcision of your flesh, hath he quickened together with him, having forgiven you all trespasses; Blotting out the handwriting of ordinances that was against us, which was contrary to us, and took it out of the way, nailing it to his cross; And having spoiled principalities and powers, he made a shew of them openly, triumphing over them in it.*
>
> **Colossians 2:13–15**

Satan cannot touch a child of God without permission, and this truth should give us comfort that we can always take refuge in God. But still, this victory doesn't stop the thief from seeking to rob us of the blessings of God's best in this life.

Just as the robber tempted Jesus in the wilderness, he tempts the followers of Christ in an effort to rob us of God's best and fullest life for us. In this effort to pickpocket us, he is always looking for a way to take advantage, but God instructs us on how we can protect ourselves from thievery—"Lest Satan should get an advantage of us: for we are not ignorant of his devices" (2 Corinthians 2:11). The key is not to be ignorant of those devices. Bitterness, compromise, unforgiveness, and pride are probably the most obvious open doors to thievery, but according to Paul, even ignorance is just as dangerous! God also warns us of ignorance in Hosea 4:6: "My people are destroyed for lack of knowledge." The ignorance or lack of knowledge God is referring to here is ignorance of the Word of God, revealed by the Holy Spirit. This is why living out the knowledge and understanding of the eight topics addressed in this book is critical for walking in God's best.

In worship, the psalmist declared,

Delight thyself also in the Lord; and he shall give thee the desires of thine heart. Commit thy way unto the Lord; trust also in him; and he shall bring it to pass.

Psalm 37:4–5

Will you delight in the Lord during this process of equipping? Will you commit to His way, no matter how challenging His Word might be? If so, you can receive the desires God places in your heart, and you will walk free from thievery.

The Time to Act Is Now

The world is changing at an alarming rate, and with each passing year, hostility toward Christians and godly principles increases. Without a major move of God bringing mankind to repentance, I believe things will continue to get worse. The need for basic training is now, and this book will help equip Christians for what is looming on the horizon.

Walking in the fullness of a prosperous life isn't about living in luxury and fame. Rather, it is about the necessity of living with purpose and walking in victory, despite the odds. It is about being a light in the darkness and drawing others toward Jesus Christ. As the darkness grows darker, God calls His people to shine His light into it. When we realize the true prosperity gospel, our desire for ending spiritual robbery will change our goal from getting all the physical things that we can in this world to passing through it as overcomers who are aiming toward another destination, not of this world.

Don't wait to walk in God's promises until it becomes a necessity for survival. Choose to take up the challenge now and be a light and a blessing in this fallen world. As you obey God, He will use you in ways you could never imagine, and by His grace you will be blessed and prosperous.

CHAPTER 1:

Our Identity in Christ

If ye then be risen with Christ, seek those things which are above, where Christ sitteth on the right hand of God. Set your affection on things above, not on things on the earth. For ye are dead, and your life is hid with Christ in God.

Colossians 3:1–3

In many places, it is the law to carry state-issued identification in public. This identification provides information about you that can be used to confirm who you are. It also grants you certain rights and privileges in society. Your spiritual identity is somewhat similar but with greater significance and eternal consequences.

I have asked many Christians over the years about their identity, and most of their responses are linked to the things of this world. What you do, who you listen to, the people you hang out with, and even how you dress are not your identity, and if you treat these things like they are, then you are being ripped off! Some Christians say our identity is simply that we are forgiven sinners, but while we are sinners saved by grace, that is not our identity. This misconception of our identity grieves me because it robs us of so many layers of identity. It oversimplifies the truth and leaves people in bondage to the perishable things of Earth, rather than accepting the eternal, fulfilling, victorious life that comes from knowing who Christ says we are in Him. This is why we must address the identity crisis at work in the lives of people today with the spirit of truth, in love.

Now, some identity issues can be controversial. It is not my intent to be callous and disregard people who are dealing with very real feelings and struggles, but the fact remains that there is truth in

God's Word, and there is power and healing in the name of Jesus. It is my prayer that every Christian will walk in the fullness of his or her identity in Christ and that every unsaved person who struggles with his or her identity will come into the total healing and peace that can only be found in Jesus Christ.

Understanding our identity in Christ is a powerful key to spiritual breakthrough that countless believers around the world need to understand. Jesus said clearly in John 8:31–32 that "if ye continue in my word, then are ye my disciples indeed; And ye shall know the truth, and the truth shall make you free." The opposite of truth is a lie, and the king of all lies will use deception to entrap us in unnecessary bondage. If Christians are not walking in the identity of Christ, they will not be able to boldly exercise their authority in Christ to the fullest. When we as Christians walk under a false identity, we are denying the work of Jesus Christ in our lives. The robber knows this. He can't undo the finished work of Christ on the cross or negate the promises that come with it, so he will work to keep it hidden. By the power of Christ's blood, we are a new creation in Him, and with this new birth through Him comes a new identity that is not of this world.

> *Therefore if any man be in Christ, he is a new creature: old things are passed away; behold, all things are become new.*
> **2 Corinthians 5:17**

So, the real question for Christians is: Did you give up your old identity in the world when you accepted Jesus as Lord and Savior, and are you walking in the fullness of your new identity? The robber can't steal away the promises of your new identity, but he can rob you from walking in that identity through doubt, deception, and ignorance. For the non-Christians, the question is: Do you know that your identity is readily available if you believe in your heart and confess with your mouth that Jesus Christ is Lord and Savior? This new identity is the only one that will bring healing to your soul because wholeness is a defining factor of our identity in Christ.

The robber will bombard believers and nonbelievers alike with identity options from this world in hopes that they will never walk in the powerful and glorious privileges available through Jesus Christ. In this chapter, we will look at some of the most common questions concerning identity I have received in my years of ministry, as well as the keys to walking in the richness of our true identity. First, we will examine the path to finding our true identity in Christ and the powers at work in the world that seek to keep it hidden. Second, we will examine the mysteries of who we truly are and the truths from Scripture for equipping us with what it takes to walk in our true identity. Third, we will examine the eternal consequences that come from the identity we choose. Finally, we will review the tools given to us for maintaining our true identity.

The Path to Identity

Identity theft has become a common crime in our world of electronic commerce. Anyone who has ever fallen prey to this crime can attest to the frustrations and inconvenience that come with having to clear your name and reestablish your credit, banking, and personal information. So this leads me to a question: If criminals seek to steal another person's identity because of its monetary value, how much more is your identity worth when it has eternal value in Christ? To what great measures would the robber go to steal it? There is nothing the robber will hesitate to do in his attempts to pickpocket your real identity and replace it with a false one. He has set up a worldly system that seeks to steal your identity and to create panic and confusion. The result is an identity crisis!

Our world is full of people seeking an identity in all the wrong places. People look to find their identity in fashion, music, sports, gangs, gender, race, politics, ancestry, chronic illnesses, work, and more. The recent explosion in the popularity of using DNA testing to reveal ancestry is one great example of this,[1] while the increase in suicides during the 2008 recession associated with sudden unemployment is another.[2] The music industry has a powerful influence that lures people with a fictitious lifestyle emphasizing perishable goods. Many people, especially youth, will dress like those they look up to and assume an identity associated with rock, rap, jazz, goth, country, and other genres. Each of these identities is so distinctive that a significant portion of the population can picture what each type of musician looks like. There is nothing wrong with being fashionable, but when fashion becomes our identity, we cheapen the value of who we are.

Every human being is a clay vessel, and the hands at work shaping us are either God's hands or the fallen world's. With only two options, there are three states we can be living in at any given time according to Revelation 3:16: First, we can be "hot" in the hands of God, being molded into His image; second, we can be "cold" in the hands of Satan, the temporary prince of this fallen world, being molded into his alternate image; or third, we can be "lukewarm," bouncing back and forth in a constant state of ambiguity. I pray your decision is to be the work of the Father's hand, with your identity rooted in Christ. There is great and lasting value in the identity of Christ. When we are completely surrendered into the work of the Potter's hands, beautiful things come about.

> *But now, O Lord, thou art our father; we are the clay, and thou our potter; and we all are the work of thy hand.*
> **Isaiah 64:8**

An Altered Image

Imagine yourself as a robot, with a mechanical system for a physical body and a program for a spirit. Your Creator is spirit, too, so He is also a program. Because you are His creation, He loves you and has made you in His image by sharing programming code that comes from Him. This gives the two of you a close and personal bond. Now imagine that one day, someone tells you that if you add this additional code to your software, you will be equal to your Creator. So you choose to add this code from an outside source to your perfect program that is running in harmony with your Creator's code. Unfortunately, this new code is corrupted, and the second you download it into your system, everything becomes contaminated and starts to crash. Your Creator must now remove His identity program from you in order to keep his program perfect and virus-free. He also has a moral obligation to do so because you rejected the framework of your relationship. So now, not only is your code corrupted, but the file containing your identity is also missing.

From a young age, we all have a need to discover who we are and find our identity. The longing for identity is inherent in us from birth, but it wasn't always this way. When God created Adam and Eve, they walked naked with God and were not ashamed. Their identities were pure in God. They were complete human beings in need of nothing and without sin. In Genesis 3, we read about the fall and the repercussions of sin. One of those repercussions was death and the sinful nature Adam and Eve chose to take on. The sinful nature imposed on them as a separation from God as God cannot dwell with sin. This separation from God brought about an identity crisis in man. The loss of identity has led to such a strong longing for its restoration because we are missing a part of ourselves that we once had. From then until today, the robber has offered many counterfeits and substitutions to fill the need for identity. But only the original can bring complete restoration to a person; the original man is Jesus Christ.

The first step on the road to walking in true identity is accepting Jesus Christ as Lord and Savior. True identity can only be found in Christ. When you surrender yourself into the Potter's hands, He will shape you into His good work. The promises for our identity are conditional to the acceptance of His lordship over our lives and the salvation from sin that comes with it. Without Jesus Christ, people will walk in spiritual blindness, and the identities they walk in will be molds cast from the fallen nature of this world. This world is perishing; everyone who self-identifies with it will perish too. Choose to walk in the identity that is not of this world.

Abandoning the Paths to Counterfeits

I am thankful to have grown up in a Christian home. My mother was Pentecostal, and my father was Lutheran, so I was able to experience the full spectrum of Christian faith and traditions. Despite having a good foundation from a young age, I was never totally sure of my identity in Christ until much later in life. Growing up, I was constantly bombarded with offers, opinions, and pressures to create my identity using the things of this world. I never realized my identity in Christ was even an option.

The pressures to create our identity can be subtly laced with good intentions, directly infused with sinister intent, or anything in between. Our true identities as Christians who are to be found in Jesus Christ are kept hidden behind the smoke and mirrors that the robber has set up. He seeks to keep people from the wholeness and truth found in God.

With technology, the all-out assault on identity has reached an unprecedented level. One of the clearest examples of this social reengineering is in the area of gender identity. There have been many legislative bills in California regarding assigned gender. The overall summary of these bills is that gender identity is not biological but based on feelings; therefore, technically speaking, there can be as many genders as there are people in the world. This idea not only brings about confusion, but it is contrary to God's design.

In 2018, I was given an opportunity as a pastor to speak in front of the California State Senate on bill SB 179 regarding the right for a person to choose whatever gender or non-gender a person wanted on their driver's license. The argument for this bill was that gender is not biological but mental, so anyone should have the right to self-identify. The Bible is very clear: God made gender identity simple. In Genesis 1:27, we read, "So God created man in his own image, in the image of God created he him; male and female created he them." God is not a God of confusion; He does not make accidents or leave things to chance. Simply put, there are only two options, male or female. The desire to pry that sovereignty out of the hands of God and push it into the hands of mortal man shows the level of confusion, depravity, and rebellion at work. If anyone ever has a true doubt about his or her gender, a chromosomal test can give an answer.

> *"For God is not the author of confusion, but of peace, as in all churches of the saints"*
> **1 Corinthians 14:33**

God is the author of order and peace, but the robber is the author of confusion. The recent push in some states to normalize gender dysphoria by teaching non-biological genders in kindergarten with an ever-increasing list of pronouns is the very blueprint for authoring confusion into the precious lives of children at a critically young age. The attack on gender identity is a spiritual one that goes straight to the core of humanity's identity, which was created by God in the Garden of Eden. It is an attempt to usurp God's commandment for parents to "train up a child in the way he should go" (Proverbs 22:6).

It is my conjecture that this subtle reprogramming of society to accept non-gender specific identity is paving the way for the mark of the beast by removing the moral objections to introducing genetic modifications to humans. These modifications will have eternal implications by permanently altering man's image from the image of God to the image of the beast. This is the primary reason why everyone who takes the mark of the beast will be irredeemable.

Some Christians believe people who take the mark of the beast can't be redeemed because they worship Satan, but in Scripture, as is the case today, there are people who are redeemed from worshiping Satan all the time. When I read Scripture, I find support for my conjecture in the stories of the Nephilim because they were the only other beings in Scripture that were irredeemable, and they were the seed of the serpent. Satan seeks to cause chaos, disorder, death, and destruction, all the forces of sin at work.

Ye are of your father the devil, and the lusts of your father ye will do. He was a murderer from the beginning, and abode not in the truth, because there is no truth in him. When he speaketh a lie, he speaketh of his own: for he is a liar, and the father of it.

John 8:44

As a cunning wolf on the prowl, the robber seeks to steal people away from God and mold them into his own perverted image by taking advantage of humanity's vulnerability. The robber was in the garden, and he knows the voids that inherently exist in our identities that need to be filled. The choices for our identities may appear to be complex, but when stripped back to the root, there are only two choices: an identity in Jesus Christ (the way we were intended) or an identity in the ruler of this temporary world, Satan (eternal separation from God). The robber's strategy is to convince your soul to assume a perverted identity, and he does this by gaining access to it through the windows of your eyes and ears.

The fight for our eyes is intense because that is the robber's window of opportunity. Satan will often tempt us through our eyes with something that will satisfy our flesh and appeal to our pride. When Satan tempted Adam and Eve in the garden, it was first through their eyes!

And when the woman saw that the tree was good for food,
and that it was pleasant to the eyes, and a tree to be desired
to make one wise, she took of the fruit thereof, and did eat,
and gave also unto her husband with her; and he did eat.

Genesis 3:6

And many years later, when Satan tempted Jesus Christ in the wilderness, his strategy didn't change; once again, he started first through the eyes.

Again, the devil taketh him up into an exceeding high
mountain, and sheweth him all the kingdoms of the world,
and the glory of them; And saith unto him, All these things
will I give thee, if thou wilt fall down and worship me.

Matthew 4:8–9

The eyes are an access point that needs to be heavily guarded, and we are the ones who have total control over them. We need to exercise wisdom, discernment, and discipline constantly. In the words of Jesus Christ,

The light of the body is the eye: if therefore thine eye be
single, thy whole body shall be full of light. But if thine
eye be evil, thy whole body shall be full of darkness. If
therefore the light that is in thee be darkness, how great is
that darkness!

Matthew 6:22–23

This vulnerability is real, and the robber is fully committed to using its weaknesses. Now that we know there is a battle for our eyes—and our imaginations—what are the robber's tools to break in through our windows?

The Tools of Identity Theft

The robber's tools are used to bring rebellion against God, His nature, His order, and His laws. Satan entices us with sin and with lies. He is the author of confusion. One major way he accomplishes deception today is through programming. The programming of our minds has the power to create change through social engineering, globalist agendas, antichrist philosophy, and counterfeit identities. These identities are tied to the temporal things of this world. Some people will laugh or scoff at the idea of social programming, but it is a legitimate issue that has been a means of molding us throughout human history.

Just as a pastor has a pulpit to preach from, the robber has a pulpit also, and that pulpit is media! As Christians, the question that we always need to ask is: Who is speaking to us when we watch what we are watching? Thievery is disguised, working in various ways within news, movies, music, the internet, and television. As Christians, we are called to discern and fight this agenda with prayer and by speaking the truth in love. Our eyes are the windows to our souls. We are warned throughout Scripture of the imperative need for us to guard our eyes!

> *"Turn away mine eyes from beholding vanity; and quicken thou me in thy way"*
>
> **Psalm 119:37**

This is a call to God to help govern our eyes from worldly and meaningless things that seek to redirect us from God's truth and priorities. These distractions many times unknowingly come in the form of programming, subconsciously planting suggestions and ideas with the deliberate intention of molding our opinions and luring our identities away from Christ and into an image of this world.

Studies have shown that when we watch television, movies,

and internet content, our minds become more suggestible than normal because we go into a semi-dissociative state.[3] This evidence only bolsters the reasoning for why God warns us so often about guarding our eyes and ears, the windows for gaining access to our souls. Scoffers might say that watching television has no effect on people. If that were true, then why would companies spend millions of dollars for thirty-second commercials during the Super Bowl? The answer is that advertisements truly have the power to influence people watching.

The power of media is so great that just the power of radio alone was able to convince some people all across America that the world was being invaded by Martians! It may be difficult to believe, but during a certain event years ago, people were heading to the hills and calling police stations in a total panic.[4] This happened during Orson Welles' broadcast of H. G. Wells' 1898 novel, "War of the Worlds," on CBS radio on October 31st, 1938. The event led many people to start paying close attention to the potential power of programming through media. Even today, we have an entire department in our military dedicated to using these and other classified tools for psychological warfare.[5] If this power to convince people that Earth was being invaded by UFOs was simply accomplished through radio, imagine the power of persuasion at use today through modern technology.

Today, there is a consolidation of power throughout society, and it is increasing at a rapid pace. Back in 2010, 388 people in the world had as much wealth as the poorest half of humanity, but since then, that number has been steadily falling and is now down to just sixty-two.[6] At this pace, Oxfam is projecting that in a few years, a single person will have as much money as the poorest half of the global population combined.[7]

This same trend can be seen in the corporate media and entertainment world. Thirty years ago, fifty different corporations dominated what, today, we call the mainstream media and entertainment. Now, that control has been concentrated around six major corporations: Time Warner, Walt Disney, Viacom, Rupert Murdoch's News Corp., CBS Corporation, and NBC Universal. Together, the "big six" absolutely dominate news and entertainment in the United States.[8]

Even the way we find information online is dominated by one company: Google. In 2013, the entirety of Google's services went offline for just a few minutes. During that time, GoSquared, a real-time analytics company, was able to determine approximately what percentage of the internet Google dominated at the time by finding that there was a 40 percent drop in overall internet traffic.[9] That is a lot of power behind one company that is allowed to control what you see and what you don't see, and their dominance is far greater today! The Nielsen report also showed the importance radio still plays in our lives too, often due to long commutes in our cars to work. On average, people listen to the radio 2.75 hours per day.[10] Looking back at the television in the 1950s and comparing it to today; we can see the dramatic moral decline of our society. How many of us do not spend thirty minutes in prayer daily with Jesus yet spend two hours in front of a television or online?

These statistics should remind all of us as Christians of the importance of learning to think for ourselves and to do our due diligence with any information we are consuming through news sources or entertainment. Seek the Lord for wisdom and discernment because the majority of television shows, news outlets, and music do not have God as their source of inspiration. As Christians, we are called to see all things through the filter of biblical truth. The devil wants to keep the truth of the gospel and of our identity in Christ contained within the walls of the church. The robber will do anything to ensure that people, including Christians, are not even aware of the option of having an identity in Christ.

If you are feeling a little convicted right now, that's okay. Conviction isn't for the sake of condemnation but for the sake of sanctification. In Hebrews 12:8, we read, "But if ye be without chastisement, whereof all are partakers, then are ye bastards, and not sons." God will bring correction to us because He loves us and because we are adopted by Him as sons and daughters when we confess that He is Lord and Savior. Being selective with what we watch and listen to has nothing to do with legalism; it has everything to do with wisdom. We are to recognize what glorifies Christ and what clearly does not and to choose accordingly. What are you allowing into your household?

Adam was given dominion over the garden, but at some point, under his watch, he allowed the serpent access. We don't know how long the serpent was allowed to linger, but eventually, the robber got to Eve and was able to work his deception. My point is this: We all have areas that we have "dominion" over: our homes, our cars, our workplaces. Wherever your responsibility is, have you allowed serpents in to linger? The unavoidable truth is that many people, including precious children, are becoming desensitized to murder, molestation, violence, and lust because their windows are open, and the robber is allowed to linger in people's gardens. When the Holy Spirit no longer fills hearts and minds with a passion for purity and holiness, there is a general lack of conviction that sets in.

Satan is a master of legalism, and I would argue that aside from God, there is no better lawyer than him. The robber will take advantage of every right we give him. If we have occult materials in our homes, then the devil has a right to be there because we are watching, reading, or listening to his covenant there. He will rob us of our true identities if given a chance. The answer to the problem is simple: Kick the robber out of your dominion! Once the input stops, it isn't reinforced. The best method of undoing any damage is by repenting of our sins and replacing the negative messages with the truth and by renewing our minds with God's Word daily.

What We Are

And the Lord God formed man of the dust of the ground,

33

> *and breathed into his nostrils the breath of life; and man became a living soul.*
>
> **Genesis 2:7**

As we read in Genesis, Adam's physical body came from the dust of the ground, his spirit entered through God's breath into his nostrils, and with life came a soul. Adam and Eve were made perfect, without sin, and in the image of God, but things changed after the fall in the garden. Because of the consequences of sin, all mankind would be born in the image of Adam and bound by sin, but the chains of death are severed when we are covered by the blood of Jesus Christ. Accepting Him as Lord and Savior is how we are born again into life forevermore. Even though our physical body still dies because of its corrupted nature, we will receive an incorruptible body as its replacement.

It is interesting to note that the Hebrew term *bnei HaElohim*, which literally means "the sons of God," is only used for Adam and angelic beings; it is never used for believers in the Old Testament.[11] After the fall, the word *bnei HaAdam*, meaning "sons of man," is used in its place for fallen mankind.[12] We don't see the former term used again until we get to the salvation that is made available through Jesus Christ in the New Testament. After we are born again, the term "sons of God" is applied to man once again. This is when our new identity is given!

So let us examine the fact that we are created as triune beings consisting of body, spirit, and soul. First, we have the body. There are many Hebrew words for "body" in the Old Testament; one of them is *beten*, meaning "bosom, belly, within, womb, or body of anything;"[13] another word is *nebelah*, meaning "body, corpse, or carrion."[14] The Greek word often used in the New Testament is *soma*, meaning "the physical body" that is made up of matter.[15] The physical is both temporary and perishable. In other words, the body has a guaranteed expiration date. For the believers in Christ, a non-perishable, incorruptible body awaits, but not for the lost.

Next, we have the spirit. In Hebrew, the word for "spirit" in the Old Testament is *ruach*, meaning "spirit, breath, wind, the will; it can be a disposition or attitude."[16] *Ruach* can also be used to describe good and bad angels, disembodied spirits, and God's Spirit, the Holy Spirit. "Spirit" in the New Testament Greek is *pneuma*.[17] This is where the word "pneumatics," meaning air-powered tools, is derived from. As for the human spirit, it was God's wind that had the power to give life to the body. *Pneuma* can also be more precise in its definition, as it refers to the simple essence of the power of knowing, devoid of all matter. Because the spirit is not matter, it is not bound to the laws of entropy, "the death force." This is an important distinction to remember.

Last, we have the soul. The Hebrew word for "soul" in the Old Testament is *nephesh*, meaning "soul, self, person, mind, emotion, passion, reason, and worship."[18] It's also a figure of speech called a synoptic. An example of a synoptic would be this: When I ask you to lend me a hand, I'm not just asking for your hand but am also requesting that the rest of you comes along with it. A soul is likewise a piece of you that is attached to and automatically comes with the rest of you. In the New Testament, the Greek word for soul is *psuche*, specifying that the soul is not equated to physical life but is invisible and immortal.[19] Why is that important? Because it confirms that the soul, like the spirit, is eternal after creation and does not cease to exist because it is not physical matter.

Everyone's body will perish one day because it is physical, but God designed our spirits and our souls to live forever. The question is, where will you spend eternity? Scripture is very clear: The only two options are eternity with God in the new heavens and the new earth or eternal separation from God in the lake of fire. Your true identity is suited for your eternal outcome. Identity in Christ is not of this world. Identity in this world perishes along with it.

Psuche is also where the word "psychology" is derived from. This is why I believe modern-day psychology is doomed to failure on many levels: because it no longer looks at the nonphysical but looks purely at the physical! Rather than dealing with the issues of the soul and spirit, psychologists tend to focus on the physical issues of the body. The first step of treatment for the body will try to mask or suppress one's struggles through pharmaceuticals that may provide some relief but will never deal with the root. Total healing never comes because the spiritual issues of the soul are never addressed. Only God can heal the soul, and without Him, restoration is impossible. It is time for psychology to return to its roots, the soul *psuche*. The body is a physical shell. If you are a true Christian, then your body is a temporary temple of the Holy Spirit, and one day it will be transformed into a glorious, perfect, incorruptible eternal body. The "real you" is not physical, and your physical body is not your identity.

The Real You

The real you is not your body, and it cannot be seen with the eyes because it is not physical. Whenever we look at people, we can make assumptions about them based on observable clues. Given enough time, we can "get to know them," but we cannot really see who they are without the opening of our spiritual eyes by God.

In many ways, computers are a simplistic example of how God designed us. On the macro level, a computer is broken down into two basic parts: hardware and software. Hardware is made up of things that are physical, like the motherboard, computer case, and processor. The software is the operating system that brings the computer to life; it is nonphysical. A computer program has varying degrees of complexity, and the more advanced the program, the more complicated the code becomes. The complexity of code proves that it is organized, ruling out any chance of randomness. The fact that the code is error-correcting reveals that the source must also be of intelligent design.

Just as computers show evidence of a creator in their design, the same can be said of us. Imagine a standard desktop computer taken completely apart down to its smallest individual units. Next, imagine the thousands of pieces in a large plastic Ziploc bag. Now the theory of evolution tells us if we shake that bag long enough, then eventually, given enough time, all the pieces will come back together to form a perfectly reassembled computer again. Now, most people will realize that that is statistically absurd, and indeed the technical mathematical term for such a low probability is "absurdity!" I think most people would agree that computers just don't come together without a designer and a builder, yet even though we are infinitely more complex than computers, we have been conditioned by evolutionary teaching to believe we are somehow different. So for the sake of argument, let us just say that given enough time, we can see a computer randomly come together; there is still one fundamental necessity that evolution leaves out: the origin of information. Even after a computer is plugged in and given power, it does not function without the information called software.

The question evolution can never answer is where the origin of the information is. The most common teaching of the beginning of the universe is that in the beginning, there was nothing, and the nothing exploded into the universe today. This may seemingly explain how matter got here, but it still doesn't explain the origin of the information that came with it. Many leading physicists are accepting the truth that there must be an outside source for the information (programming) that is at work in the universe, but they continually struggle to come up with a theory because they cannot accept that God's Word clearly explains that He is the origin and the programmer. In the account of the creation of the universe in Genesis 1, God gives instruction with His voice: "In the beginning, God said..." This tells us that at the beginning, God introduced information first by speaking, and with that information, the creation of the universe followed.

Computer software has no mass, just like our spirit and soul, but it is needed to bring life to the hardware (body). A computer loaded with software weighs the same as one that has no software installed. It cannot be directly seen or understood without an interface with the code through which its purpose can be viewed. For a computer, the tools for understanding the code are a monitor and its owner's manual. The human equivalent would be the Holy Spirit and the Bible. The Holy Spirit can give us spiritual eyes to see someone spiritually, and the Bible is our owner's manual to life. But they do not give us access to the entire code, as Deuteronomy 29:29 plainly states that: The secret things belong unto the Lord our God: but those things which are revealed belong unto us and to our children for ever, that we may do all the words of this law.

In many passages, the Bible talks about mysteries that God reveals in His timing and says that total understanding is known only to Him, the master programmer who has written all the code. This is why things like our hearts and our intentions are only truly known by God, as Psalm 44:21 says: "Shall not God search this out? for He knoweth the secrets of the heart."

In the beginning, God created man to live forever, but things changed when sin invaded man. Like a computer virus, when Adam and Eve disobeyed God, they allowed sin to corrupt their programming. God's incorruptible, sinless nature could no longer dwell with man in his sin, so He had to remove Himself from what became infected by sin. Man's identity in God changed from His sinless nature to a corrupted body that would be plagued with pain, suffering, and death. From then on, every human would be born in the image of Adam. The consequence of this has left a void in us that can be restored through Jesus Christ by being born again and filled with our new identity.

The physical body is condemned to death because of sin, but the real you, your spirit and soul, doesn't die because it is not physical, and God created it that way. Unless we are born again, our "corrupted programming" and our identity do not change, and that default programming leads us to hell. The new programming and identity through Christ will be compatible with the new upgraded glorified bodies given to Christians after our existing sinful bodies die. So the question is: If you are headed for an upgrade, then what is your identity now in Jesus Christ?

Who We Are in Christ

Who are you in Christ? I ask many lifelong Christians this question, but often they cannot give an answer. If you are not walking in the identity of Christ, then you will not be able to boldly exercise your authority in Christ to the fullest. Why? Because you are living life under a false identity. Jesus died for us so that we can live in forgiveness, abundance, and victory. These things characterize our new identity in Christ, but if we do not take ownership of them, we will continue to live in ignorance of who we are. Now, even while we are living in the fullness of our new identities in Christ, our lives will still not be perfect on Earth as we experience suffering and pain. Still, our hope is solidified in Christ's victory over death.

There are fifteen points in Scripture that outline our true identity in Christ. These points describe who Christ says we are in Him, and they are a great blessing with eternal benefits. At first glance, they can seem simple, but the depths of their ramifications are extraordinary. Walking in their truth will give you greater peace and confidence in who you are. Pray and ask God to help you realize them. Take ownership of them because they are yours, and they are true! Finally, walk in the peace and power that comes with your real identity.

Let's look at the fifteen truths of our identity in Christ declared in Scripture.

1. We are known by God.

Nevertheless the foundation of God standeth sure, having this seal, The Lord knoweth them that are his. And, Let every one that nameth the name of Christ depart from iniquity.

2 Timothy 2:19

Imagine all the people living on Earth right now suspended in the vastness of space and time. In the midst of it all, you are known by God because you are His. The Greek word used for "knoweth" in the above passage is *ginosko*, meaning to "know absolutely."[20] God knows your struggles, your dreams, your physical disabilities, your pain, the way you talk, and the motives of your heart. There isn't anything about you or concerning you that God does not know completely. We are known, cared about, and watched over from the very beginning of our creation. That means that there is not one day that God has not cared for you. You can't hide from God; He knows who you are and where you are before you do. Our true identity means that the Creator of the universe knows us personally!

2. We are chosen.

Moreover whom he did predestinate, them he also called: and whom he called, them he also justified: and whom he justified, them he also glorified.

Romans 8:30

We have been handpicked by God for salvation even though we do not deserve it. The Greek word used for "predestinate" is *proorizo*, meaning to "determine in advance and ordain."[21] Our salvation is not accidental. God had always intended it, even before we were created. If you ever question whether or not you are valuable, just remember that you are valuable enough to Him that God chose you to be reconciled back to Him. Even though there is nothing we can ever do that would make us deserving of salvation, the fact remains: our true identity means we are chosen.

3. We are reconciled with God.

And all things are of God, who hath reconciled us to himself by Jesus Christ, and hath given to us the ministry of reconciliation; To wit, that God was in Christ, reconciling the world unto himself, not imputing their trespasses unto them; and hath committed unto us the word of reconciliation.

2 Corinthians 5:18–19

Because of the finished work of Jesus Christ, we have free access to God and have been reunited with Him by the power of the blood of Jesus Christ. The Greek word used for "reconciliation" is *katallasso*, meaning "to change mutually, to compound a difference and reconcile."[22] Everything that stood between Him and us is now powerless in our new identity, destroyed by the power of the blood. Our true identity means we are now part of God's family of brothers and sisters in Christ.

4. We are rescued.

For there is one God, and one mediator between God and men, the man Christ Jesus; Who gave himself a ransom for all, to be testified in due time.

1 Timothy 2:5–6

We have been rescued from death! The Greek word used for "ransom" is *antilutron*, meaning "instead of, or substitution for, a redemption price."[23] Jesus paid the ransom for our lives with His own so that sin no longer holds our lives hostage to the consequences of sin, which are eternal death to the body and eternal separation from God. Our true identity means we are no longer people who are being held hostage to death. We should be living a life of gratitude and should be making decisions based on the fact that we have been rescued.

5. We have been forgiven.

To the praise of the glory of his grace, wherein he hath made us accepted in the beloved. In whom we have redemption through his blood, the forgiveness of sins, according to the riches of his grace; Wherein he hath abounded toward us in all wisdom and prudence.

Ephesians 1:6–8

Everything that we have ever done that does not follow the character of God has been forgiven. The Greek word used for "forgiveness" is *aphesis*, meaning "freedom, pardon, deliverance, forgiveness, liberty, remission."[24] Every sinful action, thought, or spoken word, as well as the good things we did not do though we should have, are forgiven. Knowing we are forgiven by God through Christ means that we can walk in our true identity, free from the shame and guilt of our past.

6. We have been redeemed.

Looking for that blessed hope, and the glorious appearing of the great God and our Saviour Jesus Christ; Who gave himself for us, that he might redeem us from all iniquity, and purify unto himself a peculiar people, zealous of good works.

Titus 2:13–14

We can look forward to a rich, meaningful, and purposeful life because all of our debts have been covered. The Greek word used for "redeem" is *lutroo*, meaning "ransomed, to loosen with a redemption price, redeemed."[25] God's future plans for us are totally accessible because our redemption is paid for by the blood of Jesus Christ. We now qualify for the total inheritance of God because we are no longer in debt with sin. Our true identity means we are not in bondage in debtor's prison and destined toward hell anymore but are free to live eternally with Christ Jesus.

7. We are justified before God.

Being justified freely by his grace through the redemption that is in Christ Jesus: Whom God hath set forth to be a propitiation through faith in his blood, to declare his righteousness for the remission of sins that are past, through the forbearance of God; To declare, I say, at this time his righteousness: that he might be just, and the justifier of him which believeth in Jesus.

Romans 3:24–26

Jesus has won our court case by paying all of the penalties for us. The Greek word used for "justified" is *dikaioo*, meaning "to render, show or regard as innocent, free, justify, be righteous."[26] As a result, we have been acquitted of all of our crimes. God, the ultimate judge, has ruled us innocent because of Christ's finished work on the cross. In our true identity, we are innocent of all charges before God!

8. We are bought at a price.

What? know ye not that your body is the temple of the Holy Ghost which is in you, which ye have of God, and ye are not your own? For ye are bought with a price: therefore glorify God in your body, and in your spirit, which are God's.

1 Corinthians 6:19–20

We no longer belong to ourselves but to God. The Greek words used here for "bought" and "price" are *agorazo* and *time*, meaning "to purchase, to redeem," and "money paid, valuables, of highest degree, precious, price, or sum."[27] God has redeemed us through the payment of Christ's blood, which has the highest degree of value. As a result, our old way of life no longer owns us. Our true identity means we are now God's.

9. We are sealed.

Now he which stablisheth us with you in Christ, and hath anointed us, is God; Who hath also sealed us, and given the earnest of the Spirit in our hearts.

2 Corinthians 1:21–22

God has sealed us and has put His Holy Spirit in our hearts as a guarantee. The Greek word used here for "sealed" is *sphragizo*, meaning "to stamp, with a signet or private mark, for security or preservation, to seal up."[28] His seal of ownership is placed over us, and He has anointed us for His purposes. The truth of our identity is that God's mark of ownership over us gives us security in knowing that nothing can steal us from Him and that our souls will be preserved for eternity with Him.

10. We are received.

Wherefore receive ye one another, as Christ also received us to the glory of God.

Romans 15:7

We are no longer rejected nor considered outsiders because we have been welcomed by God. The Greek word used here for "received" is *proslambano*, meaning "to take to oneself, lead or admit to friendship or hospitality, receive, take unto."[29] Our real identity means we are friends with God and that He is a gracious host in all of His glory.

11. We are saved.

But God commendeth his love toward us, in that, while we were yet sinners, Christ died for us. Much more then, being now justified by his blood, we shall be saved from wrath through him. For if, when we were enemies, we were reconciled to God by the death of his Son, much more, being reconciled, we shall be saved by his life.

Romans 5:8–10

We have been saved from God's justified anger toward sin. The Greek word used here for "saved" is *sozo*, meaning "to save, deliver, protect, and heal, preserve, do well, be whole."[30] We are now saved from the robber's sinful system that leads to death and separation from God. We are even saved from ourselves. Our true identity in Christ means that we are living in a constant state of salvation, being made whole and eternally protected by His blood.

12. We are called with a purpose.

And we know that all things work together for good to them that love God, to them who are the called according to his purpose.

Romans 8:28

God works out all of our circumstances for good because we are called, and we are purposeful. The Greek word used here for "called" is *prothesis*, meaning "a setting forth for purpose, proposal, intention."[31] The Greek word *kletos* that translates to "purpose," means "an invitation, invited, appointed, a saint called."[32] Regardless of how we are treated or valued by others in this world, our true identity means that the Creator of everything values us enough that we have a purpose in Him. Let your godly purpose be your identity.

13. We are loved.

For God so loved the world, that he gave his only begotten Son, that whosoever believeth in him should not perish, but have everlasting life.

John 3:16

45

God's love for us is so great that He displayed that love by giving up the most valuable thing He had: His Son. It is Christ's priceless blood that covers our debt so that we may have everlasting life. The Greek word used here for "loved" is *agapao*, meaning "to love much in a social or moral sense."[33] God tells us how much He loves us in His Word. He loves spending time with us by His Holy Spirit. His action on the Cross shows us His love, the greatest gift of eternal life proves His love, and His work through other Christians gives us His physical love here on earth. Every benefit of our true identity exists because God first loved us, and all the love we have to give comes from Him as the source of true love.

14. We are free.

But now being made free from sin, and become servants to God, ye have your fruit unto holiness, and the end everlasting life. For the wages of sin is death; but the gift of God is eternal life through Jesus Christ our Lord.

Romans 6:22–23

We are no longer slaves to sin because we have been set free. The Greek word used here for "free" is *eleutheroo*, meaning "to liberate or to exempt from moral liability, deliver, make free."[34] That does not mean we no longer fight against sin but that we are no longer bound to the damnation of sin. If we still sin, it is because we choose to sin; we are no longer made to sin. Our identity in Christ means that we now have authority over it.

15. We are truly alive.

Likewise reckon ye also yourselves to be dead indeed unto sin, but alive unto God through Jesus Christ our Lord.

Romans 6:11

Our mortal bodies will be made new and immortal after we die. The Greek word used here for "alive" is *zao*, meaning "to live, life, lifetime."[35] Our spirits have been brought to new life, as we have received that life from God, along with new meaning and new purpose that give us a new way of looking at life itself. Our true identity means we are alive forevermore.

Do you accept these characteristics as part of your new identity in Christ? Ask the Lord to deepen your understanding and your desire to walk in the fullness of these truths. When we embrace our true identity, we will live our lives in a way that will reflect it. We absolutely must think this way about ourselves and about others who are in Christ Jesus. It is in our new identity that we can be ambassadors of God! The more we live in the truth of who we are, the more will be revealed to us about God.

Our Identity Fits Our Destination

Our identity in life has long-term implications. If we have been born again, covered by the blood of Jesus, and He is our Lord and Savior, our identity is in Jesus Christ, and heaven is our destination. If our identity is anything other than Christ, then we will live for all eternity separated from Him. The question to Christians is: Are you walking in that identity, or are you being robbed? Even if you have been saved and your destination is heaven, you can be robbed of your identity in Christ, and you can be missing out on your privileges now.

Many people ask, "If God is so loving, then why does He send people to hell?" It is important to remember that hell is the default destination for mankind. This makes heaven the only option that can be freely chosen. So God does not send people to hell; He only sends people to heaven. Scripture tells us that hell is like a pit without walls where everyone can be cast into it but can't get out, while heaven is surrounded by impenetrable walls containing twelve gates guarded by twelve angels, who only allow those with the correct identification to enter. Counterfeit identities will not work; only originals will be accepted at the gates, and only Jesus Christ issues them. So let's look at heaven and hell, the two destinations your identity gives you access to.

The Reality of Hell

There is a falling away from the truth of the Word of God regarding hell. Many spiritual teachers are proclaiming that there is no hell or eternal punishment, and even more, they are fearful to even talk about the subject because it offends people. It is a biblical fact that hell is a reality, and any preacher who tells you otherwise is lying to you. To reject the reality of hell is to discard the Word of God. The verbiage used throughout Scripture discussing hell in both Greek and Hebrew is specific and definite. The contexts leave no wiggle room to interpret hell as being anything other than an actual place with a specific location and very real consequences.

Some people say that hell is too scary to think about, and others set up a defense using the idea that if someone preaches on hell, it is only fear-mongering for the purpose of playing on people's emotions in order to manipulate them to commit to Christ. The truth is that Jesus spoke more about hell than He did about heaven. If it was an important topic to Him, it should be for us, too.

Despite the constant changes in culture, many surveys show that the majority of people still believe that there is a heaven and a hell and that we have souls that continue after death. Even with this belief, many Americans confess that they are uncertain about their personal fate after death.

One study found that 81 percent of Americans believed in an afterlife of some kind, 9 percent were unsure what they believed, and only 10 percent felt certain that there was no afterlife. Seventy-one percent of people believed that hell exists as a place of eternal separation from God or a place of actual torment and suffering after death. Thirteen percent believed hell is only symbolic. Sixteen percent were either unsure or did not believe in hell. [36]

So, if 71 percent of Americans have some form of certainty that there is a hell, then why aren't preachers preaching about it, and why aren't Christians talking about it? If we are to be like Christ, then we need to follow His precedent and discuss hell with both believers and nonbelievers, as He did.

The same study by the Barna Group found that almost 1 percent of Americans think they are going to hell, but the true number of the unsaved is far, far greater than 1 percent.[37] That alone should compel us to talk about the reality of hell and the need for a Savior.

In the Bible, hell is mentioned fifty-four times, the lake of fire is mentioned four times, and hellfire is mentioned three times. Scripture tells us that the inhabitants of hell will be those that are wicked and those that have turned from God, as Psalm 9:17 says: "The wicked shall be turned into hell, and all the nations that forget God." It also describes it as a place full of sorrows and pain: "The sorrows of death compassed me, and the pains of hell gat hold upon me: I found trouble and sorrow" (Psalm 116:3).

Unfortunately, hell is a place that will never be full. Proverbs 27:20 says, "Hell and destruction are never full; so the eyes of man are never satisfied." Until the day of the Great White Throne Judgment, when the lost are cast into the lake of fire, mankind's sinful lineage will come to an end. Until then, people will still be going to hell, and we have a responsibility to let people know. It is our job as Christians to warn them and let them know that there is an option to change their identity to what it was originally meant to be.

Jesus takes the reality of hell very seriously. He warns that hell is a destination to fear and that both the body and soul are sent there. In the words of Jesus in Matthew 5:30,

And if thy right hand offend thee, cut it off, and cast it from thee: for it is profitable for thee that one of thy members

should perish, and not that thy whole body should be cast into hell.

And we hear in His words again in Matthew 10:28,

And fear not them which kill the body, but are not able to kill the soul: but rather fear him which is able to destroy both soul and body in hell.

In these verses, the Greek word that is translated as "destroy" is *apollumi*, meaning "to be delivered up to eternal misery."[38] Nowhere in Scripture is it ever used to mean "annihilate." So hell is a place to fear where both the body and the soul go for eternity.

The Bible has much to say about hell being a real place that has an address. It is not just some obscure metaphor; it is physical, it has boundaries, and it has locality. Some of the scriptures that talk about this are:

1. *"It is as high as heaven; what canst thou do? deeper than hell; what canst thou know?" (Job 11:8)*

2. *Let death seize upon them, and let them go down quick into hell: for wickedness is in their dwellings, and among them (Psalm 55:15)*

3. *"But he knoweth not that the dead are there; and that her guests are in the depths of hell" (Proverbs 9:18)*

4. *"The way of life is above to the wise, that he may depart from hell beneath" (Proverbs 15:24)*

5. *Hell from beneath is moved for thee to meet thee at thy coming: it stirreth up the dead for thee, even all the chief ones of the earth; it hath raised up from their thrones all the kings of*

the nations (Isaiah 14:9)

So, hell is described as deep, beneath, down, below, and in the opposite direction from heaven. Scripture makes it clear that hell is a place of sorrow, torment, and pain. The boundaries of hell are also always able to expand in order to accommodate more lost souls.

> ***Therefore hell hath enlarged herself, and opened her mouth without measure: and their glory, and their multitude, and their pomp, and he that rejoiceth, shall descend into it.***
>
> **Isaiah 5:14**

There have also been recent discoveries in physics that could be giving us a glimpse at the physical building blocks of hell. Ultimately only time will tell what is going to happen, but my concern is that as technology increases, the possibility of mankind opening a gateway to hell (the bottomless pit), willingly or accidentally, may happen in our lifetime. The potential repercussions are talked about in Revelation chapter nine, where the locusts came upon the earth from the bottomless pit with power to hurt anyone who did not have the seal of God on their foreheads. The bottom line is: without the redemption of our identity, all humanity is bound to hell. To put this in perspective, estimates from 2011 indicate that globally, 6,316 people died each hour.[39] Another estimate indicates that in 2015, 31 percent of the global population called themselves Christians.[40] So if we take the best-case scenario by assuming that everyone who identifies themselves as Christians is truly saved and will go to heaven, and if those numbers are still approximately the same, then in the last hour, an estimated 4,358 people have made the transition to hell.

The Reality of Heaven

As difficult as this topic can be because of the unfamiliar

51

nature of this "alternate reality," our ability to grasp the complete fundamentals and nature of heaven is limited for the time being because of our mortal bodies and minds. We are also plagued by a plethora of literary works and other forms of entertainment such as television, music, and movies that feed into our imagination of what heaven should be like. These images often begin as early as childhood in the form of cartoons, comic books, and toys. But the only ultimate authority that is the source of our true information on heaven is the written Word of God, and it is totally accurate. The facts of heaven alone should compel us to share with others the truth of the Word of God and the benefit of a new identity in Christ. There are four points about heaven that will be discussed here. First is the world's view of heaven and how that should motivate us. Second, we will discuss the insights from physics and astronomy that may be giving us a glimpse into the reality that heaven exists. Third, we will look at what the reality of heaven is. Last, we will read in Scripture about how rewards are given out in heaven.

What the World Believes

In a 2003 poll of Americans, participants were asked to identify whether they believed in heaven.[41] A surprising 46 percent believed heaven was a state of eternal existence in God's presence. Thirty percent believed heaven was an actual place of rest and reward. Fourteen percent said they believed heaven was just symbolic, followed by 5 percent who believed that there was no such place. Finally, 5 percent expressed that they are not sure. This pretty much correlates with the same proportion of people who also had the same views on hell.

This same poll of Americans also asked what they believed their ultimate destination was going to be. Sixty-five percent believed they would go to heaven, and 24 percent said they had no idea. Five percent thought they would cease to exist, while another 5 percent believed in reincarnation. Surprisingly, as mentioned in the previous section, 1 percent of the people asked believed that they were going to hell. Even more interesting findings were indicated when the 65 percent of people who believed they were going to heaven were questioned. Forty-three percent of them said they would because they had confessed their sin and accepted Jesus Christ as Lord and Savior. Fifteen percent believed it was because they had tried to keep the Ten Commandments. Another 15 percent claimed that it was because they were basically good. Lastly, 6 percent believed that God loves all people, and therefore no one will go to hell.

Maybe these results don't surprise you, but what is truly shocking to me is that among self-professing Christians, as much as 50 percent believe there are multiple options for gaining entry into heaven! This is despite the fact that Jesus Christ Himself said that the only way into heaven was salvation through Him (John 14:6). About 50 percent also believe that a person can earn salvation based upon good works, even though Scripture clearly claims that it is by grace through faith that we are saved, not by works (Ephesians 2:8–9).

Furthermore, 29 percent believe it is possible to communicate with the dead—and although the question isn't whether it is possible to communicate with disembodied spirits, Scripture is very clear (in 2 Corinthians 11, Leviticus 19, Deuteronomy 18, Isaiah 8, 1 Corinthians 10) that necromancy, or communication with the dead, is absolutely forbidden. Lastly, 10 percent of Americans believe in reincarnation (in the traditional sense) after death, even though God's Word says that "it is appointed unto man once to die, and after this the judgment" (Hebrews 9:27). For me, what these statistics clearly indicate is that not only is there a mission field out in the world, but there is also one within the heart of the American church!

As we will see in the chapter on deception, there is a significant portion of people in church who need to know the truth of the Word of God and are being robbed. The church needs to have a Holy Ghost encounter, to be filled with the refining fire of God, and to walk in its true identity in Jesus Christ! For people to believe that God is so set on rescuing people from the default destination of hell that He would change His perfect nature and guiding principles is foolishness. It detracts from the very nature of who God is! It is clear that Jesus Christ, who is the Word of God made flesh, is "the same yesterday, and to day, and for ever" (Hebrews 13:8).

Going back to the study, the survey found that 12 percent of atheists and agnostics believed that accepting Jesus Christ would most likely make life after death possible.[42] So why don't they choose Jesus? It is my belief that they are so dissatisfied with this life that the idea of eternal life to them is unacceptable because Satan has them so bound that it is impossible for them to perceive the glorious and purposeful identity that God has waiting for them. Share the good news of Christ and walk in your identity. It's time to bring truth to this identity crisis!

Now, these numbers are from 2003, but a more recent study regarding these same beliefs indicates that there has been surprisingly little change among Americans on this issue.[43] Seventy-two percent believe in heaven, as opposed to 76 percent in 2003, and 58 percent believe in hell, as opposed to 71 percent in 2003. I believe a significant part of the 13 percent decline in the belief in hell is due to the "seeker-sensitive" church model's rejection toward preaching on hell mentioned earlier in the chapter.

Clues from the Natural World

For the invisible things of him from the creation of the world are clearly seen, being understood by the things that are made, even his eternal power and Godhead; so that they are without excuse: Because that, when they knew God, they glorified him not as God, neither were thankful; but became vain in their imaginations, and their foolish heart was darkened. Professing themselves to be wise, they became fools.

Romans 1:20–22

This verse sounds a lot like the times we live in today. If you watch some of the big yearly debates in the scientific community, like the 2016 and 2018 Isaac Asimov Memorial Debate at the American Museum of Natural History, there is now so much evidence that our physical universe was designed that the arguments have moved from evolution versus creation to the introduction of the idea that whatever we see is just a simulation running on a computer in an alternate universe.[44] Despite being faced with overwhelming evidence of a master designer, many scientists still cannot accept that there is a God to whom they will be held accountable. The scripture above tells us that, at the very least, God will hold us all accountable to Him by the proof of His sovereignty in creation itself. [45]

One amazing property of heaven is that it is limitless in many ways. I think one of the best ways for us to understand the vastness of heaven is to grasp the limits of our finite reality. A great example of this is the fact that the concept of infinity does not actually exist in our universe, but we know from Scripture it is a personal attribute of God—and it would appear to be one of the fundamental laws of heaven.

For thus saith the high and lofty One that inhabiteth eternity, whose name is Holy; I dwell in the high and holy place, with him also that is of a contrite and humble spirit, to revive the spirit of the humble, and to revive the heart of the contrite ones.

Isaiah 57:15

As we grow up, most of us are taught in school that time is like a straight line starting at point A and moving toward point B. Because of this, we have a tendency to imagine God as someone who has lots of time, but God is completely outside of the restrictions of time

55

altogether. This is one of the major ways God authenticates His Word to us because of His unique position outside of time altogether. Only He can write the future before it happens! Heaven is also outside linear time, as the death force is confined to our physical universe. The laws of thermodynamics support the biblical narrative. Death, which is the consequence of sin, is not playing out in heaven, as heaven is a place where there is no death or decay.

The laws that govern the universe prove it had a beginning and that it will ultimately have an ending as well. Just as Isaiah says in chapter 46, verse 10, God is:

Declaring the end from the beginning, and from ancient times the things that are not yet done, saying, My counsel shall stand, and I will do all my pleasure.

So, the physical universe is encapsulated by a beginning and an end, and it is also confined by physical limits in size too.

What we would call our physical reality has limits in all directions. In other words, we are the ones who are currently living in a box. As large as the universe is, it is just a box within the expanse of heaven. There are limits to the size of our reality: In scientific terms, it is referred to as the macrocosm. The macrocosm ranges from the finite, observable edge of the universe down to 10^{-33} centimeters. Anything smaller is called the microcosm. The microcosm isn't in a single small space, but it's all around us. This term just means that everything in this realm consists of extremely small things where the physics of death and decay don't exist, and time on that level works differently.[46] This is the area of quantum physics that is unseen, and the Bible calls the unseen more real than what is seen:

While we look not at the things which are seen, but at the things which are not seen: for the things which are seen are temporal; but the things which are not seen are eternal.
2 Corinthians 4:18

To me, it appears that the microcosm's description and properties match what the Bible calls the spiritual realm. If this is the spill-over from heaven, only imagine how much grander it is at the source where God is seated.

There are also limits to the time we experience now. These limitations to linear time are regulated in length from the inception of sin (when the death force mechanism was activated in Genesis 3) to the appointed end of the heavens and the earth in Revelation 21. There is also a limit to how small-time can be recorded: 10^{-43} seconds. In James 1:17, the author writes that:

Very good gift and every perfect gift is from above, and cometh down from the Father of lights, with whom is no variableness, neither shadow of turning.

These same attributes that are specifically phrased in this order are also repeated seven other times throughout Scripture. The emphasis means that God is outside time (literally stating that He is above) and that He never changes.

The Truth of Heaven

Scripture tells us that there is a perfect city residing in heaven, called the New Jerusalem. It is also an environment devoid of all moral evil. Because of this, the consequences of sin and death are absent, and we will have resurrected bodies free from these corrupting forces. We will have fellowship with every believer who has ever lived. We will still have our will to choose but with the absence of sin, along with intellectual and emotional abilities and personal knowledge from our life experiences. What I look forward to the most is that we will also have no barriers from knowing and loving God to the fullest! Amen.

Our identities in Christ, including our genders and unique characteristics, will remain a part of us. Some people question whether there will be genders in heaven because Matthew 22:30 states that after the resurrection, we will "neither marry, nor are given in marriage, but are as the angels of God in Heaven." However, just because people will not marry in heaven doesn't mean that people become genderless; in fact, Scripture doesn't talk about people losing their gender at all. Even the angels of God in heaven are spoken of using masculine pronouns (not neuter in Greek), indicating that angels are not genderless beings. I would also point out that Jesus Himself also retained His gender after His death and resurrection.

In the book of Revelation chapters 21 and 22, God's plan for making all things new again is revealed, and this plan doesn't just restore everything back as it was before the fall in the Garden of Eden but makes everything even better. Gender was a good thing that was part of God's perfect design before sin. God created Eve because Adam needed a helpmate, and this union between man and woman is an example of Christ and the church, as seen in Ephesians 5:25–32. Our gender is part of the identity God created for us, and it is also the perspective by which we relate to God, so it would seem logical that our gender will be perfected and glorified in our resurrected bodies.

In Scripture, we can see slight hints as to what our resurrected bodies will be like.

Beloved, now are we the sons of God, and it doth not yet appear what we shall be: but we know that, when he shall appear, we shall be like him; for we shall see him as he is.
1 John 3:2

John tells us we will be like Christ is in His resurrected body! After Christ's resurrection, He was able to eat, and He was able to be touched and appear solid, yet at the same time, He could walk through walls, and He was even able to fly into the clouds. In other words, we will be able to experience all the other spatial dimensions available to Christ, and thanks to God, we will no longer be infringed upon by sin, death, and pain.

Additional insight can be found when examining the word John used in Greek for taking on this new body, *oiketerion*. This word is used only one other time in Scripture, in the book of Jude.

And the angels which kept not their first estate, but left their own habitation, he hath reserved in everlasting chains under darkness unto the judgment of the great day.

Jude 1:6

This verse is discussing the mischief of the fallen angels in Genesis 6 and gives clarity to how they were able to engage with women, resulting in the race of giants called Nephilim. When we expound on the Greek, we see they were able to disrobe from their spiritual, multidimensional bodies and become more physical. Sin lured the fallen angels down into flesh, perverting this transformation process, but our identity in Christ will draw us up into glorious bodies using the transformation process, the way God intended it.

The Rewards Given in Heaven

Now he that planteth and he that watereth are one: and every man shall receive his own reward according to his own labour. For we are labourers together with God: ye are God's husbandry, ye are God's building. According to the grace of God which is given unto me, as a wise masterbuilder, I have laid the foundation, and another buildeth thereon. But let every man take heed how he buildeth thereupon. For other foundation can no man lay than that is laid, which is Jesus Christ. Now if any man build upon this foundation gold, silver, precious stones, wood, hay, stubble; Every man's work shall be made manifest: for the day shall declare it, because it shall be revealed by fire; and the fire shall try every man's work of what sort it is. If any man's work abide which he hath built thereupon, he shall receive a reward. If any man's work shall be burned, he shall suffer loss: but he himself shall be saved; yet so as by fire.

1 Corinthians 3:8–15

This passage does not seem to be preached in church much, but it is extremely important. The things we do to build upon the foundation Jesus Christ laid do matter, not because they save us (only Christ does that) but because they lead to everlasting rewards in heaven. If every good and perfect gift we receive on earth comes from above, then the rewards we will receive in heaven are unimaginable! We cannot enter into heaven based on works, but when we are saved by grace through faith in Christ, our works built on His foundation lead to rewards. Similarly, there are varying degrees of eternal punishment for those separated from God in hell, as Jesus illustrated in His parable of the wicked servant in Luke 12:42–48, in Revelation 20:12–13, and in other passages in Scripture.

In the passage above from 1 Corinthians, we clearly see that there will be those who barely skate by into heaven simply because of the fact that they are covered by the blood of Jesus Christ. These will receive no rewards. How sad is that? We also see that the works will be divided between the things that can burn (wood, hay, stubble) and the things that can survive fire (gold, silver, precious stones). Only the works that survive the fire will be accredited on the day of the test.

Maintaining Our Awareness of Our Identity

God is redeeming all of His creation, and part of His redemption plan, according to the book of Revelation, is that He will make all things new. In this new creation, He is restoring things back to the way they should be, and we are a part of this journey. The road to perfection is illuminated by God's Word. He guides us with His Word (*logos*) and His voice (*rhema*). He takes us from glory to glory as we walk in faith, discipline, obedience, and discernment. Our identity doesn't need maintaining—that is always there—but our carnality can struggle with accepting and walking in it. We need to remind ourselves of our true identity and take ownership of it by maintaining our walk in it.

We must walk in victory. We are on the side that has already won, and it is finished. The robber cannot beat you, death has lost its sting, and neither can stop us from crossing the finish line. We are winners because God is for us. The question is, will you live life in this truth? Will you have any rewards waiting for you in heaven?

> *Nay, in all these things we are more than conquerors through him that loved us. For I am persuaded, that neither death, nor life, nor angels, nor principalities, nor powers, nor things present, nor things to come, Nor height, nor depth, nor any other creature, shall be able to separate us from the love of God, which is in Christ Jesus our Lord.*
>
> **Romans 8:37–39**

We must walk in purity. Life will get messy at times, and sometimes we will choose sin, but God cleanses us continually. It is an ongoing process. We may desire not to sin, but as long as we are in our flesh, we will be at war with carnality. So having grace for yourself, be intentional in your fight. Declare with your mouth that you choose not to sin, resist the devil, and ask the Lord to forgive you. Remember that we are being made clean and holy for God by His Spirit's work in us.

> *If we confess our sins, he is faithful and just to forgive us our sins, and to cleanse us from all unrighteousness.*
>
> **1 John 1:9**

We must walk as living pieces of God's workmanship. We are all works of art being created by the greatest artist ever. His work in us is only completed at the moment we take our last breath in these mortal bodies. Imagine that you are clay in the Potter's hands. To remain moldable, the clay needs to have water continually added to it. The water is the Holy Spirit; fellowship with Him and His work keeps us moldable. But if we stay away from the Spirit, we can become dry and brittle. I have seen this so many times: When believers neglect the living water, they become brittle, and they crumble because they can no longer move within the Potter's hands. Luckily, God makes beautiful things out of broken pieces of clay, so no matter where you find yourself, the truth remains that you are His masterpiece.

For we are his workmanship, created in Christ Jesus unto good works, which God hath before ordained that we should walk in them.

Ephesians 2:10

We must allow ourselves to be blessed with every spiritual blessing. The imperishable things that are not tied to the physical things of this world are made available to us; these are the things of the Spirit. They are the unfathomable treasures of God. These treasures are so great that Scripture tells us that it will take the rest of eternity to unfold the vastness of the blessings. Do you know and recognize your spiritual blessings? Have you ever given thanks to God for them?

Blessed be the God and Father of our Lord Jesus Christ, who hath blessed us with all spiritual blessings in heavenly places in Christ.

Ephesians 1:3

We must maintain our membership in Christ's body. You are not a family of one. Your identity in Christ means you are part of a much larger living family, the body of Christ, and in that body, you have a purpose and a function. You have a place in the body that requires active engagement and participation. What body part are you? The chapter on the five callings will help you determine that. Know who you are, and don't rob others of your gifts.

"So we, being many, are one body in Christ, and every one members one of another"

Romans 12:5

A True Testimony of Identity Theft

Identity theft is possible when we do not actively walk in our true identity. In order to experience healing of our identity, we might have to surrender some things that we have been holding onto. Here is a story where someone's identity was compromised and how he was healed.

Back when I was leading a prayer ministry at a large church, we had a designated area where people who needed prayer could go. One Sunday, a young man in his mid-twenties came to me for prayer. I could tell that he was very upset, an impression he quickly confirmed when he told me that his life was a mess and that he needed prayer. When I asked him to tell me what was going on, he proceeded to tell me about a whole list of problems: he struggled with drug addiction that he could not stop, he did not have a relationship with his dad, he had been living on the streets, and he was struggling with his sexuality. He also mentioned that the only person he could talk to was his best friend, a girl he knew from high school. As I listened to the Lord's voice for direction, I heard God say that this young man was experiencing an identity crisis and that I needed to pray for his mind to be healed.

Out of the many times I had people come to me wanting prayer, there were some times when people didn't really want healing. Either they were unwilling to make the changes necessary and exercise the discipline needed for healing, or they just wanted God's approval to keep living the way they wanted without the consequences. But that is not how God works; sometimes, God will only bring healing in our lives when we are willing to submit to His will and give Him permission to take control and work within us. I knew this would be the case for this young man, and I could tell he was at the point of surrender. I asked him if he wanted God's perfect will for him and if he wanted to be healed, and he said yes. So with a sense that God was about to do something amazing, I started to pray for his true identity to be restored.

Just as the Holy Spirit began to lead me in prayer, I saw in a waking vision God's hand reaching into the young man's brain and beginning to untangle it. As I watched, there was a snake that was wound throughout his mind that had a stronghold on his thoughts. When the snake was untangled from his brain, God crushed it and pulled it out. Just as I was seeing this, the demeanor of the young man changed. He looked up suddenly with a glow on his face, and I knew that his mind was healed. He said he could understand his situation from a spiritual perspective and knew the robber had a hold on his thoughts. God had just released him from a false identity that was tied up in lies and worldly things. He ceased to have a desire for drugs or an attraction to men, and he now had an incredible sense of peace and purpose. Supernaturally through prayer, God healed him and brought him into his real identity.

The following week, he came back to church looking for me in the prayer corner. He was so excited and wanted to tell me about all the amazing things that had happened that week. He told me that for the first time in years, he had not used nor even had a desire to use drugs. He had gone on a date with the girl whom he had considered his best friend. He had signed up for counseling. He had also reconciled with his dad, which led to his moving back home. This healing of his true identity was drastic and instant. I want to emphasize again that the fact that he wanted God's perfect will and that he gave God permission to restore his true identity were, I believe, the major factors in his receiving instant total deliverance and healing. In light of this story, I encourage you, if there is anything you are struggling with or if you are in need of a miracle, first surrender to God and give Him permission to do whatever needs to be done. Be prepared because He will lead you through whatever challenges you need in order to have victory and to receive His best and perfect will.

In Closing

Thank God that because of what He has done, we have a new identity in Jesus Christ that is not of this lost and dying world. Just think of all the promises and characteristics we have as a result. Think about how much God has changed you and will change you. What have you given up to follow Christ? Was it worth it? Let this reflection of your past and your potential encourage you in your growth.

Accepting Christ brings change, and with change comes greater transformation. This transformation underlies what we think about and how we think concerning others, our jobs, the future, God, life, and everything. This is all part of the renewing of our mind mentioned in Romans 12:2:

And be not conformed to this world: but be ye transformed by the renewing of your mind, that ye may prove what is that good, and acceptable, and perfect, will of God.

Our minds need to be renewed to take on and live out our new identity in Christ to the fullest. Where are you now in this process?

What do you spend your time thinking about the most? Do your thoughts glorify God? Remember that even though we may not have a perfect thought life yet, we are no longer slaves to sin. If you are discouraged, and you know there are areas of your thought life that need to be renewed, ask God for help. He will give you strength and healing. It is God's will for you to walk in the fullness of your true identity; He died to give you that gift. So choose to walk in the fullness of your identity, and the next time someone asks you to tell him or her about yourself, start by sharing your real identity in Jesus Christ.

Closing Prayer

Dear heavenly Father, thank You that, because of Your finished work on the cross, You have provided a new identity in Christ for those who believe in You as Lord and Savior. Thank You that our real identity is secure and imperishable in You. Thank You that You have prepared a place for us in heaven. Thank You for Your love. Thank You for changing us to be more like You.

Help us to walk with confidence in all the glorious privileges of who You say we are. Help us to identify and relinquish the perishable things in this world that we may attach our identity to, and keep us safe from the strategies of the thief. Restore everything that is intended for us that has been taken by the robber. Remind us daily to store up riches in heaven. Remind us that because we are not of this world, there is nothing here to fear. In the precious name of Jesus, amen.

CHAPTER 2:

The Five Callings

And he gave some, apostles; and some, prophets; and some, evangelists; and some, pastors and teachers; For the perfecting of the saints, for the work of the ministry, for the edifying of the body of Christ.

Ephesians 4:11–12

In my years of ministry, I have always been sad to see people who have been Christians their entire lives struggling, discouraged, and unfulfilled, pursuing careers they are unhappy with because it was not their calling. The very definition of *career* means "an occupation undertaken, with opportunities for progress," but in these cases, it often leads to emptiness and stagnation.[47] Whenever I have a chance to talk with them, I ask, "What is God's calling for your life?" Usually, they either struggle to answer, or they simply have no idea. When I follow up by asking them about the five callings the Bible describes, most do not understand what I am referring to. How can this be? These are Christians who have spent their entire lives in churches of various denominations. In contrast, when I talk to those who know their callings and purposes in Christ, I find that they are already walking in their callings and have the satisfaction that comes through continual spiritual growth and being who God made them to be. It is regrettable that there are churches unable to teach their congregations to walk in the fullness and provision of God's calling for their lives.

One example of the wrong way to attempt to bring fullness into people's lives can be observed in some segments of prosperity gospel theology. Some churches will take this type of teaching beyond what the Bible says. They will encourage Christians to act according to their fleshly desires instead of encouraging them to surrender those desires and actions to God. In churches like these, Christian terms like "blessings," "fullness," and "provision" tend to be bandied about without mentioning the conditions for those promises. True blessings and fullness do not come from selfishly seeking the riches of the earth by manipulating the King of heaven. They come from obeying the King, and provision comes with doing what we were made to do.

Human beings can be compared to tools, each uniquely created for a specific purpose. Do you think a screwdriver can fulfill its purpose if it is being used as a hammer? It may show limited competence when used this way, but over time and with repeated use, the screwdriver will likely become damaged, and the handle may chip and eventually break. At that point, it will need to be restored before it can be used again, even for its purpose as a screwdriver. But when a screwdriver is used for its designed purpose, it functions properly: it performs its tasks efficiently and quickly, and it stays intact.

Our callings are placed within us at birth. It is the deeply-felt passion to fulfill those callings that the devil tries to steal from us. Our callings gratify our souls, fill our spirits, and allow us to accomplish what we were made for. Although the scope of biblical authority has changed, all five of the callings are alive and well in the world today because God's design is perfect and because He understands humanity's nature perfectly. The system has been handed down over generations because it works. You may be called to operate in church ministry, or God may desire you to be His light in the area of business, education, research, or anything else. Whatever the Lord has for you, it will be fulfilling. Each calling is just as important as any other calling. Do not be hasty as you identify which calling may be yours. The purpose of understanding the five callings and knowing your calling is to fulfill God's perfect will for your life and to be who He designed you to be so that you can gain wisdom and learn how to interact with members of the other callings. Once you know these things and walk in them with a complete team effort, as Paul said, you will surpass all your successes of the past.

The Concern

Christians fall into one of four categories when it comes to the five callings:

1. They know their calling and are walking in it.
2. They know their calling but are afraid to walk in it.
3. They are ignorant of their calling because they have not been taught it.
4. They do not believe the five callings apply today.

No matter what category you find yourself in, it is my prayer that this chapter will encourage you to operate within God's perfect will and to accurately pursue His calling for your life. I understand that some people do not believe that the five callings are applicable today or that they all apply to everyone. If you find yourself to be one of these people, please take the time to read through the chapter. Once you have finished, ask yourself: "Do I see these callings in members of the church today? Is one of these callings speaking to me?" Take your questions to the Lord in prayer. I have total confidence that you do have a calling from God, and once you begin walking in it, your life will change. I have seen so many Christians who have blossomed and come alive once they have recognized their callings and started operating in them. My heart's desire is for you to be able to do the same.

As Christians, it is essential that we know and understand the calling God has for our lives. God has a destiny, a plan, and a purpose for us. He also has an incredible love for us. David, the king, knew the truth of this in his own life, as he declared to God,

> *My substance was not hid from thee, when I was made in secret, and curiously wrought in the lowest parts of the earth. Thine eyes did see my substance, yet being unperfect; and in thy book all my members were written, which in continuance were fashioned, when as yet there was none of them.*
>
> **Psalm 139:15–16**

How amazing is that? The one who holds all things together and created all things with His voice alone is so closely involved with our lives, despite His separation from sin. Just imagine how much He longs for us to choose to walk in the callings for which He created us. From our very conception, we are designed to operate in one of the five callings. To identify these callings for ourselves is not meant to be a chance to create titles for ourselves for the sake of our own pride or to justify actions contradictory to Scripture; these callings are simply our commission as Christians to do something. If you can grasp the significance of this chapter and identify your calling, you will be turned in the right direction so that you may walk forward and fulfill your destiny.

Why So Few?

In Matthew 22:14, Jesus declared to his disciples, "Many are called, but few are chosen." Why are there so few representing Him if many are called? The calling is the invitation to salvation through Jesus, and the chosen are the ones who accept the invitation and comply with its terms. The invitation is either heard, not heard, or rejected. The term for accepting the calling is submission to Christ as Lord and Savior. This includes surrendering to God's calling on your life. What is most important is the answer we give God.

Let's look at the word "called" (*kaleo* in the original Greek), as used in Matthew 22:14. It derives from the same root word as

70

the word "calling."[48] This is an active word indicating that one is continually being summoned or invited to participate; it is not a one-time invitation. Some teachers believe this verse is saying that God only chooses a few people to have a calling, but I believe a strict hermeneutical study, taking into account the context of the totality of Scripture, easily shows this teaching to be inaccurate and ultimately destructive to the order God has designed. Only a few are chosen because only a few respond.

Next, let's look at accepting the invitation to the calling. Have we accepted Jesus Christ as Lord and Savior? If so, we are being called by an all-knowing God Who has had our purpose in mind forever! There are no time limits on God, and our purpose is not just now popping into His mind. It has been there for eternity. Since our creation, we have had purpose and unique value. His desire is for us to walk out our purpose through sanctification, from glory to glory, into eternity with Him.

You are being called. Are you willing to surrender to the Lord to be chosen and used by Him for your perfect purpose?

The Five Callings: Each Is Essential

The five callings, according to the Apostle Paul in Ephesians 4:11–16, are:

1. The apostle
2. The prophet
3. The evangelist
4. The pastor
5. The teacher

Paul describes the church as a human body and illustrates that the entire body of Christ is joined and held together by every supporting ligament. Each part must do its job so that the body can function and grow. When all the callings work together in unity, the church is built up, protected, encouraged, and strengthened in love. Of the many churches I have worked with, the ones that have this God-designed system in place thrive and prosper the most; they tend to grow more easily and even seem to be more theologically sound in all areas. In fact, without all of these callings in place, ministries within the church will sometimes struggle or even fail completely. A balance of the callings within a church makes it more complete and takes it to the next level of effectiveness, blessing, and success.

The Apostle Paul also tells us how the different callings should work and interact with each other:

> *For as the body is one, and hath many members, and all the members of that one body, being many, are one body: so also is Christ. For by one Spirit are we all baptized into one body, whether we be Jews or Gentiles, whether we be bond or free; and have been all made to drink into one Spirit. For the body is not one member, but many. ...But now hath God set the members every one of them in the body, as it hath pleased him. And if they were all one member, where were the body? But now are they many members, yet but one body. And the eye cannot say unto the hand, I have no need of thee: nor again the head to the feet, I have no need of you. Nay, much more those members of the body, which seem to be more feeble, are necessary. ...That there should be no schism in the body; but that the members should have the same care one for another. And whether one member suffer, all the members suffer with it; or one member be honoured, all the members rejoice with it.*
> **1 Corinthians 12:12–14, 18–22, 25–26**

Unfortunately, sometimes pride in church leadership can get in the way of reaching the next level of spiritual success. Pastors who struggle with pride are not always willing to acknowledge

72

they may need help from the other callings, or they may have difficulty admitting that they are not walking in their true calling. Some pastors will try to operate as apostles out of a desire to hold greater power than a pastor is meant to have. Yet by doing so, these pastors compromise their ability to grow their churches properly. While members of any of the five callings can preach, not everyone is called to be a preacher. I know some "preachers" operating in the calling of the pastor who are miserable, burnt out, depressed, and unsatisfied. They think this is due to stress, busyness, or having too much to manage. These may be true, but I would suggest that the real reason for their fatigue may be that they are walking in the wrong calling. If we are operating in callings that do not line up to how God designed us, then we end up working against ourselves and neglect the importance of each calling.

Callings in the Secular World

The five callings are made for the building of the church, but they can also be observed wherever organizational structure is needed: in the military, in entertainment, in government, and in technology, to name a few. Roles in the business world can be used to illustrate the five callings, as most people are familiar with their positions and have to interact with them in everyday life. In a corporation, the top position is the CEO, and under him are the VP, the CFO, HR, and the sales department. Each of these is critical in the function of a business. When working with people in the business world, understanding these callings helps us to interact well with them and may also help us identify those who are not operating in their intended callings.

These are the business roles corresponding to each of the five callings:

1. 1. The CEO (chief executive officer) is the apostle. For the CEO to perform well, he must have a good understanding

of all the other callings. A CEO can be referred to as the "Jack of all trades." The CEO loves to build things; he works best starting with nothing but a dream and then making it a reality.

2. The VP (vice president) takes the same role as the prophet does in the church. The VP has the ability to look beyond the horizon to see the future and warn the CEO of potential problems that need to be avoided. The VP can be considered as the one who rides upon the bench beside the driver on a stagecoach, keeping a lookout for danger, recommending a safe direction, and, if necessary, defending the stagecoach. A VP loves truth. He feels most fulfilled when speaking truth, thinking about truth, or searching truth out.

3. The CFO (chief financial officer) is the teacher. He has the responsibility of gathering and keeping track of all the details. When the CEO comes up with great and impressive dreams, the CFO brings the focus down to earth and searches out what is available to make it reality. CFOs are known to operate at the ten-foot level to see the details, while the CEO is flying at thirty thousand feet so he can see the big picture. CFOs are fact-oriented and realistic, and they have difficulty settling with open-ended dreams.

4. Those in HR (human resources) are the pastors. They are the ones who interface with people. They have big hearts that desire to make everything better, but they tend not to do well with confrontation. They are always there to hear others' problems and offer sincere empathy and advice. Members of HR are motivated by people.

5. The salespeople are the evangelists. They are energetic and always on the move. Salespeople give their all but can sometimes push themselves too hard and run out of energy suddenly. They are commonly referred to as the "go-getters." Salespeople are highly focused and determined once they lock onto a target. They are motivated by fun and will not

miss an exciting meeting.

Now that we have a better idea of what each of the callings means, let's look at each calling in more detail.

A Closer Look - Apostle/CEO

The apostle loves to build things. He (or she) has the gift of taking ideas or dreams and making them reality. An apostle with a calling to ministry will be a kingdom builder, starting churches, organizing outreach events, and creating ministry projects. In the business world, the CEO can operate as the head of a corporation or of a small startup business. In the entertainment industry, this role would be fulfilled by the producer, who oversees the many different departments working on a film. The apostle's passion is motivated by the desire to create a kingdom, so the most important question for him is, whose kingdom is he building? An apostle walking with God builds an extension of God's kingdom, as we see in Paul's desire to go places where no one had yet preached.

Apostles are natural leaders, and because of their authority and understanding of all the other callings, people are more likely to take directions from them. Their understanding of all the callings is usually developed over time by practical learning experiences acquired while holding roles in some of the other callings. A desire to learn and walk in all the callings is necessary in order for apostles to become more effective, balanced leaders. Although they can do any one of the callings well, they only truly thrive on building the kingdom and making dreams and ideas into reality.

Because apostles like to work at the thirty thousand-foot level, they are able to see the general spiritual landscape and see where and how the Lord is working. With this comes the gift of networking people together to make existing ministries more effective or the ability to bring together teams capable of making ideas into reality.

A good apostle or CEO understands the importance of each calling because he can relate to all of them. He appreciates the need for each calling in order to build the kingdom.

Aside from the lack of proper structural leadership within churches that do not recognize the calling of apostles, another resultant casualty is their relationships with other churches. In these cases, the relational networking gift of the apostle is not allowed to operate, so instead, churches tend to become isolated and build their own kingdoms. They tend to be unwilling or unable to see the other parts of the body they could team up with; as such, they do not utilize the power of unity that God's Word describes. Jesus Himself gave reason for the importance of unity:

> *That they all may be one; as thou, Father, art in me, and I in thee, that they also may be one in us: that the world may believe that thou hast sent me.*
>
> **John 17:21**

When the body of Christ comes together in unity, then the world will believe God sent Jesus Christ. The apostolic calling is the position God designed to bring this unity about; it is no surprise, then, that the devil has worked so hard to diminish it.

When an apostle is walking with God and moving in submission to His perfect will, he will excel in starting ministries and expanding the kingdom of God with the good news of Jesus Christ. Apostles are the generals leading the charge into the enemy's territory; therefore, they tend to face the toughest attacks. It is important that apostles walk in discipline, be covered with prayer, and keep the full armor of God on. The apostle who is not walking in full submission to the Lord can become very hardheaded, controlling, and fixated on building his own personal kingdom. He may introduce "new revelation" that is not supported by Scripture.

If you are an apostle, you must take the reins of whatever stagecoach team God has to give you. Without a driver, the goods are never delivered to people in need, and the needy suffer. There is potential within you to change entire industries or affect entire regions of the world for the better. Walk in and accomplish your calling.

> *For unto whomsoever much is given, of him shall be much required: and to whom men have committed much, of him they will ask the more.*
>
> **Luke 12:48**

Prophet/VP

The prophet is intuitive, discerning, and focuses with single-minded intensity on truth. A prophet thrives when working closely with an apostle, who can work together with him (or her) to help prevent others from falling into unnecessary or difficult circumstances. Because prophets hate to see people go through hardships they see as avoidable, they will operate with wisdom and quickly make decisions. They love it when building a kingdom goes smoothly.

Prophets are like moths to a flame when it comes to seeing any attacks or distractions from the enemy. They respond to these attacks by making an effort to resolve issues without delay. When a prophet is allowed to operate in his gifting unhindered, he can usually fix or divert a problem before most people even know it is there. If sin is an issue in the situation, the prophet will not tolerate it for long. He feels he must deal with problems quickly, and he tends to do so with little mercy or compassion to prevent unnecessary interruptions to the process. A prophet knows that there are enough legitimate difficulties in life to navigate without having to take on extra problems. When a prophet says, "I told you so," it is not because he loves being right, but because he does not want to see people go through difficulties that can obviously be avoided.

Apostles and prophets work well as a close team. The prophet always has the apostle's back and is ready to defend God's territory and to call out dangers beyond the horizon. The prophet can also supplement the apostle's ministry with visions and dreams. He can, however, tend to be very narrow-minded and preoccupied with one small part of the bigger picture. That laser focus is a part of his discernment and is a needed gift to accomplish his job. His voice is his tool, and when a prophet is prevented from using it, he will either blow up from a buildup of revelations or will stop speaking because he has been robbed by bitterness or hurt.

When prophets are free to speak truth, they are indispensable. They are willing to say what needs to be said, even if no one else will say it. Prophets are the ones who speak tough love, so their friends tend to consist mostly of people who appreciate truth. Their words of truth tend to be short and to the point. They usually only expound upon what they have already said when prompted to do so. They are great at giving orders, which they usually do briefly and bluntly.

Prophets are resilient and do not easily give up, fail, or accept defeat. For them, a problem is to be solved, not dismissed. This is why they make excellent VPs in the corporate world, as they can handle the more specific issues, allowing the CEO to focus on the larger picture with more freedom.

The loss to the church body that rejects the calling of the prophet is clear. Without prophets, there is no one to bring warnings to the church through visions and dreams, to strengthen, to encourage, and to comfort believers in the unique way that prophets do. Prophets are also needed to bring conviction of sin and call out wickedness within the church. Spiritual warfare is the prophet's specialty. The devil seeks to diminish the role of the prophet in the church because he does not want to be exposed or threatened by the work of the Holy Spirit through the prophet.

When a prophet is walking with God and surrenders to His perfect will, he is used powerfully as he works closely with an apostle. If he is not allowed to speak out, or if he already has bitterness in his life, he can become negative, controlling, hyper-critical, resentful, and unpleasant to be around. Compromised prophets are a poison to the church.

If you are a prophet, you need to realize that not all Christians are aware of the same things you are. God has chosen you to be at the forefront and to see the visions, dreams, and warnings. It is very important that you share these if God asks you to do so. Your job is to ask the Lord when, where, and how to share them. It may be that the leadership in the church needs to know what the Lord is saying. As the person riding in front beside the stagecoach driver, it is your responsibility to tell the driver what you see so that he can make the necessary adjustments in steering the stagecoach.

> *Before I formed thee in the belly I knew thee; and before thou camest forth out of the womb I sanctified thee, and I ordained thee a prophet unto the nations.*
>
> **Jeremiah 1:5**

Pastor/HR

Pastors love people generally with more compassion and warmth than the members of the other callings and are friendly with just about anyone. People feel comfortable going to pastors for comfort or advice because they will always be welcomed with understanding. A pastor is more concerned about people than about rules or systems to live by, and he (or she) chooses mercy over condemnation. The pastor, like an HR representative, thrives on conflict resolution and keeping the peace. When a fight or disagreement is avoided, he has accomplished his calling for the day.

Because pastors are great listeners and struggle with maintaining discipline, people often take advantage of them, especially people with addictions. Pastors are willing to sacrifice their own best interests to a great degree for the people they care for, yet it can take a very long time for them to get to a point where they are willing to have confrontation over an injustice. Pastors also tend to bottle up their emotions, which can, unfortunately, lead to an explosive release.

It is said because the Bible is what it claims to be, the inspired, inerrant, and infallible Word of God, then preaching is the highest calling known to man. As pastors fall under this high calling, they are also called to love the sheep. However, this love may take them too far if they become tolerant of wickedness. An overabundance of tolerance can allow evil to subtly soak into pastors' homes and relationships, wreaking havoc on their lives. When this happens, they need an apostle or prophet to remind them of the truth. True love is strengthened by truth; compassion alone can lead to complacency that may result in destruction.

The church body universally accepts the calling of a pastor, so one of the devil's most common strategies against pastors is to attack their character. He will try to frame them as faithless hypocrites or tempt them to fall into a secret sin so that they can easily be blackmailed. A pastor whose integrity has been violated cannot teach all of Scripture or confront sins in the church without risking exposure. Pastors often have only a few trustworthy people to talk to because gossip is rampant in the church. Pastors need extra prayer and encouragement to protect against the strategies of the enemy.

When a pastor is walking with God and surrenders to His perfect will, he brings healing, understanding, and the peace of Jesus to any situation. A pastor can speak wisdom with understanding into a divisive situation to help bring resolution. When he is unbalanced or excessively codependent, he will tend to be too tolerant of evil or abuse. He can also become very one-sided, showing favoritism to one party over another. A pastor who has fallen into this pit is not in a position to fulfill his potential as his calling requires.

If you are a pastor, preach the Word with a heart full of Christ's love. Know that your calling is close to the heart of God because

80

the heart is where His love rests. Without love and compassion, this world would be a much darker place. As the darkness rises, the carnal love of the world has no real power. Only true love has the ability to leave a lasting impression. Rise up and take your place in this world of confusion and loneliness.

> *And I will give you pastors according to mine heart, which shall feed you with knowledge and understanding.*

Jeremiah 3:15

Teacher/CFO

Facts, details, and accuracy are the heart of a teacher, and this is a great gift when it comes to gathering everything there is to know about something. The teacher has the gift of seeing the small details that most people overlook. When you tell a teacher something, he (or she) will usually ask for more information. When the teacher tells you something, he will tend to be a little more verbose than others would be. He is excited and passionate to find explanations for things and feels the need to share with others what is on his mind. A teacher looks at everything from the ten-foot level and expects others to see that way, too. Because of the teacher's drive to search out the details, he can be hard to live with for those who are not also teachers. In fact, it seems to be a trend that most teachers marry other teachers.

Teachers/CFOs are important to an apostle/CEO if he wants to build kingdoms or projects successfully. Teachers excel in bringing the facts of reality to every situation, and if they don't know the facts, there is no one better at doing the research to discover them. Teachers are analytical and love order and logic. As a result, they can have difficulty putting faith in the unseen. Of the people in all of the five callings, teachers have the most difficult time understanding and walking in the supernatural. Doing things in blind faith naturally seems ridiculous when there is an entire world of physical objects and ideas to understand and analyze.

When it comes to change, teachers are the last to accept it. Teachers find comfort in keeping lists and being able to check items off those lists. They thrive on routine. Most teachers are introverted. Although they love to share information, they can quickly be drained in social settings. To overcome this, teachers can be asked to research whatever changes are being considered, which gives them time to process the idea of change.

There is a saying: "Ignorance is bliss." In reality, ignorance can be deadly. This is why the devil seeks to keep teachers from operating in the body of Christ. Teachers are needed to remind us of the details in Scripture that expose false doctrine. Because most Christians glance over the details, or the details get lost with time, the devil is sometimes able to slip demonic doctrine into the church without resistance. The enemy's details fill in the gaps where sound doctrine has been rooted out. Without a teacher to utilize the details in Scripture to correct the errors or the prophet to call out deceiving spirits, the growth of false doctrine in the church is inevitable.

When a teacher is walking with God and surrenders to His perfect will, he discovers new things and brings a better understanding of knowledge that is beneficial to kingdom-building or to organizations. If he is bitter, resentful, and operating in unforgiveness, he may believe himself superior to others and to the position God has ordained for him. He may even attempt to operate as an apostle or pastor, with very little success.

If you are a teacher, you are living in the greatest time in history to walk in your calling. There has never been a time when information and resources were so easily accessible as they are now. At this point in history, the details and facts of Scripture are overlooked in favor of personal feelings and fantasies. Take your place, and help round up the lost and the delusional!

In all things shewing thyself a pattern of good works: in doctrine shewing uncorruptness, gravity, sincerity, Sound speech, that cannot be condemned; that he that is of the contrary part may be ashamed, having no evil thing to say of you.

Titus 2:7–8

Evangelist/Sales

Evangelists are the easiest of all the callings to recognize. They love social settings, going on hikes, and exploring exciting new places. They are always full of energy and ready to go anywhere as long as it grabs their interest. The evangelist's personality is fun and energetic and easily attracts attention. He (or she) likes to move fast and bring in new recruits to the church rather than work with those who are already in the church and struggling. Evangelists can sell anything when they have the motivation, and their motivation is usually to have fun. For evangelists, one of the most thrilling things to do is to win souls for Jesus Christ, just as it is the ability to persuade people that excites the salesperson in the corporate world.

As long as evangelists are feeling entertained, they are excellent at starting up new projects for kingdom-building or selling ideas to raise support. However, the moment things start to slow down and become mundane, evangelists tend to be the first to jump ship and move on to another project. Once a kingdom or business has been established, its success will be determined by whether evangelists/ salespeople will continue to function within them. Bringing positive evangelists together as a team brings great rewards. When the team loses interest and the fun is over, the evangelists' charismatic natures draw other team members out of the project with them, especially if they leave on bad terms.

Newton's first law of motion is often stated as "a body in motion stays in motion, but a body at rest stays at rest."[49] The devil will attack evangelists in order to keep the church body at rest. When a church is at rest, it becomes like stagnant water, which is undrinkable due to the growth of bacteria. A stagnant church will eventually dry up and die. Evangelists are the explorers who discover exciting new things and new ways to do old things. They help give the other callings the momentum to keep them moving to keep them from becoming stagnant.

When the evangelist is walking with God and surrenders to His perfect will, the kingdom will be energized and refreshed. People who are not currently being reached with the good news of Jesus will hear of salvation and a greater purpose for their lives for the first time. An evangelist can carry a lantern into a city enslaved to fog, and his light will give direction to all the inhabitants trapped within it. However, when the evangelist is not walking with God, his social nature may draw him to get involved with things that may seem exciting, like sex, drugs, and late-night parties. The evangelist must be aware of himself; he is intended to be an influencer of the world, not to be influenced by it.

If you are an evangelist, please jump into your calling and help bring life back to the dead in the church. Stir the stale waters, and if the water doesn't start to flow, take the people who are on life support with you to a place where they can flourish. Our society is full of people who have no ambition and who are slaves to apathy because of the thievery of the devil. You can make a difference by selling them the hope and future God desires through salvation in Jesus Christ. What could be more exciting than seeing the power of God change a life like that?

But watch thou in all things, endure afflictions, do the work of an evangelist, make full proof of thy ministry.
2 Timothy 4:5

Four General Aspects of Our Callings

While there are five different callings, there are four universal aspects of all of our callings as Christians. These aspects are: the calling to believe in Jesus Christ, the calling to be a disciple of Jesus Christ, the calling to be a witness of Jesus Christ, and the calling to be an active member of the body of Christ. These are all parts of our daily walk as followers of Jesus Christ. Now that we have discussed the five main callings, let's highlight the four aspects:

1. The calling to believe in Jesus Christ

God is faithful, by whom ye were called unto the fellowship of his Son Jesus Christ our Lord.

1 Corinthians 1:9

We are called to believe in the faithfulness of God, that He provided redemption through Jesus Christ, His only Son. It is by this faith that we are saved and enter fellowship with Him as our Lord and Savior.

2. The calling to be a disciple of Jesus Christ

And he said to them all, If any man will come after me, let him deny himself, and take up his cross daily, and follow me.

Luke 9:23

If Jesus Christ is our Lord, then we are called to become His disciples. We do this by denying our sinful nature and choosing to be obedient to Him on a daily basis. Jesus leads each step, and we are to follow.

3. The calling to be a witness of Jesus Christ

And Jesus came and spake unto them, saying, All power is given unto me in heaven and in earth. Go ye therefore, and teach all nations, baptizing them in the name of the Father, and of the Son, and of the Holy Ghost: Teaching them to observe all things whatsoever I have commanded you: and,

85

lo, I am with you alway, even unto the end of the world. Amen.
Matthew 28:18–20

Once Jesus has saved us, and we are in a relationship with Him, it becomes our responsibility to share our testimonies of Christ to the world around us. The robber adds many external pressures to our environment in an attempt to silence our testimony, but that should give us all the more reason to witness.

4. The calling to be active members of the body of Christ

For as the body is one, and hath many members, and all the members of that one body, being many, are one body: so also is Christ. For by one Spirit are we all baptized into one body, whether we be Jews or Gentiles, whether we be bond or free; and have been all made to drink into one Spirit.
1 Corinthians 12:12–13

Regardless of the existence of man-made denominations, Jesus makes it clear that there is only one body of Christ and that each of us has a critical part to play. Whatever our callings are, we all get our gifting and strength from the same source, the Holy Spirit.

Now that we know what all of us are responsible for, let's walk in the individual calling that makes each of us unique in how we are meant to serve the Lord.

Are Our Motives Pure?

Let us not therefore judge one another any more: but judge this rather, that no man put a stumblingblock or an occasion to fall in his brother's way.

Romans 14:13

When someone is walking in bitterness, unforgiveness, or has a critical spirit, his frustrations will often play themselves out according to what his calling is meant to be. For example, an evangelist will judge all the other callings for taking religion too seriously and for not enjoying life enough. An apostle will judge all the other callings for not taking on the world with the same passion and conviction that he does. A teacher will judge everyone for not being as knowledgeable as he is and for not researching as well as he is able to do. A pastor will judge prophets for being too harsh and lacking in compassion, and a prophet will judge pastors for not being stern enough.

Too often in the church, I have seen people who judge and belittle others simply because they are not similar enough to them in their personalities, their roles, or their actions. We need to recognize that people with callings different from ours will go about doing things differently than we will, and that is how God intends it to be. If you are someone who judges and belittles others because they are not like you, I urge you right now to go before the Lord and ask for forgiveness. Pray for understanding to be able to see them the way God sees them. Recognize that God has designed them that way for a purpose. It is good that each calling thinks, works, and handles things differently because when we come together, we will be healthier and more balanced as one complete body. Each calling is a spoke on a wagon wheel. When all five spokes are in place, the wagon can move forward and carry a heavy load much farther than if a spoke or two is missing. A wheel with a missing spoke may work for a time, but eventually, the added stress will cause first burnout and then total failure if not fixed. Let's recognize each other's callings and encourage one another to unite in victory with our Lord Jesus Christ. The time for ignoring or misusing others' callings and our own must come to an end!

We must move forward in our callings with humility, free from pride. It's time to serve the Most High God in our callings with the gifts and tools given to us and to be ambassadors reflecting His light here on earth with the hope, love, truth, and grace He provides for us. So move forward in the spirit of peace, unity, and blessing to be all that God made and called you to be. Surrender to His calling and walk into your purpose!

> *Let every man abide in the same calling wherein he was called. Art thou called being a servant? care not for it: but if thou mayest be made free, use it rather. For he that is called in the Lord, being a servant, is the Lord's freeman: likewise also he that is called, being free, is Christ's servant.*
>
> **1 Corinthians 7:20–22**

Why We Are Robbed

> *Hope deferred maketh the heart sick: but when the desire cometh, it is a tree of life.*
>
> **Proverbs 13:12**

The robber (devil) does not want us to know that there is a thriving life to be had walking in our callings. He prefers that we continually live with sick and depressed hearts. Why? Because when we function in our callings and operate under our anointings, we thrive and become who God made us to be. This is a threat to the robber's kingdom. When we walk in God's perfect calling for our lives, things do not automatically become easier, but we come to experience fulfillment, satisfaction, and the production of much fruit.

What is the result of a successful attempt of the devil to hide our true callings from us? For nonbelievers, this manifests as continued bondage. As for believers, a lack of purpose locks them into an anemic state. Spiritual anemia leaves a Christian drained, weak, exhausted. Anemic Christians are never able to get ahead because they cannot exercise the spiritual authority they have in Christ Jesus when they surrender to His will. We, as Christians, will always be drained when we consistently do what we were not made to do! It is quite agitating that the secular world generally operates under the system God designed for the church with success, while many churches do not preach it, teach it, or believe in it. As long as the five callings will not be recognized universally in the church, portions of the church will remain anemic. Due to this pernicious disease, these portions will be incapable of growing to the level to which they aspire. This should not make us feel incapable of change but should instead motivate us to bring emphasis to all five callings in the church.

The robber has no legal right to shut the door between God and us, nor can he prevent us from accessing our purpose. Despite his best efforts to hide the door from us, only we can put up a block against God. Yet God is faithful to be found by those who seek Him and His purposes. Jeremiah wrote to the captives in Babylon, prophesying God's word to them:

> *For I know the thoughts that I think toward you, saith the Lord, thoughts of peace, and not of evil, to give you an expected end. Then shall ye call upon me, and ye shall go and pray unto me, and I will hearken unto you. And ye shall seek me, and find me, when ye shall search for me with all your heart.*
>
> **Jeremiah 29:11–13**

How beautiful this promise was, and how much more does the promise of access to God and the plans He has for us mean today in the time of the finished work of Jesus Christ on the cross? "What shall we then say to these things? If God be for us, who can be against us?" (Romans 8:31).

A Testimony of Obeying the Call

In 2010, I transitioned from architecture into full-time ministry.

One area of my ministry at the time was to lead the prayer and disciple ministries at the singles' group at a local megachurch. On occasion, the Lord would highlight people in the group to me and would allow me to sense their callings, which prompted me to make an effort to get to know them and to listen to their life stories. Once I had asked them questions about their spiritual walk and what their dreams and desires were, I would look for opportunities to encourage them to discover God's calling for their lives. Sometimes, simply praying with them would open the door for God to touch their lives and give them direction; other times, their callings had not yet emerged, and patience with God's timing became necessary. It is always best for Christians to discover their callings on their own, with God's help. I am of the belief that as long as one's heart is desiring God's best, seeking after Him, and willingly surrendering to His Lordship, one will either discover his calling or unknowingly walk into it.

I once met a lady at this singles' group who was a hard-working mother of three. She had recently gone through a divorce and was dealing with depression. She attended church, but she wasn't walking in victory with Jesus; in fact, Jesus wasn't even a priority to her at the time. After talking with her, I could see that she was burdened with inner pain, but I could also see that God had a great calling on her life to be a pastor to women. Eventually, I was able to pray for her and talk to her about God. From that point on, I used every possible opportunity to encourage her to seek God's calling and to introduce her to other people I knew in ministry who could inspire her and speak words of life into her. She had an amazing heart full of compassion and love for people, and it was that heart that the devil wanted to kill the most. She was on depression medication to numb her pain and hold her back even from the feelings that she was meant to have. Pastors are known for their big hearts, so it is no coincidence that the enemy wanted to make her ineffective by robbing her of one of the most precious gifts God had given her to fulfill her calling: her capacity for deep emotion. Fortunately, the devil's schemes are no match for the power of the blood of Jesus!

Because this woman was submissive to God, He began a great work within her. God delivered her from depression so that she no longer needed medication. She began to feel again, and along with these feelings, she had a hunger for the Word and a desire to grow close to God. A fire started to burn down in her soul for the hurting and the lost. A holy boldness began to build up, and she began witnessing to people at her workplace. She started to pray for people. This was when I knew the time was right to confront her about God's calling on her life, so I described the five callings and asked her if she identified with one. Immediately she identified with the pastor's calling. At the time, she was working as a teacher. Because she was operating outside of what God made her to be, she was continuously feeling drained. Now was the time for her to turn away from a calling that was not hers; now was the time for her to walk into her true calling. So together, we began praying specifically for God to open doors for her in full-time ministry as a pastor to women.

Over the course of the next year, as this friend of mine began to follow her calling in faith, God answered her prayers. She met an amazing man of God, whom she eventually married. In the months leading up to their wedding, God was faithful to provide in amazing ways. My friend left her job to pursue her calling as opportunities in ministry began to open. Her husband started a new business that quickly became successful, which made up for the financial loss that she took when she left her paying job. Now, her ministry is blossoming. She regularly speaks at women's retreats and leads Bible studies. She is a testament to God's grace, love, and provision to all of us when we decide to accept God's best for us by choosing to walk in our callings.

Are You Still a Doubter?

There are some who believe the five callings aren't for today. The gifts mentioned in the New Testament are intended for us to display His power, love, grace, and mercy. The robber (the devil) would love for us to believe the spiritual gifts and five callings are no longer active today. The devil can't steal the callings God has for our lives, so instead, he does his best to keep Christians from walking into those callings with a campaign designed to convince us that they no longer apply today.

Now, every Christian I know admits there are still pastors, evangelists, and teachers in existence today. If that is the case, why would God cease creating Christians with the other two callings, those of the prophet and the apostle? All five of these callings can still be seen operating in the areas of business and government today. Does God not say in Acts 2:17 that in the last days, the young will prophesy? And when were apostles no longer needed to plant churches and to provide leadership and organizational structure? Men and women are doing apostolic ministry all around the world right now, but very few recognize it or call it by name. Should it surprise us to learn that the New Testament identifies more apostles than the twelve men who followed Jesus?

You see, just as in warfare, if you remove the generals (apostles) and the intelligence officers (prophets), no matter how powerful your army is, it will be incapable of taking, or even sustaining, ground. If we are honest with ourselves, this is the state of the church today. There can be no doubt that, in a war where so many are being deceived, consequences are deadly and casualties great.

For we wrestle not against flesh and blood, but against principalities, against powers, against the rulers of the darkness of this world, against spiritual wickedness in high places.

Ephesians 6:12

Be Encouraged

Some of us are wondering if we have a purpose or if we will ever accomplish something of value in life. I'm telling you right now, these answers will be found on the road to God's calling for your life, where every necessity is met, every tool is provided, and all the power and anointing necessary for success lies waiting for you. We have only to press in toward our callings with persistence, as Peter encouraged in 2 Peter 1:10: "Wherefore the rather, brethren, give diligence to make your calling and election sure: for if ye do these things, ye shall never fall." Peter wanted us, the church, to be diligent in discovering our callings and to be active in developing the gifts within those callings. If we do these things, we will not stumble in our spiritual growth.

What is your calling? Who did God create you to be? What drives you to get out of bed every day? What is God telling you? He desires us to know and walk in our callings with all confidence and security in whom He made us to be. God never calls us to a place we can never reach. Anything that comes between where we are now and where He is calling us to be cannot ultimately keep us from arriving at our destination. On the contrary, because of God's powerful work in our lives, any obstacles we may face will only benefit us for our good.

God moves through people to accomplish His will; this can be seen in every great movement of God. What is God planning to do through your calling? Recall the stories of God's people found in the Scriptures. Remember that when God got ready to lead His people, He raised up Moses. Remember how God prepared to feed His people who were suffering from famine by placing Joseph in the opportune position to provide food for them. Recall how God prepared to restore Israel by calling Nehemiah to rebuild the wall of Jerusalem. Finally, to prophesy His coming, God raised up Isaiah. Who is God raising you up to be? He is calling for you.

Recognizing your calling can be a profound revelation. More importantly, choosing to walk into that calling will lead you into a closer relationship with God. This, more than anything else, is His perfect will for your life. This is the time to quit stumbling in the desert of God's permissive will and to thrive in the river of His perfect will for your life: the river that flows from the throne room of Almighty God. When you pursue your calling according to God's perfect will, you will meet the desires of your heart that God placed there, you will succeed in being who you were made to be, and you will complete your journey of being made perfect through the sanctifying power of the blood of Jesus Christ. No more buts, no more excuses. Don't let fear hold you back because fear is of the devil, and the devil is the robber.

Seek God first for direction. Is your calling in full-time ministry, or is it in the public workplace, or perhaps both? If you're an apostle, then start building. If you're a prophet, then keep a lookout. If you're a preacher, then listen and love. If you're a teacher, then teach, and if you're an evangelist, then energize the church! Know your calling, and trust God's plan to get you there. Walk into your commission and be a light in a dying world that needs Jesus.

And we know that all things work together for good to them that love God, to them who are the called according to his purpose.

Romans 8:28

Closing prayer

Oh Lord God in heaven, thank You that You have given us life with meaning and purpose. I pray, Lord, that You will reveal the callings You have on our lives. Please bring clarity and direction to all those who do not know how to walk in their callings. For those who are walking in them already, I ask that You would bring a new level of anointing and vision in this season of their lives. I ask that all of us will be given the ability to fulfill our destinies and callings as you make us complete. May we surrender our lives to You so that we may be confident in our commissions. Raise our faith to supernatural levels as we trust in You to fulfill our purposes and callings. To You be all the glory, honor, and praise. In the mighty name of our Lord and Savior Jesus Christ, amen.

CHAPTER 3:

Knowing the Shepherd

The Lord is my shepherd; I shall not want. He maketh me to lie down in green pastures: he leadeth me beside the still waters.

Psalm 23:1–2

What would you do if you suddenly lost access to your Bible and were no longer able to read it? Would you know it well enough to be able to refer to it in your heart? Do you know the Lord's voice? Can you hear Him clearly enough to be led beside still waters?

As we will cover in the chapter on hearing the voice of God, we are mandated to hear God as Christians. Jesus, the great Shepherd, leads us with His voice. As in all relationships, the more familiar we are with Him, the more we will recognize His voice and character. In this chapter, we will go over Psalm 23 to take a closer look at the responsibilities of a shepherd, as well as the promises that come from being in the flock under the responsibility of Jesus Christ, the Chief Shepherd: promises of a relationship, covenant, provision, protection, refreshment, restoration, and hope.

The Lord really wants us to understand how critical it is that we hear His voice for direction because His direction is specific to the changing circumstances of the times in which we live. Electronic devices can fail us, and Bibles can be taken away or destroyed. There are still many countries in the world where Bibles are banned, and to be in possession of one can lead to death. Though God has protected His sovereign Word to endure through the generations, it has not always been available to everyone on a micro-level. It is altogether possible that we in America could lose our access to the written Word of God, perhaps even in this very generation. Some may think a statement like that is foolish, but history has proven otherwise. That is why it is critical that we read and study the written Word of God now, so it is in our hearts. With the written Word of God in our hearts and the spoken word of our Shepherd in our ears, we can have valuable direction. God's Word can provide direction through the daily volumes of fake news, lies, and deceptions. These will likely become more and more prevalent until Jesus returns.

There may be a day that comes when the Lord calls you to run for the hills for preservation or run into the wasteland to minister to the sick and dying clinging to life. If that day were today, would you have the ears to hear and the heart willing to obey? Is the written Word of God alive in you to draw upon? Remember, if your heart isn't soft and willing to obey, you will not be able to hear God.

Jesus the Chief Shepherd_

The Lord is my shepherd. ...He restoreth my soul: he leadeth me in the paths of righteousness for his name's sake. Yea, though I walk through the valley of the shadow of death, I will fear no evil: for thou art with me; thy rod and thy staff they comfort me. Thou preparest a table before me in the presence of mine enemies: thou anointest my head with oil; my cup runneth over. Surely goodness and mercy shall follow me all the days of my life: and I will dwell in the house of the Lord for ever.

Psalm 23:1, 3–6

Psalm 23 is a psalm of David and is one of the most recognized passages in Scripture. It speaks directly to the heart and soul, addressing the dreams and anxieties we may have. It is a reminder that the Lord is caring and compassionate toward us. Just as sheep depend on their shepherd, we need to depend on the protection and provision of Jesus Christ, our Chief Shepherd.

Many Christians have a difficult time understanding the metaphors and concepts of what it means to be a shepherd. This is understandable. It wasn't until recently in the history of humanity that the majority of people no longer needed to seek out their own food, so many of the concepts and ideas of shepherding have been lost. Let's explore the words and images of the shepherd to give us a better understanding of the message God is conveying to us here.

When Psalm 23 is broken down, we see thirteen individual statements. I find this fascinating because, in Scripture, the number thirteen is significant. The dragon who is behind all rebellion against God is found thirteen times in Revelation; Nimrod, who tried to take the place of God, was the thirteenth descendant of Ham; and in Romans 1, where the Apostle Paul listed twenty-three characteristics of sinful people, the thirteenth characteristic was that they were haters of God. These and many other examples reflect the recurring theme that the number thirteen represents rebellion against God and the fallen state of mankind. Psalm 23 starts with the Redeemer of that fallen state, Jesus Christ, the Chief Shepherd, and the psalm ends with the promise of eternal life with Jesus. How amazing it is to see the fingerprints and master plan of God woven into this scripture!

Let's look at these thirteen duties and promises of the Chief Shepherd found in Psalm 23 and explore line-by-line verses one through six. It is my prayer that each one of these will draw you closer to Jesus, and your faith, knowledge, and relationship with Him will increase as you go.

The Shepherd's Responsibilities

Psalm 23 makes these thirteen statements about what the Shepherd does:

1. "The Lord is my shepherd."

First, we must have a commitment to Jesus Christ as our Lord. If we accept Him as our Lord and Savior, we become part of His flock, and He becomes our Shepherd. All of the conditional promises that follow this statement are yours only if you are in His flock. If you are in His flock, then you are of His sheep. If you are of His sheep, then you will recognize the Shepherd and follow His voice. In the physical world, a shepherd only cares for the sheep that are his, meaning those over which he has ownership. If Jesus is our Shepherd, then we belong to Him. If we belong to God, then we are the sheep under His care. We no longer have ownership of ourselves. Unfortunately, many Christians struggle with this because our flesh does not want to surrender.

2. "I shall not want."

This statement alludes to the promise that God will meet our deepest needs. If we are not content with His provision and timing, then we can become like sheep that wander off in search of greener pastures. When we wander off alone, the danger is that we can become easy prey for predators. The robber will seek to tempt you with grass that looks greener on the other side of the fence to isolate you from the flock. The grass outside your pasture can have an attractive appearance, but it can be quite deadly. The reality could be that the grass is greener there because that is where the neighbors' septic system is. If you see greener pastures on the other side of the fence and wonder why the Shepherd hasn't led you there Himself, you can be confident that it is in your best interest that He does not because you know that He is good.

3. "He maketh me to lie down in green pastures."

In the world, sheep will never rest in the presence of predators, conflict, or hunger. For sheep to rest and lie down, it is critical that the shepherd offers an environment of protection and peace. When we are following the voice of the Shepherd, we are free to rest because we have the power, the peace, and the provision of Christ Jesus. Stay with Jesus, and rest assured during the most difficult times in life that you are under His protection.

4. "He leadeth me beside the still waters."

The Hebrew word for "still" here can also mean quiet.[50] This draws a parallel to 1 Kings 19:12, where God speaks on the mountain to Elijah with a still, quiet voice. As Christians, we can drink deeply of the Holy Spirit, the only water that can quench our souls. The significance of being by still waters as a sheep is that staying beside those still waters can avoid the danger of drowning. A fast current can sweep sheep away. Because of their heavy wool coats, sheep are not good swimmers and drown easily. Jesus will always lead us to places of safety for refreshment that will also be quiet enough to hear His voice.

5. "He restoreth my soul."

God has made it possible for us to be restored back to Him through Jesus Christ. He cares about the deep things in our hearts and desires to renew our minds. In the world of shepherding, it is possible for sheep to get stuck on their backs in such a way that it is difficult for them to get back up. Over time, they can become dehydrated, weak, and can even die trying to get back on their feet. It is the shepherd's responsibility to tend to a sheep that is stuck on its back and help it stand back up again. We are fallen in sin from birth, but through Jesus Christ, we can be restored; when we fall in our walk with Him as Shepherd, He will always be there to help us back up.

6. "He leadeth me in the paths of righteousness for His name's sake."

Sheep are creatures of habit. They can destroy their own pasture by overgrazing if left alone too long. This is why sheep need to be led to new pastures in order to survive. The shepherd is responsible for knowing where the best pastures for food are, as well as the safest ways to get there. The Word of God is "the lamp unto our feet and a light unto our path" (Psalm 119:105). Remember, He leads us with His voice, and He is the one holding the lantern. If Jesus is leading you to a new place, trust Him because your provisions may be running out. The new resources for your next season are ahead.

7. "Yea, though I walk through the valley of the shadow of death, I will fear no evil; For Thou art with me."

Valleys often have the best grass to graze on because they are rich with water runoff from the surrounding mountains. At the same time, valleys do present inherent dangers to sheep. The lowness of their location can expose sheep to predators that hunt from the higher ground. Valleys can also be dark places, as the surrounding mountains cast huge shadows; they are the first to see a setting sun and the last to see the sunrise. Despite the looming dangers, we don't need to fear that Jesus will ever leave us. When you find yourself in a valley, there is always a river nearby to jump into. So when you hit rock bottom, trust the river—the Holy Spirit—to lead you.

8. "Thy rod and Thy staff, they comfort me."

The promise of God's discipline and guidance should be comforting to us because Scripture tells us that God disciplines the children that He loves. In the world of shepherding, the purpose of the rod is for discipline, to help give guidance and direction. If necessary, it can also be used for protection against prey. Take comfort in knowing that God loves us so much that He is willing to do whatever He needs to keep us from becoming orphans once we have accepted Him.

9. "Thou preparest a table before me in the presence of mine enemies."

If I am surrounded by enemies, my first thoughts are going to be about strategies for survival—but God is above and beyond all that. Even when we are surrounded by enemies, God still has the time and the means to tend to our needs while holding off our enemies and displaying His power before them. When a shepherd leads his flock to a new pasture, it is his responsibility to make sure both that the pasture is clear of any poisonous vegetation that his sheep could eat and that it is capable of providing adequate protection against any potential predators.

10. "Thou anointest my head with oil."

Shepherds will use oil for both a bug repellent and medicine for healing wounds. In Scripture, anointing oil is a symbol for the Holy Spirit. Catch this revelation that both healing and bug repellent are available with the Holy Spirit. Do you need healing? Then pray, worship, and move in the Holy Spirit. Do you need bug repellent to wipe out the biting lies of the enemy? Then pray, worship, and move in the Holy Spirit. The anointing of oil also symbolizes God's work to prepare us for His service. Are you in His service?

11. "My cup runneth over."

Our provision from God exceeds our needs so that we always have some measure that can be given out to others. We can easily get fixated on finances, but there are many other ways our cup can run over: for example, in talents or in time. Do you have time to spend with someone who is lonely? Do you have talents that could be a blessing to someone in need? Where is your cup spilling over? If it isn't overflowing, could it be because you are in your own pasture away from the Shepherd? The good shepherd always leads the flock to more lush and fruitful areas for grazing. A natural shepherd has to always weigh the cost/profit margin when planning for provision, but Jesus doesn't need to worry about additional costs because He already paid all the costs for us.

12. "Surely goodness and mercy shall follow me all the days of my life."

God's goodness and grace will not only be upon me, but they will follow behind me for the rest of my life. When the shepherd leads his sheep to the next pasture, the sheep tend to leave a lot of manure behind. That manure helps transform the consumed pasture into a fertile field that will grow again. What are you leaving in your wake: devastation and drought, or goodness and mercy?

13. "And I will dwell in the house of the Lord for ever."

The great promise for all Christians is that we will live in eternity with God. After spending the summer traveling with sheep to different pastures, the shepherd always leads his sheep back home during the fall, where they will rest for the winter. We will go through many pastures in life, but through it all, the final destination lies ahead. Jesus is the only one who can lead us there where His house awaits.

The Shepherd and Jesus

Let's dive deeper now by looking into the comparisons between the requirements of a shepherd and the character of Jesus. Looking into the life and responsibilities of shepherding can help us better grasp the attributes of Jesus as our Chief Shepherd.

1. A shepherd always leads the sheep to safe pastures with food and water. Jesus calls His disciples to follow Him wherever He leads.

And when he putteth forth his own sheep, he goeth before them, and the sheep follow him: for they know his voice. And a stranger will they not follow, but will flee from him: for they know not the voice of strangers. ...Then said Jesus unto them again, Verily, verily, I say unto you, I am the door of the sheep. All that ever came before me are thieves and robbers: but the sheep did not hear them. I am the door: by me if any man enter in, he shall be saved, and shall go in and out, and find pasture.

John 10:4–5, 7–9

2. A shepherd will always protect the sheep from predators and all natural dangers. Jesus rescues us and warns us. Jesus intercedes for us continually and without ceasing.

While I was with them in the world, I kept them in thy name: those that thou gavest me I have kept, and none of them is lost, but the son of perdition; that the scripture might be fulfilled. And now come I to thee; and these things I speak in the world, that they might have my joy fulfilled in themselves. I have given them thy word; and the world hath hated them, because they are not of the world, even as I am not of the world. I pray not that thou shouldest take them out of the world, but that thou shouldest keep them from the evil.

John 17:12–15

3. A shepherd is responsible for feeding the sheep. Jesus is the bread of life who fed the multitudes.

[Jesus] said, Bring them [the loaves and fishes] hither to me. And he commanded the multitude to sit down on the

grass, and took the five loaves, and the two fishes, and looking up to heaven, he blessed, and brake, and gave the loaves to his disciples, and the disciples to the multitude. And they did all eat, and were filled: and they took up of the fragments that remained twelve baskets full.

Matthew 14:18–20

4. A shepherd has the responsibility to tend to the weak and sick sheep. Jesus cares for and heals the weak and the sick.

And Jesus went forth, and saw a great multitude, and was moved with compassion toward them, and he healed their sick.

Matthew 14:14

5. A shepherd will discipline the difficult sheep, and he will pursue the sheep that wander from the group. Jesus rebukes the disciples and goes after the lost.

What man of you, having an hundred sheep, if he lose one of them, doth not leave the ninety and nine in the wilderness, and go after that which is lost, until he find it? And when he hath found it, he layeth it on his shoulders, rejoicing. ...I say unto you, that likewise joy shall be in heaven over one sinner that repenteth, more than over ninety and nine just persons, which need no repentance.

Luke 15:4–5, 7

6. A shepherd needs to keep the sheep from overgrazing

the land so it can provide food for the next year. Jesus shows the disciples how to care for others.

But I say unto you which hear, Love your enemies, do good to them which hate you, Bless them that curse you, and pray for them which despitefully use you.

Luke 6:27–28

He saith unto him the third time, Simon, son of Jonas, lovest thou me? Peter was grieved because he said unto him the third time, Lovest thou me? And he said unto him, Lord, thou knowest all things; thou knowest that I love thee. Jesus saith unto him, Feed my sheep.

John 21:17

I have had the opportunity to visit several farms and ranches in my life, and I have always been amazed by the striking parallels between shepherding and the Shepherd. Seeing it firsthand brought a deeper level of appreciation for what Jesus is doing in my life. I pray that this exercise has been as meaningful to you as it was to me standing in the midst of a shepherd's handiwork.

A Testimony of Knowing the Shepherd

As a child, my wife, Shanee, didn't know or follow Jesus as the Shepherd, but that didn't keep Him from tending to her needs. When she was just six years old, she became very ill. Her illness would be diagnosed as an autoimmune disease with no cure, and she would later undergo hundreds of procedures and five major surgeries starting at the age of ten years old. Her parents were always there for her, but when things were really difficult, she knew that there was a "god" to pray to. She missed quite a bit of school during this time. Whenever she was able to be there, she was teased for being "moon-faced" from steroid treatment. In her teen years, as she was still struggling with health issues, she tried to fit in by doing things she shouldn't have been doing.

Looking back on her life, she now sees that there were many instances when she could have chosen to go down the wrong path or, worse, she could have been killed in some dangerous situation. Now, as a Christian, she recognizes that Jesus was with her all along, watching over her as the Good Shepherd. The Shepherd protected, provided, and guided her. When asked how she knows it was Jesus, she says, "There really is no other explanation of how I remained safe and alive."

Spending so many years in the hospital as a young person gave Shanee the desire to be a baby nurse. Many people thought she couldn't make it through nursing school because of her constant sickness. Yet again, prior to even having a personal relationship with Jesus, God carried her through schooling and then positioned her into the dream job that perfectly fit her God-created design. In this job, she was able to use her extensive experience from being sick as a child to help parents understand what their children were experiencing.

According to Romans 8:28, "we know that all things work together for good to them that love God, to them who are the called according to his purpose." Shanee was growing in her love for God and was unknowingly walking in His calling and purposes. It wasn't until age twenty-eight, five years into her career, that the Lord brought a nurse to her unit who would be an amazing friend and would ultimately lead her to Christ.

Shanee began attending church, and soon after, she accepted Jesus Christ as Lord and Savior. When she was born again, her relationship with God started to change. She began hearing His voice and realized that not only did God have a plan for her life, but He had been leading her in His plan since she was born. Now, she is getting to know the Shepherd who has always known her.

Her experiences and health issues have made her who she is today. They are part of her testimony of Jesus' love for her and for all of us who don't deserve it. After having walked with Christ for over nine years, she has now learned to listen for His leading and is so grateful to have a personal relationship with Him as He continues to be the Good Shepherd in her life.

Conclusion

For whom he did foreknow, he also did predestinate to be conformed to the image of his Son, that he might be the firstborn among many brethren. Moreover whom he did predestinate, them he also called: and whom he called, them he also justified: and whom he justified, them he also glorified.

Romans 8:29–30

The Good Shepherd never neglects His responsibilities. As long as you are still breathing, it is never too late to follow Him. Just as He has done for my wife, who has been through much in her life from a young age, the Lord is always leading us out of the darkness and into the light. Have you struggled through hardships in life? Has the Shepherd been trying to lead you out from a poisonous, unprotected pasture to a place of provision and purpose?

In the Garden of Eden, there were two trees: the tree of the knowledge of good and evil and the tree of life. After the fall of man, the Lord no longer permitted access to the tree of life because to have allowed fallen man eternal life in a fallen, sinful state would have been to assign him to hell. Fortunately for us, God already had a plan to bring us back into reconciliation with Him through the sacrifice of the perfect Lamb, Jesus. Now is the time to truly know Him. Take the time to listen to His voice! Read the Word and keep it in your heart to stay! Let Jesus be your Chief Shepherd Who leads you beside still

ARE YOU BEING ROBBED?

waters to new fields of opportunity! You won't regret it.

Closing Prayer

Lord, thank You for revealing Yourself to us in Your Word. Thank You for purchasing us with Your blood and looking after us. Help us to desire more of You. Help us to surrender to You, listen to You, and obey Your voice as You lead us through life until the day we come face to face with You in glory. Amen.

CHAPTER 4:

Knowing the Will of God

For ye have need of patience, that, after ye have done the will of God, ye might receive the promise.

Hebrews 10:36

There are many Christians who are being robbed of God's perfect will for their lives. This statement often elicits very passionate and spontaneous responses, most based on very limited or misunderstood teachings on what God's will actually entails. Has the enemy robbed you because you have little to no knowledge of God's will, or are you robbing yourself by ignoring the obligation we have as Christians to seek it out? There are two extreme views about this. One is the carefree attitude that thinks God is in control, so there is no need to seek out His will because it will happen anyway. The other is the paralyzing fear of the consequences of choosing God's will incorrectly. Either of these creates the opportunity for thievery to take place.

For example, some people believe that everything that happens is God's perfect will, regardless of our decisions. They say that we do not have to worry about seeking God's direction or exercising godly wisdom in our decisions because God's perfect will always plays out. Some have even used this belief to the extreme as an excuse to say that we do not need to reach the lost with the good news of Jesus Christ! Does that not sound like teaching from the devil?

Unfortunately, this mindset will lead to significant long-term repercussions, as not every facet of God's will produces a blessed outcome. The real battle of the wills is the one between our own will and God's. We need to be set free from the bondage of our own excuses. If you believe everything is God's perfect will, then I can guarantee you are being robbed.

I have observed that some Christians, including some pastors, believe this teaching that God's perfect will always plays out despite our choices. Friends of mine who believe this struggle deep inside when confronted by its incompatibility with the totality of Scripture and its application that is inconsistent with the reality of day-to-day life. The fear of backlash from man's traditional teachings within their denominations keeps them from having fear of the Lord and accepting God's true Word. Others may fear hearing from God and learning what His perfect will is because their flesh is resistant to God's will.

If God is my ruler, would it not make sense to obey His commands? But if I am my own ruler, the more attractive option would be to neglect the search for God's perfect will and be happy living in my own will, based on my fleshly desires. I might argue that to deny my desires poses a risk of pain and inconvenience to me. Ignorance is bliss; I would rather believe that everything that happens is within God's perfect will and that He is responsible for everything. But this kind of thinking can lead to thievery. The Bible makes it clear that living in the flesh is not as safe as we might think. Hosea, the prophet, recorded God's lament: "My people are destroyed for lack of knowledge" (Hosea 4:6). Here, the knowledge God is talking about is the Law that reveals His perfect will. The ignorance of that will brings destruction, death, and rejection.

Do not live life under the lie that choosing to seek out and walk into God's perfect will is not an option! It may seem more comfortable to believe all our decisions will result in God's perfect will, but comfort and truth do not often lead to the same conclusion. The real comfort comes with the promised blessings, fulfillment, and protection of walking in the perfect will of God.

We have a tendency to default to comfort because we all have been afflicted with some degree of laziness since the fall of man in the garden. The consequence of sin is death, which manifests as the physical law of entropy, the winding down of everything in the universe. Doing work requires the input of energy. It takes work and discipline to overcome laziness, work which will result in God's best. Seeking God for direction in His Word, both written and heard, requires the work of reading, praying, and listening carefully for His voice on our part.

God's Perfect Will Is Best

And be not conformed to this world: but be ye transformed by the renewing of your mind, that ye may prove what is that good, and acceptable, and perfect, will of God.

Romans 12:2

There are three key components to God's will in this verse. First, we have the directive not to conform to this world, and as Christians, we are called to be in this world but not of it. The Greek word used here for "world" is *aion*, meaning "age or period of time."[51] This word emphasizes that it's not just about the physical world around us but also about the promise that all fallen creation has an expiration date. Jesus is both coming back for us and is redeeming all of His creation, and the fallen state of this world is just temporary.

The second component is the transformation by the renewing of the mind. This isn't just a one-time experience but a daily need for us. Just as we must put on the full armor of God daily, we must also continue in the renewing of our minds by reading the Word of God and praying for the mind of Christ as He is making us a new creation in Him.

Last is the promise that comes as a result of meeting the conditions so that we may discern what is good, acceptable, and perfect. The word "good" in Greek is *agathos*, which means "beneficial."[52] "Acceptable" in Greek is *euarestos*, meaning "permissive and acceptable;"[53] "perfect" in Greek is *teleios*, which means "of full age and completeness."[54]

According to Paul, turning our backs on the world and having our minds renewed by God enables us to discern and experience God's perfect will for ourselves. The robber has done his best to obscure and twist our understanding of this blessing and the tools God has given us to make the necessary course corrections. God's perfect will is good, beneficial, and highly suitable. It has no flaws and no missing pieces; it is totally complete. Because God is omniscient, He knows what He will accomplish in us. He knows what we will do and what we will not do in any situation we may face. This is why His plans for us can never fail and are perfect. They are not flawed with missing information, unknown details, or bad timing because He is above all that. God's plans and purposes for every believer in Jesus Christ are for our good and for His glory!

Our carnality is the most vulnerable point of attack on this issue. The robber knows that our pride, rebellion, and ignorance will keep us from the blessings God has for us in His perfect will, as long as we continuously choose our will over God's. Satan will do everything he can to keep us in the dark. We must choose to rebuke the enemy and seek the light. As Christians, we are called to surrender our lives to God and submit to His will. It is within our free will to do so. Pursuing His perfect will and intentionally choosing it results in decisions that are good and pleasing to God.

The decision to follow God's perfect will also results in the very best God has for us. This doesn't just include the blessings God gives us out of His grace for us, which are wonderful and serve to display His mercy. The specific blessings of obedience come from a place of overflow. They bring treasure in heaven and additional gifts on earth. Will you seek the understanding needed to receive them?

Understanding in Part

The idea that our free will to make decisions contrary to God's will can still operate within God's will is a difficult concept to grasp. There are things we can only understand in part because we are limited by physical laws placed on us because of sin. These temporary limits restrict our physical mind from understanding a limitless God.

Despite this, I remain convinced that every Christian needs to grasp in part the significance of knowing God's perfect will and how to choose to walk in it to receive the fullness of blessing available to us and please God. God has given us free will to make decisions in life, and these decisions generate both positive and negative consequences, according to the three categories of His will. These categories are His perfect will, His sovereign will, and His permissive will. Knowing these will give clarity to Scripture and some understanding of why things happen the way they do around us. It sheds some light on the decades of denominationalism because of human misunderstandings of Scripture. Rather than taking God's Word for what it specifically says, some people have reinterpreted Scripture to make it more relatable to them. Sometimes when we do this, as in this case, we do a disservice to God's Word and put God in a box. We need to be careful not to forget who God is. His locality is everywhere, yet He is separate from sin; He sees everything but isn't always directly seen; He knows everything because He created everything, and He has no beginning and no end.

Just as we need to remember who God is, we also need to remember who we are. "For we know in part, and we prophesy in part," Paul explained in 1 Corinthians 13:9. We only know fragments of reality, our knowledge of things is incomplete, and our understanding is limited. God has designed it that way for our protection. Yet, in the same passage, Paul went on to tell us that these limitations are temporary and will end when we receive our eternal bodies with Jesus. Yet, for now, we need to reach the level of understanding that God has made available to us to do the best we can to follow God's will.

So as you read this chapter, understand that we are taking an attribute from the heavenly realms that is limitless in time, space, and colors and compressing it down to black ink on white paper in order for our limited minds to try and understand. Ask God to speak to you as you read this chapter, and don't be discouraged if you don't completely understand how His will functions because it is the understanding of the principles that matters most. When you are finished reading this entire book, remember to come back to this chapter one last time to read. I believe that after combining this information with the concepts from the rest of the book, you will be able to come to a sufficient understanding of the will of God.

The Three Wills

The stories and scenarios of the Bible indicate that the will of God works in different ways. The three subcategories of the will of God are:

1. His sovereign will (sometimes called the will of decree)
2. His permissive will (sometimes called the will of desire)
3. His perfect will (sometimes called the will of direction)

We need to understand the differences between these three. Let's look at each of them in more detail. As you read, think about what areas of your life may fall into each category. Then ask yourself, "Am I where God wants me to be? What decisions have I made lately that may fall under His permissive will?" The choices we make may be permissible to God, but we miss out on an incredible opportunity if we do not choose His perfect will.

We will look at the differences between the subcategories of God's will using the Scriptures.

1. The sovereign will of God

The sovereign will of God is His eternal, foreordained plan and purpose that cannot and will not be prevented. His sovereign will has been set, and God Himself cannot change it because it is finished. This can be difficult for us to understand. We tend to think about things through our mental timeline, linear time, meaning that we envision time as a straight line with a starting point going in one direction. But God is outside of time altogether, and He knows the beginning from the end. He can place finished works simultaneously at different points throughout time. Though to Him these works are already finished, we may still have yet to encounter them. Solomon wrote with much wisdom and understanding of this complex principle in the book of Ecclesiastes. "Consider the work of God: for who can make that straight, which he hath made crooked?" (Ecclesiastes 7:13).

It is difficult to comprehend, but God's sovereign works are set in place from outside linear time. It has multiple dimensions, like a crooked line, which can be converted only by God back into our straight line, linear time. This is a quality that is uniquely His. One example of these sovereign finished works is our salvation. Paul wrote a letter to the unified believers in Christ at the city of Ephesus, telling them how God chose us before we were born through the finished work of Jesus Christ:

> *Blessed be the God and Father of our Lord Jesus Christ, who hath blessed us with all spiritual blessings in heavenly places in Christ: According as he hath chosen us in him before the foundation of the world, that we should be holy and without blame before him in love: Having predestinated us unto the adoption of children by Jesus Christ to himself, according to the good pleasure of his will.*
>
> **Ephesians 1:3–5**

115

Because of God's omniscience in regards to time, He can predestine us without compromising our free will to choose to accept salvation through Jesus Christ. It is the sovereign finished work of Jesus on the cross that makes it possible for God to reach through that fixed moment in our linear time to reconcile us with Him.

This quality also means God will not and cannot change His mind about covenant promises and purposes. These are part of His sovereign will. A great example of this can be seen in the conversation between God and Moses. When the people of Israel turned from God and began to worship a golden calf, Moses reminded God of His covenant promises:

> *Remember Abraham, Isaac, and Israel, thy servants, to whom thou swarest by thine own self, and saidst unto them, I will multiply your seed as the stars of heaven, and all this land that I have spoken of will I give unto your seed, and they shall inherit it for ever. And the Lord repented of the evil which he thought to do unto his people.*
>
> **Exodus 32:13–14**

The text says that God "repented" of contemplating the destruction of Israel and the making of a new nation of Moses. Some people will argue that God can and did change His mind, but He did not as it pertains to His sovereign will. Moses interceded for Israel by declaring the covenant God made, knowing He could not change His mind because He was God. The idea that God changed His mind about destroying Israel is really more about how He didn't change His mind despite the consequences of sin. God was so grieved by the level of sin in humanity in the time of Noah that He wished He never created mankind (Genesis 6:6). Yet He was still pleased with Noah and made a covenant with man that they could be redeemed through Jesus, which kept Him from changing His mind toward His creation.

In addition, there were two purposes that God was able to

impress upon Moses by expressing His anger to him. The first was to develop Moses' level of faith and intercessory prayer for his people. The second was to highlight the seriousness of the sinful condition of the people. Ultimately, their sin would deprive them of the many privileges they thought were secure.

God's sovereign will is often hidden from us until after it comes to pass. This allows us the opportunity to choose our will or His will. However, our free will does not change the fact that God in His sovereignty ordains everything that comes to pass. This means that nothing happens outside of God's will as it encompasses both His perfect will and permissive will. Paul shared this aspect of God's will in his letter to Ephesus:

> *In whom also we have obtained an inheritance, being predestinated according to the purpose of him who worketh all things after the counsel of his own will.*
>
> **Ephesians 1:11**

God "works" (meaning that He puts energy into) "everything" (that means all of His creation) so that it comes into agreement with His will.

In the Old Testament, Job described how God's plans are unstoppable: "I know that thou canst do every thing, and that no thought can be withholden from thee" (Job 42:2). Because God is sovereign, His will can never be thwarted. There is nothing that can ever happen that is beyond His control. This does not suggest that God causes everything to happen; that choice is given to man and lies within His permissive will. Job acknowledged that because God is sovereign, He must allow whatever happens to happen. Even when God permits things to happen, we must understand that it is His choice to do so. God always has the power and authority to intervene, but when He does not, it can be frustrating for our Christian walk. Despite this, we must remember that His ways are not our ways, and God knows what is best. We must have faith and peace in His decisions.

2. The permissive will of God

The next aspect of God's will is His permissive will. This is easier to understand because God has chosen to reveal some of His permissive will in the Bible. The permissive will is defined as God's will regarding principles and precepts He has given to us concerning what we should or should not do in a moral sense. God's commands not to murder and not to steal, for example, inform us that it is God's will for us not to do those things. If a Christian brother were to tell me, "God's will for me is to murder or steal," I can say with absolute certainty that this is false because the Word of God contradicts any such statement. The will of God in this example is clearly stated in Scripture. It is called the "permissive will" only because we have the ability to choose to do what is contrary. We can choose to disobey His permissive will and suffer the consequences. I have met many people in my years of prayer ministry who seek answers to what God would say about particular issues, not realizing that those very answers can already be found in the Word of God. For example, we do not have to pray about God's will regarding sleeping with someone we are dating when God has spoken clearly on the issue:

> *Flee fornication. Every sin that a man doeth is without the body; but he that committeth fornication sinneth against his own body. What? know ye not that your body is the temple of the Holy Ghost which is in you, which ye have of God, and ye are not your own? For ye are bought with a price: therefore glorify God in your body, and in your spirit, which are God's.*
>
> **1 Corinthians 6:18–20**

Under God's permissive will, He lets us know what gives Him pleasure and what does not. Moses wrote about how God loves to show mercy and grace when we choose His ways in His permissive will, but when we choose to sin against God, He will execute judgment.

And the Lord passed by before him, and proclaimed, The Lord, The Lord God, merciful and gracious, longsuffering, and abundant in goodness and truth, Keeping mercy for thousands, forgiving iniquity and transgression and sin, and that will by no means clear the guilty; visiting the iniquity of the fathers upon the children, and upon the children's children, unto the third and to the fourth generation.

Exodus 34:6–7

God does not take pleasure in pouring out His eternal wrath on sinners, but He does take pleasure in the salvation of sinners. In the words of Jesus, we read:

How think ye? if a man have an hundred sheep, and one of them be gone astray, doth he not leave the ninety and nine, and goeth into the mountains, and seeketh that which is gone astray? And if so be that he find it, verily I say unto you, he rejoiceth more of that sheep, than of the ninety and nine which went not astray.

Matthew 18:12–13

Whenever we have decisions to make that are not clearly sinful or do not fall under a commandment of God, our desire should always be to do that what pleases God. Seek Him for direction, and if His voice isn't heard, always choose to imitate God by asking yourself, "What would Jesus do in this situation?"

Just because something comes into agreement with God's sovereign will and foreordained plan, that doesn't necessarily mean it is pleasing to God. It merely means that it is permissible to Him at the time. Because of the freedom within God's permissive will, God even allows sin. God allows us to reject the gospel, willfully disobey His commandments, and even persecute the righteous. His permissive will keeps Him from obtaining what He really desires; all men must freely choose His gracious offer, and only the ones who do are predestined by Him in His sovereign will. All three areas of His will are covered by His sovereign will, yet only two have pleasing outcomes. Other examples of the permissive nature of God's will are found in the books of Matthew, Luke, and Revelation, to name a few. These demonstrate great sorrows, sins, and wickedness foreordained by God in the prophecies concerning the latter days before Jesus' return and are therefore unfortunately unavoidable according to His sovereign will, until such a time as Jesus is set in place to reign with justice.

At the same time, God's permissive will is never outside of His control. God allows things under His permissive will that may even be sinful because they will eventually lead to the accomplishment of His sovereign will. The crucifixion of Jesus Christ is a perfect example of His sovereign will, despite Judas' choice to betray Christ under God's permissive will.

> *For of a truth against thy holy child Jesus, whom thou hast anointed, both Herod, and Pontius Pilate, with the Gentiles, and the people of Israel, were gathered together, For to do whatsoever thy hand and thy counsel determined before to be done.*
>
> **Acts 4:27–28**

There will always be people who will choose not to follow God's principles and precepts, but this does not change the fact that God is always in control, and His purposes are always accomplished. Judas, Herod, and Pontius Pilate fulfilled God's sovereign will in betraying Christ, but that does not justify their sins. They were still held accountable for condemning Christ to death. Understanding this aspect of God's permissive will holds us accountable for the fact that although we have the free will to disobey God's commands, we do not have the right to do so. There is never an excuse for our sin. We cannot claim that by choosing sin, we are simply fulfilling God's sovereign will and are, therefore, actually in the right.

3. The perfect will of God

The role of the perfect will of God is to reveal to us His personal guidance in our lives. His perfect will does not violate His sovereign or permissive will. There are times when God wants us in a certain place, doing a certain thing at a certain time. The most effective way to receive this direction is through a sensitive heart with a hearing ear that is turned toward God. The written Word of God is seldom the source that will provide us with this personal revelation of His perfect will, but we can look to the Word to find examples of how God reveals His perfect will. We can see one such revelation in the direct guidance of Philip:

> *And the angel of the Lord spake unto Philip, saying, Arise,*
> *and go toward the south unto the way that goeth down from*
> *Jerusalem unto Gaza, which is desert.*
>
> **Acts 8:26**

Because Philip obeyed the direction from the Lord to do a certain thing at a certain time, he experienced a divine appointment to tell an important Ethiopian about Jesus.

We can also see God's perfect will at work with Peter and Ananias in Acts 10:1–23. Because both men were able to receive God's direction and were obedient in choosing to follow it, they both walked into blessings that resulted in many people being baptized in the Holy Spirit. Both men had to take a step of faith. Their obedience and faith led them to the overflow that was in God's perfect will.

God does guide us personally and directly, just as Jesus said:

But he answered and said, It is written, Man shall not live by bread alone, but by every word that proceedeth out of the mouth of God.

Matthew 4:4

In this statement, "word" means a spoken word in a moment, not the permanent forever written Word of God. Many Christians say that they cannot hear God's voice or that they do not hear from Him as often as they would like. This may be because they are not taking the time to listen or to seek God out. Sometimes, we can be so focused on hearing the things of this world that we are totally deaf to the still, small voice of God speaking to us.

Being able to hear or discern God's perfect will for blessings, provision, and protection is a requirement at certain points of our Christian lives. There will be times when specific guidance is needed to walk into the best God has for us. When we cannot hear God directing us, we need to discern what His perfect will is. Through wisdom and maturity in Christ, we can have a perception of God's will for our lives to help us in these times. We can see this at work in Paul and Silas in the Macedonian call.

I have discovered that when the Holy Spirit does not "show up" in a situation where someone needs to hear His words, it can be a waste of time for me to speak because I would be speaking from my own carnal nature. Sometimes the Holy Spirit may even be moving on me to restrain my mouth. Paul went through something similar in one of his missionary journeys:

Now when they had gone throughout Phrygia and the region of Galatia, and were forbidden of the Holy Ghost to preach the word in Asia, After they were come to Mysia, they assayed to go into Bithynia: but the Spirit suffered them not. And they passing by Mysia came down to Troas. And a vision appeared to Paul in the night; There stood a

122

man of Macedonia, and prayed him, saying, Come over into Macedonia, and help us. And after he had seen the vision, immediately we endeavoured to go into Macedonia, assuredly gathering that the Lord had called us for to preach the gospel unto them.

Acts 16:6–10

In the Bible, we can see God's permissive will and perfect will fitting together like puzzle pieces at times. Using the example from earlier, His perfect will desires that all be saved (God's best for us) (see 1 Timothy 2:4), but His permissive will allows people the choice to reject Jesus and face eternal separation from Him. While God takes no pleasure in the eternal separation of those who reject Jesus, He is also the one who regulates their judgment. God's perfect will is for all men to be saved, and yet His sovereign will only allows salvation through the choice of accepting Jesus Christ as Lord and Savior, as it is written in John 6:44:

No man can come to me, except the Father which hath sent me draw him: and I will raise him up at the last day.

When we desire God's best for our lives, we can easily become obsessed with seeking out the perfect will of God. We need to remember that God has not chosen to reveal all aspects of His perfect will to us ahead of time. What we can seek to know at this time is His revelation through the Word of God concerning His sovereign will and parts of His permissive will. A true mark of spiritual maturity is when we have a hunger to know and live according to the revelation in the Word of God and have an available ear to hear His voice when He speaks.

His Perfect Will Is Not Always Easy

Although it isn't popular in some churches to talk about

suffering, the fact is that suffering and tragedy will come to each of us sometime in our life. When this happens, it does not mean we are necessarily outside the perfect will of God. His perfect will also includes hardships. We will be refined and defined through the process, and the outcome will be for our betterment and salvation. Paul wrote about how God comforted him and the Corinthians:

> *Blessed be God, even the Father of our Lord Jesus Christ, the Father of mercies, and the God of all comfort; Who comforteth us in all our tribulation, that we may be able to comfort them which are in any trouble, by the comfort wherewith we ourselves are comforted of God. For as the sufferings of Christ abound in us, so our consolation also aboundeth by Christ.*
>
> **2 Corinthians 1:3–5**

In these writings, we can see how we will be a blessing to others by giving them comfort as they go through similar hardships because God first comforts us in ours. We can also see that in order to help us stay effective, powerful Christians in the perfect will of God, He will use hardships, if necessary, to keep us on the right path. As we read in Paul's revelation from the Lord, he wrote to the Corinthians that God allowed Satan's messengers to torment him in order to keep him from being conceited:

> *And lest I should be exalted above measure through the abundance of the revelations, there was given to me a thorn in the flesh, the messenger of Satan to buffet me, lest I should be exalted above measure. For this thing I besought the Lord thrice, that it might depart from me. And he said unto me, My grace is sufficient for thee: for my strength is made perfect in weakness.*
>
> **2 Corinthians 12:7–9**

It is important to recognize that although God allowed the robber to torment Paul for his own betterment, nothing was stolen; in fact, there was nothing but gain. God has a conditional promise to work all things for good if we love Him and continually walk in His calling and perfect will for our lives.

> *And we know that all things work together for good to them that love God, to them who are the called according to his purpose.*
>
> **Romans 8:28**

God's Perfect Will Gets Us Across the Battlefield

We all have a battlefield to cross in our lives. This battlefield can represent many things and may serve multiple purposes, but it is best crossed by our choosing God's perfect will. Doing so will help us get to our destination more quickly and with fewer battle scars. In Ephesians 6:12, we read that our battle [our struggle] is not against flesh and blood, but against the rulers, against the authorities, against the powers of this dark world, and against the spiritual forces of evil in the heavenly realms.

The path that traces our personal testimony is the road of God's perfect will and calling for our lives. When we are obedient to make the right choices and walk in faith to His perfect will, we reach our destination intact and are better able to serve others who are attempting to cross the same field.

There are three ways we can cross our battlefield, and one way we can die there. First, we can choose to walk into it knowing we have victory by trusting in God and in His perfect will for us. Second, we can stumble through the battlefield in ignorance and become significantly wounded along the way. Third, we try to fly over it in a useless attempt to avoid it, thinking we can still reach the other side. Fourth, we can die there by simply staying in the trenches and refusing to cross.

In the case of the third option, we attempt to fly over our battlefield by seeking out every route that appears easier than the one God has for us. This attempt is as foolish as claiming that all roads lead to heaven. If I told you to go somewhere you have never been, you would ask for a map or directions. If I told you not to search for directions because all roads would lead you there, what do you think your journey would look like? Trying to fly over the battlefield by choosing our will instead of God's will effectively have the same results. We cannot get ourselves high enough on our own to know how to get out of the battlefield. The plane will be shot down by the robber, who is the ruler of the air—unless God in His mercy first pushes us out of the plane with a parachute before it crashes. Alternatively, if we stay still in our own hole, denying that God's perfect will exists, we miss out on the many blessings awaiting us. Eventually, the enemy will dial in our position and take us out with the artillery. It is absolutely critical that we move forward into God's will, for our sake as well as for His.

The battlefield is a very dangerous place, and the best way to cross it is to be directed by God, step by step. God's direction to us will always be His perfect will. Sometimes we may make choices that fall only under His permissive will, and when we do, we can expect delays and injuries. This does not necessarily mean we will not reach our destination.

The battlefields we are confronted with are usually the most valuable territory in our lives. This is why it is even more critical at these times that we seek and obey the perfect will of God. The level of the enemy's attack at these times is proportional to the level of anointing that God has for us. If the battle is strong, it is because there is a lot at stake. While crossing the battlefield, we will sustain cuts and bruises that will ultimately give us character.

What lies at the end of every battlefield is victory and promotion. When promotion comes, we are lifted up to a higher level. Through the victory, we can see further and reach back to help lift others up out of the same battlefield we had victory in. One of the ways we can do that is through the sharing of our testimony of overcoming, as the tribulation saints.

> *And they overcame him by the blood of the Lamb, and by the word of their testimony; and they loved not their lives unto the death.*
>
> **Revelation 12:11**

You see, the devil does not want you to cross your battlefield because it brings defeat to him and glory to God. Walk in God's perfect will, and cross that battlefield in Jesus' name.

Do Not Fear

Since there is a perfect will, does that mean there is an imperfect will of God? Do not fear that you will miss His perfect will and be forever cursed to live out a life of regret, failure, and frustration. God's perfect will takes into account our ignorance, weakness, and sins. Even the sins of others against us cannot derail the perfect will of God. In Joseph's account, he told his brothers that even though they had sold him into slavery, that sinful act had led to the perfect will of God to bring them provisions to survive many years later:

> *But as for you, ye thought evil against me; but God meant it unto good, to bring to pass, as it is this day, to save much people alive.*
>
> **Genesis 50:20**

God is not caught off-guard by anything. He is creative and can make openings back into the flow of His perfect will at any time. As long as you are still breathing in this world, there is still time to receive directions and get back on track. Do not be robbed of time and blessings; do not miss the opportunity to glorify God and reach your destination. Now is the time to be intentional. God is waiting for you.

Be Guided by the Holy Spirit and by the Word

As Christians, it is our responsibility to obey the will of God—however it is revealed to us. It is a waste of time to speculate about what His hidden will might be for us when we can and should seek guidance from the Holy Spirit. Remember that the Holy Spirit will always lead us to righteousness. This journey to righteousness will mold us into the image of Christ so that our lives will glorify God. Let us be holy in every aspect of our lives. I think Peter summarized this principle best:

> *But as he which hath called you is holy, so be ye holy in all manner of conversation; Because it is written, Be ye holy; for I am holy.*
>
> **1 Peter 1:15–16**

Living our lives according to God's sovereign will, making the best choices under His permissive will, and always following His perfect revealed will are collectively the chief purpose of the Christian life. Paul summarizes this truth as we are called to dedicate our lives to God:

> *I beseech you therefore, brethren, by the mercies of God, that ye present your bodies a living sacrifice, holy, acceptable unto God, which is your reasonable service. And be not conformed to this world: but be ye transformed by the renewing of your mind, that ye may prove what is that good, and acceptable, and perfect, will of God.*
>
> **Romans 12:1–2**

God will allow hardships to happen. That means that God allows us to reap the fruit that we sow. Choosing to walk in the footsteps of God's perfect will through His Word and being guided by the Holy Spirit will bring greater blessings and fullness of life. While walking in the will of this world robs us by reaping the fruit of decay, destruction, and death. We make our choice, then the choices we make affect us. Don't develop a history of making wrong choices.

Choose to live a life of God's best. Choose to understand and know the permissive will of God. Choose to walk in the perfect will of God and choose to accept the sovereign will of God. We can start by immersing ourselves in the written Word of God. Our minds must be saturated with it. Then, we need to pray that the Holy Spirit will transform us through the renewing of our minds. He will give us eyes to see, ears to hear, and hearts that align with the cares of Christ's heart.

Pray the Will of God

It is possible to pray against the will of God. When our thoughts, wills, and emotions subvert the voice of God, and we ignore our spiritual discernment, prayers will produce nothing.

> *Ye ask, and receive not, because ye ask amiss, that ye may consume it upon your lusts.*
>
> **James 4:3**

When we pray for something and nothing happens, regardless of how hard we pray, there are three considerations. First, it may not be God's timing. The prayer will be answered, but God has an appointed time for His perfect purposes. Second, we ask for something contingent on another requirement. For example, He will not heal us from a physical impairment that we will use to either ignore or go deeper into a repetitive sin without first leading us in healing and victory over that sin. And third, we might be praying amiss. We need to evaluate our prayers in these situations and ask ourselves, are we praying against God's will? Are we praying against God's Word? Are we praying with unrighteous motives? As James explained in chapter 4 of his book: when we pray for things outside the will of God, we can expect nothing in reply and risk hindering God's work in us as we actively push against God's will.

It can be very difficult to pray God's will, especially when it appears contrary to what we think is best in our own minds. But we must remember that we only know in part and understand in part, while God knows everything. He can determine what is best, but we cannot.

A few years ago, I was visiting a Bible study for the first time. After a great time of fellowship in God's Word, we closed with prayer requests. A gentleman in the group asked for prayer for his aunt, who had lived a long life but was now in poor health. People started praying for her physical healing around the room, but the entire time, I was struggling because God was telling me His will was for her to go home with Him. I struggled to pray His will because it was against the flow of the well-meaning prayers of everyone else in the room. When I made a decision to pray God's will, I heard Him say that He had dispatched a royal carriage reserved just for her and was bringing her home to be with Him in paradise. So after I prayed those same words that God had given me over her, the room was understandably dead silent. When I left that night, the gentleman came up to me, thanked me, hugged me, and said the prayer really touched him. God's words brought confirmation of peace with them, and in the morning, his aunt went to be with the Lord in paradise.

Over all my years of experience praying publicly for others, some have noticed that God seems to answer most of my prayers. When they ask me what my secret is, I tell them that I have none: I am a sinful man covered by the grace and blood of Jesus who diligently seeks first the will of God in every prayer request and only prays what God reveals. I am not perfect. There are times when my flesh gets involved. But I attest that every prayer I have prayed in accordance with God's will has been answered. When we pray in accordance with God's will, our requests come into alignment with His desires and decrees, resulting in the supernatural taking place and God being glorified. Pray His will and see the things hoped for become reality.

When God Says "No"

If we look at Scripture, we can see that God most commonly responds to our prayer requests in four ways: He can give us either a definite answer, a different answer, a delayed answer, or a denied answer. When seeking God's will through prayer and Scripture, there may be times when we wonder if God hears us because we do not receive an answer or the answer we receive doesn't line up with our expectations. When the answer is "no," we can be tempted to think that it's our imagination, that we cannot be hearing correctly. Yet the truth is that God has promised that if we pray and seek His will, He will answer us. "No" is not only a valid answer, but it's also a valuable one when it comes from the God who knows everything, sees everything, and has our best interest in mind!

In fact, there were many times in Scripture when God answered His children's prayers with "no." He said "no" to people who prayed in faith, He said "no" to people who had good hearts, He said "no" to people who had relationships with Him, and He said "no" to people who were His servants. He even said "no" to Himself in Mark 14:36:

And he said, Abba, Father, all things are possible unto thee; take away this cup from me: nevertheless not what I will, but what thou wilt.

Not only did Jesus deny Himself, but the Father also said "no" by letting the Son drink the cup that He was asking not to drink.

In our pursuit of God's will, not everything we ask for in prayer will be granted. Prayer requests are just that: they are requests, not demands, nor are they magic words that can make things happen by our own power. God hears our prayers, and He makes them effective and powerful. He ultimately decides how to answer them, and sometimes the answer is "no." "No" is one of the shortest words in the English language, yet it is one of the hardest words for our ears to hear. When God says "no," it can mean many things. Often, His "no" is not a "No way, forget about it," but rather it is a "No, I have something better in mind." Let's look at some examples in Scripture when God's will was "no."

The first example is found in Deuteronomy when Moses pled with God to allow him to cross the Jordan and see the promised land. God forbade him to do as he asked to be allowed to do (3:23–27). Second, in 2 Samuel, David's great desire was to build a temple for the Lord (7:1–4). This seemed like such a selfless and honorable act, yet God said "no!" Third, John recorded in his gospel the death of Lazarus, where Mary and Martha called for Jesus to return and heal Lazarus before he died from sickness. However, much to their dismay, Jesus said "no" and waited until after Lazarus' death to visit (11:1–44). Fourth, we read in 2 Corinthians that despite Paul's prayers, God's answer to removing the thorn in his side was "no" (12:7–10). Fifth, the book of Mark recorded the most powerful "no" ever given in Scripture, the denial of Jesus' plea to be spared the cup of suffering (14:32–39).

God said "no" to Moses' prayer to cross the Jordan River and see the promised land, but God allowed Moses to view the promised land from the mountaintop. God said "no" to King David's request to set up God's temple, but God did promise to establish David's kingdom forever and to later allow David's son to build God's temple. God said "no" to Mary and Martha's request for Jesus to come quickly and heal their brother before he died, but God did raise their brother from the dead through Jesus Christ four days later for the glory of God. God said "no" to Paul's three requests that He

132

free him from the thorn in his flesh, but God did allow Paul to realize that "[His] grace [was] sufficient" and that God's power was "made perfect in weakness" (2 Corinthians 12:9). God the Father said "no" to Jesus' prayers to avoid His future suffering. This was the only prayer Jesus made to which God said "no." God did allow Jesus to die and conquer the grave, to step on the devil's head, and to nullify the contract of sin and death with His blood. Now He is seated at the right hand of the Father, praying for us continuously and without ceasing. Jesus has a scheduled appointment to return soon to earth, to rule and reign forevermore!

All these examples demonstrate that there is a greater meaning in God's answer if His answer is "no." A key Jesus demonstrated in His prayer was, "Nevertheless not what I will, but what thou wilt" (Mark 14:36). This example should teach us there are some things we ask for that may seem good, but they are not God's will for us. Jesus accepted the Father's will, and the results were powerful. In both Jesus' case and in ours, the ultimate outcome when God's will is done is that life comes out of death. Our deepest need has already been met through the finished work of Jesus Christ. We never deserved it, and we could never earn it or buy it; it is a gift that is freely given, and that is His will.

We have a responsibility to be content with His answers to prayer, even if His will is "no." We should not doubt, we should not disbelieve, and we should not get discouraged, but instead, we should be grateful. It is not easy. We can and will struggle to be content. Even the Apostle Paul said that he had to learn to be content (Philippians 4:11–12). Right now, God's will may not be a new car, a comfortable home, a spouse, or even good health, but His will is what we need. And our obedience is for God's glory.

My Testimony of Following God's Will

I know there are people who do not believe that God specifically chooses a mate for each of us, but it is my opinion that this belief diminishes the heart of God for a perfect union between husband and wife. It is entirely possible that because of our free will, we can choose to ignore His perfect will and settle for His permissive will. Working in singles ministry for ten years, I saw this principle play out over and over again. The people who listened to God and were willing to submit to God walked into beautiful marriages in which God took them to an entirely new level.

On the other side, I saw people who chose each other based on fleshly desires and on what they each thought they could get out of the other, rather than submitting to God. Many of these marriages ended in pain, sorrow, and a loss of confidence, and a few who have decided to stick it out are miserable. Now, God can still do a miracle. I once saw Him heal a marriage in a brief period of time, but the key was that both people were willing to suddenly submit to God and surrender to the other person's needs. That gave God the room and permission to do healing work in their marriage.

My view of dating started out the way the world told me: If you see someone interesting who is a Christian, you ask her out and see what happens. I did believe that dating was for marriage, so I tried to be very cautious about whom I dated. One day, a friend suggested I make a list of what I wanted. So, I wrote out the things I thought were important to me. Most of these items had to do with interests like sports, music, movies, etc. When I was done, I had a list of thirty-eight very specific requirements.

Soon after I completed my list, I began spending time with a wonderful lady from church I had known for a couple of years. After a few months as friends, we started dating. I came to realize that she met every requirement on my list. As we continued to date, something began to be off in my spirit—though not because there was something wrong with the woman herself. I was discerning that something was not right with the two of us together. One night, I was seeking the Lord in prayer when I heard Him say to me, "Do you want what you think you want, or do you want My perfect will?"

I was shocked. Here I was trying to go after my will when God simply wanted me to surrender to His will. I made a mess of things, deeply hurting my friend in the process. After that, I didn't date for six years. My focus during that period shifted toward surrendering my life totally to God.

One night after doing ministry, I ran into her, the one; God's perfect will for me. What happened after that brief encounter required me to trust in God and be patient. Several months later, we began dating; within days of the first date, she heard from God that I was the one for her too. We both would receive several other confirmations in the coming weeks. After only four months of dating, we put our trust in the Lord and stepped up to the altar to get married.

When we made the commitment to surrender to God's perfect will, everything came into place. The four months leading to our wedding were filled with miracles all along the way. We even left for our honeymoon with no plans and no clue how to pay for it, but once again, the Lord provided, and it was a week full of God's grace and blessings.

When we first met, I was not her type; my hair was always messy, I dressed like a teenager with Air Jordans, and my taste in music was scary to her. I felt she was too assertive, she didn't play tennis, and of all things, she had never seen *Star Wars*! In our natural eyes, this would never work out, but in the supernatural, it was a match made in heaven. If we had not surrendered to God's perfect will over our wills, we would never have chosen each other, but our wills were wrong! He is the perfect match-maker. We both have grown so much together. My wife's spiritual growth has been amazing, and the two of us keep each other in line. She is in every way exactly what I needed to be a better man.

As a single man, I walked the earth missing a rib for a long time. Because I chose to follow God's perfect will, I now have not only a rib but the actual rib that was missing. Do not settle for less than God's best, His perfect will for your life.

135

Closing Prayer

Dear Jesus, I pray that this chapter is a blessing to every reader. I pray that we will know Your perfect will for our lives and choose to follow it with submissive hearts. I pray that in the areas of Your permissive will, we will seek to choose what is pleasing to You through the study of Your Word and through prayer. Let us rest in the peace made available in Your sovereign will. Thank You for always having our best interest at heart. Amen.

CHAPTER 5:

Hearing the Voice of God

But this thing commanded I them, saying, Obey my voice, and I will be your God, and ye shall be my people: and walk ye in all the ways that I have commanded you, that it may be well unto you.

Jeremiah 7:23

There is a robber that actively seeks to keep us from the wisdom, guidance, and blessings of living a fulfilling and thoroughly equipped life that comes from hearing and obeying God's voice. I have learned that to hear God's voice and hear it correctly is one of the most important things to walking in God's perfect will for my life. Throughout all of Scripture, there is a consistent requirement to hear and obey the voice of God.

Hearing God's voice, obeying Him, and letting Him be our God is a commandment. The resulting positive consequence is that it will be well for us. This theme is repeated so often throughout Scripture. It should be obvious that God is trying to make an important point. Yet all too often, when I ask other Christians if they hear from God, they either do not know what I am talking about or are unsure whether they do hear from God. How can this be? If you do not know whether you can hear God's voice, then you are being robbed. God speaks to us not only through His written Word but also through a still, small voice. It is my prayer that by the end of this chapter, you will be inspired to hear and follow the voice of the Lord. We must recognize His voice in a world that is constantly competing for our attention.

Hearing God's voice and obeying His direction is one of the

ways we can be identified as Christians. We see this in Exodus 19:5:

Now therefore, if ye will obey my voice indeed, and keep my covenant, then ye shall be a peculiar treasure unto me above all people: for all the earth is mine.

What sets us apart from the rest of the world and makes us His is the ability to hear His voice and obey His commandments. Hearing God speak and following through on His commandments are some of the most exciting things in the Christian experience, providing us with supernatural opportunities and blessings. We can be absolutely confident that whatever God speaks to us, it is always in our best interest to listen and obey.

Competing Voices

We are swimming in a sea of voices competing for our attention. Television, radio, billboards, and the internet are just a few in the natural world, but there are also voices coming from the spiritual realm, as well. The robber has many tools and tactics to drown out the voice of God or even to imitate God if he thinks he can get away with it.

As Christians, we can even distract ourselves. We can spend all of our time focusing on the past, studying the days of Moses and Jesus. On the other hand, we can be too fixated on the future by seeking out a prophetic word or Bible prophecy or by dedicating so much time to thinking about what heaven will be like that we do not hear what God is saying right now. The things of the past and the future have their place, but we cannot let them consume us to such a degree that we end up missing what God is doing and saying to us right now! Don't miss out on the things of the present that will lead to the blessings of tomorrow.

Jesus leads us with His voice, and we should follow Him.

Whenever we stay close to the Shepherd, His voice is clear. Obedience to His voice will help keep us in His perfect will and protection. Some understanding of the world we currently live in can be seen in the analogy of how a shepherd leads sheep and how a cattle herder drives cattle. The devil is herding people like cattle with his voice. The devil's voice will harass you and apply pressure to you from behind to drive you in a direction that leads to rebellion against God. Jesus is the opposite, as He is the great Shepherd. A shepherd leads sheep with his voice. The sheep are to be so familiar with his voice that they are willing to follow and to obey. Are you being driven by the devil's voice, or are you being led by the voice of Jesus?

A Generation Going Deaf

There is a generation of youth being lost because of an epidemic of deafness. Many are aware of the mass exodus of Christian youth from the faith once they go to college. Some Christians believe it is because they are indoctrinated by teachers and science professors who preach a godless existence and utopian socialism, while others believe that if young people were only better equipped in apologetics, they would hold onto their faith. Even if both opinions are true, it still does not get to the heart of the issue.

The reason youths are leaving in droves is that they have no personal relationship and therefore are deaf to God's voice. Deafness prevents any who suffer from it from having a complete relationship with God. Young people do not personally know that God is trustworthy, faithful, and true. What they know is a book of rules and regulations and hearsay that God is real. It is easy to walk away from a relationship with someone you rarely talk to and don't take the time to listen to them. Think about it: If you had a friend that you never listened to and knew little about, how easy would it be to walk away? It is much harder to walk away when the relationship is built on two-way communication and even more so when the voice you hear gives you trustworthy advice, supernatural wisdom, encouragement, and blessings.

So why are there not many churches that teach about the need for us all to hear the voice of God? Some say that the subject is too controversial, or that it is too difficult to teach, or that it scares people away. Yet Scripture is full of moments when God's voice was heard. It may not be easy to learn how to hear God, but it is an invaluable skill. Regardless of the challenges, God will equip you for His purposes along the way, and He will surely teach you to know His voice because He desires you to!

> *And other sheep I have, which are not of this fold: them also I must bring, and they shall hear my voice; and there shall be one fold, and one shepherd.*
>
> **John 10:16**

It is a universal requirement for *all* Christians, regardless of their ethnicity or geographical location, to hear God's voice. The above verse suggests that the key to Christian unity is for all Christians to be listening to the voice of God. He speaks to both the Christian Jews and to all other "folds," which consist of the different groups of Gentiles. God is not fickle in His thinking, and He never changes His mind. The voice of God will never be in conflict with itself, as God the Father, God the Son, and the Holy Spirit are all one. Scripture will contradict neither itself nor God, for Jesus is the Word made flesh. If we all would listen to and obey the voice of God completely, we would walk in a unity that we have never before experienced. As a result, the world would acknowledge that Jesus was sent by God and is one with God (John 17:21).

Jesus said it plainly: "My sheep hear my voice, and I know them, and they follow me" (John 10:27). Are you His? If you are, then according to Him, there are three steps to this equation:

1. We hear God's voice,
2. He recognizes us, and
3. We willingly follow Him.

If you are a follower of Jesus Christ, then I want you to declare right now with your voice to God in prayer that you will hear God's voice, that God knows who you are, and that you will follow Jesus Christ! This is what makes us followers of Jesus.

The Mark of Maturity

The children of God desire milk, and the milk is the written Word of God.

For when for the time ye ought to be teachers, ye have need that one teach you again which be the first principles of the oracles of God; and are become such as have need of milk, and not of strong meat.

Hebrews 5:12

By this point, the Jews to which Paul was writing in this passage had not yet fulfilled his expectations of maturity; he responded by telling them that someone needed to reteach the basic principles of God's Word. They were not yet ready for solid food. They needed to continue to drink milk until they became ready.

A mother's milk is essential for brain development, strong immunity, and good gut health. Like milk, the Word of God is foundational for the first steps at the beginning of life. The brain development can be compared to the renewing of the mind, giving us the ability to grasp the truth and promises in the Word of God. The strong immunity helps us fight off attacks from the enemy with the sword that is the Word of God. Good gut health is like the Holy Spirit, who helps us to take in and absorb what is good for us spiritually.

All these are foundational for growth in the Christian life, but mature believers are also continually led by the voice of God.

There comes a time in a child's life when he is weaned off of his mother's milk and comes to rely more on solid food. All the foundational systems are in place and still remain relevant, but the time of silently taking milk for survival transitions to a time of obedience to the mother's voice, resulting in blessings:

> *Children, obey your parents in the Lord: for this is right. Honour thy father and mother; (which is the first commandment with promise;) That it may be well with thee, and thou mayest live long on the earth.*
>
> **Ephesians 6:1–3**

From day one, the mother begins talking to the child. Even though the child doesn't understand what is being communicated, he recognizes the voice of his mother and is comforted by it. This time is part of the bonding process between the two. Eventually, he begins to understand what she is saying, and a relationship is formed. This is usually around the same time that the child begins to be weaned from the mother's milk. The need to hear, understand, and obey the mother develops trust and maturity. Life for a Christian was never intended to be lived drinking milk alone, but many do drink only milk because it's easier. Do not let the devil keep you as an infant when solid foods are available through the hearing and obedience to the Shepherd's voice.

When the Lord speaks, our souls should listen for everything of value that He says that will add to our treasure trove. He speaks things of unknown knowledge and revelation, with specific direction and timing on when to act. When we obey His instructions, we can expect demonstrations of His love, authority, and grace. Anyone can walk around wearing Christian shirts or carry around a Bible to "look" like a Christian, but for those of us who have a real relationship with God, we can demonstrate the presence and power of God through obedience to His voice.

A History Lesson on Hearing God

There is a requirement throughout Scripture from Genesis to Revelation, consistent through all the different dispensations, to hear God's voice. On a macro level, there are three major dispensations in regards to this:

1. Dispensation of the patriarchs (fathers of families): Adam, Enoch, Noah, Abraham, and Isaac. God dealt directly with them and their families, and they communed directly with God.
2. Dispensation of the law, when God dealt with Israel collectively as a nation. He put them under a law that was specific to them and not other nations. It was during this time that Israel was required to have a temple and a priesthood.
3. Dispensation of the gospel, which applies to the entirety of humanity. This is the dispensation that we find ourselves in now. It requires each of us to have an individual response and interaction with God through Jesus Christ.

So let's look at some highlights of God's call for us to hear His voice from the Old Testament and work our way forward to the New Testament.

In the book of Genesis, after creation and the beginning with Adam in the garden, we see how God spoke directly to Adam, and Adam talked directly with God. Adam could be in the presence of God without the separation resulting from sin. God only gave one command to Adam:

And the Lord God commanded the man, saying, Of every tree of the garden thou mayest freely eat: But of the tree of the knowledge of good and evil, thou shalt not eat of it: for in the day that thou eatest thereof thou shalt surely die.

Genesis 2:16–17

However, Adam and Eve did eat of the tree, and the consequences of sin took place. From that time on, we see the continual distancing of man from God and the increased necessity for us to hear God by seeking His voice intentionally.

Moving forward in time to the Israelites' journey from Egypt in Exodus, we see that after three days of wandering in the desert without water, the Israelites were thirsty and complaining.

So Moses brought Israel from the Red sea, and they went out into the wilderness of Shur; and they went three days in the wilderness, and found no water. And when they came to Marah, they could not drink of the waters of Marah, for they were bitter: therefore the name of it was called Marah. And the people murmured against Moses, saying, What shall we drink? And he cried unto the Lord; and the Lord shewed him a tree, which when he had cast into the waters, the waters were made sweet: there he made for them a statute and an ordinance, and there he proved them.

Exodus 15:22–25

When the Israelites came to a pool of water, they thought they found relief for their thirst, but what they discovered was that the water was bitter and undrinkable. What they didn't understand was that they stood at the gate of their blessing and provision. To unlock the gate and step into the promise, they had to hear from and obey the Lord. The Lord told Moses to take a branch from a nearby tree and put it in the water, and the water became sweet and was drinkable. Because Moses diligently listened and obeyed God, the blessing came.

How many of us have reached the water in our life to quench our thirst, only to find it a bitter and undrinkable thing? How many of us have taken the time to listen and be obedient to His voice concerning those situations? I find that many Christians simply move on and leave the blessings behind because of deaf ears or unwilling hearts.

144

The very next verse following the above passage in Exodus explains the promised blessings for hearing and obeying His voice after they experienced it firsthand. So listen to the voice of God and obey what He is calling you to do, and He will turn the bitter undrinkable things into sweet, drinkable waters!

Now let's look at some examples of hearing in the New Testament. We read in John the words of Jesus Christ talking about the relationship between Him and His people.

> *To him the porter openeth; and the sheep hear his voice: and he calleth his own sheep by name, and leadeth them out. And when he putteth forth his own sheep, he goeth before them, and the sheep follow him: for they know his voice. And a stranger will they not follow, but will flee from him: for they know not the voice of strangers*
>
> **John 10:3–5**

Notice that Jesus didn't say He leads us with His Word here; He says He leads us with His voice. We are Jesus' sheep, and He is our Shepherd. We are to be so close and familiar with Him that we easily recognize His voice and follow His direction. The verse closes by also saying that His people will not follow a voice other than His and will, in fact, take action against the opposing voice by fleeing. How many of us run from the voice of the stranger? When a spirit other than God's starts to speak to you, run from it. We are not called to entertain it, we are not called to give it a place in our heads, and we are not called to think the lies over. We are called to kick it in the face and cast it out by the name above all names, the mighty name of Jesus Christ, and get as far away from it as possible.

The Direct and Present Voice

If it isn't spoken, it cannot be heard. As mentioned earlier, shepherds lead sheep with their voices instead of driving them from behind like cattle, as is the devil's method. It is impossible to be led by God without hearing His voice. This may be difficult to grasp for some Christians, but Jesus did not say, "My sheep follow me by reading Scripture." Some Christians hold fast to the sanctity of Scripture yet do not see that it is within Scripture itself that we learn we must hear and obey Jesus' voice.

Reading Scripture can let us know His will, His character, His promises, His future plans. It gives us tools for discernment and warfare. It tells us what God's moral will is. It even instructs us on how we can become familiar with His voice. But it is not reading the Bible that enables us to follow Jesus as the Shepherd when He is at work, actively moving and guiding us. It is not reading the Bible that enables us to follow Him to new pastures. Let me be clear that reading our Bible is absolutely essential to the Christian walk, but it is not sufficient for the totality of the walk. There are many Christians all over the world who do not have access to Bibles, but they seek the Lord, and He reveals Himself and leads them with His voice. There is no guarantee we will always have Bibles ourselves, and if that ever happens, it will be even more critical both to have Scripture in our minds and hearts and to hear God's voice.

In the chapter "Do Not Be Deceived," we will examine the words *logos* and *rhema*, which translated from Greek to mean "word." There we will focus on the word *logos*, meaning God's total purpose, written and recorded (the Bible). In this chapter, we are dealing with *rhema*, a spoken word. It is in the here and now and can be heard.

The Bible is black ink on white paper. It is physical, and it cannot have a voice if it is not read out loud or brought to life with the voice of the Holy Spirit. When I speak a word, it is *rhema*. One literal translation of the word is "an utterance or a thing that is said"[55] and "a thing spoken by a living voice."[56] The moment that spoken word is written down and becomes something physical, it becomes *logos*.

Now let us look at the word *rhema* as used by Jesus. When

Jesus was confronted by the devil and was tempted to surrender His authority, Jesus responded with Scripture.

> *But he answered and said, It is written, Man shall not live by bread alone, but by every word that proceedeth out of the mouth of God.*
>
> **Matthew 4:4**

Jesus responded to the robber with a Scripture that addressed the need to hear the voice of God personally to be sustained. His choice to use Scripture and to use that verse specifically for His first rebuttal demonstrated the importance of both the *logos* Word of God and the *rhema* word of God. Bread feeds the natural body and makes us strong, but the personal *rhema* word from God feeds our spirits and builds our faith. *Rhema* is given out to us personally. Like bread, it is given out in the portions that are needed at the time we need them.

There are three attributes to hearing God's voice:

1. It is personal.
2. It can't be touched.
3. It is in the present.

First, God's voice is personal. Just as there are no two voices the same, God's voice is also individual and unique. Remember, Jesus said that His sheep hear His voice and follow Him. That means His voice must be distinct and unique to be recognizable. Our ears should only listen, and our hearts should only respond to the voice of God. We need to cultivate a close relationship to become so familiar with the Shepherd that when the robber tries to deceive, his voice is easily recognizable as in opposition to the Shepherd's voice. There are many spiritual voices in the world, but the only spiritual voice we need to allow to speak to us is God's. Whenever a Christian opens the door to allow any other voice to speak to him, he will get robbed. Be aware: some examples of open-door invitations are tarot cards, palm reading, Ouija boards, fortunetellers, occult movies, and New Age spiritualism. If we partake in these things, we need to repent, renounce them, seek forgiveness, get deliverance and lock the door. We must ask Jesus to replace those things with hunger and the ability to hear His voice.

Second, God's voice cannot be touched. His voice is intangible, meaning that it can't be seen but only heard. It is not restricted to the physical; it is beyond space and time. There is no man-made ritual to summon God's voice, as is the case with the occult. He can speak anytime, even now. Are you listening?

Third, the voice of God is in the present. A voice can only speak right now, at the moment. When we realize a significant part of our relationship with Jesus is hearing His voice, that truth forces us into a very present and committed relationship. God expressed this very present nature when He said to Moses, "I am that I am: and he said, Thus shalt thou say unto the children of Israel, I am hath sent me unto you" (Exodus 3:14).

The Hebrew words used here for "I am that I am" are *ehyeh asher ehyeh*, which should more accurately be translated as "I will be what I will be." This expression is an idiom, so by using the translation "I will be what I will be," God clarifies that His name means "He who becometh." The phrase "to be and to become" indicates the present. The use of *ehyeh asher ehyeh* in Exodus 3:14 was God's way of pledging to Moses that He would be whatever Israel would need in the present; in this particular case, He would be their deliverer.

The Blessings of Hearing God

Living our lives with our ears tuned in to God can help us avoid some of the hardships and sicknesses in life. Too often, we make major lifelong decisions without ever consulting God or listening to His voice for wisdom and direction. This warning was given to the Jews along with specific instructions on how to walk into blessings just after the Exodus:

And [he] said, If thou wilt diligently hearken to the voice of the Lord thy God, and wilt do that which is right in his sight, and wilt give ear to his commandments, and keep all his statutes, I will put none of these diseases upon thee, which I have brought upon the Egyptians: for I am the Lord that healeth thee.

Exodus 15:26

Living life with our ears diligently hearkened (that means being quiet and using both ears to hear God) can help us steer around some of the obstacles we might otherwise face. In Exodus 15:26, we see that God lays out four requirements. It is important to note that the promise given is specific to escaping the pains and diseases God put on the Egyptians. These afflictions were above and beyond what is already at work in the state of our fallen world. There is already enough in life to deal with, so why add to it by not allowing ourselves to benefit from the blessings of hearing from God? If we pursue a close relationship with Jesus by actively following these four requirements, there is much hardship we can personally avert while limiting the robber's access into our lives at the same time.

Remember to always:
1. Actively seek out the voice of God.
2. Do what God says is right.
3. Hear and understand His directions and commandments.
4. Actively obey all of His directions and commandments.

And Moses went up unto God, and the Lord called unto him out of the mountain, saying, Thus shalt thou say to the house of Jacob, and tell the children of Israel; ...Now therefore, if ye will obey my voice indeed, and keep my covenant, then ye shall be a peculiar treasure unto me above all people: for all the earth is mine: And ye shall be unto me a kingdom of priests, and an holy nation. These are the words which thou shalt speak unto the children of Israel.

Exodus 19:3, 5–6

Do you want blessings that are waiting beyond grace, that come through obedience to God? If so, then look at the pattern set in Scripture. God only required two conditions that needed to be met for the children of Israel to be the most blessed people in all the world. These two commitments can be found in both the Old and the New Testament.

1. Obey the voice of God.
2. Be faithful to the commandments and promises of God.

Obeying God's voice means we need to hear His voice. Being faithful to His commandments and promises means we need to know Scripture. We cannot expect to have a complete Christian experience, with all the blessings God has for us, if we only rely on our knowledge of Scripture or if we only listen to God's voice. Both are not only essential for Christian maturity but are also part of God's design.

There are blessings from God that require us to hear God. Hearing God takes action and intentionality on our part.

And it shall come to pass, if thou shalt hearken diligently unto the voice of the Lord thy God, to observe and to do all his commandments which I command thee this day, that the Lord thy God will set thee on high above all nations of the earth: And all these blessings shall come on thee, and overtake thee, if thou shalt hearken unto the voice of the Lord thy God.

Deuteronomy 28:1–2

Did you notice that the word "hearken" is used both at the

opening and again at the closing of the promise in this verse? "Hearken" means to listen. We are to listen for the Lord and listen to the promise the Lord gives us. In other words, pay attention! The verse also starts by saying to "hearken diligently." Diligence requires careful, persistent work and effort. It requires action and intention to hear the voice of the Lord.

Being faithful to God's commandments and meeting the terms of His promises in Scripture will also lead to blessings. As Jesus said, "But seek ye first the kingdom of God, and his righteousness; and all these things shall be added unto you" (Matthew 6:33). The commandment is to first and most importantly seek and strive after God's kingdom in pursuit of His righteousness with the right attitude and character of God. Obedience results in the promises of all these blessings given to us. Earlier in Matthew 6:6, Jesus also urged us to take time and go to a private place and pray to God, and blessings would follow.

The blessings that come from hearing and obeying God's voice, commandments, and promises vary. In 2007, I felt like I was at the bottom of my life. On a particularly bad day, I decided to take a walk in the mall nearby, where I saw that the newest Air Jordan shoes had become available. Having collected Air Jordan shoes as a kid, I thought now was the time to buy them to improve my day. The price, however, was far higher than other Air Jordans would have been. I was told they were very limited and were made specifically for professional game use. When I tried them on, it was as if a sense of destiny came over me... but they were still too expensive.

In my own mind, I justified the purchase by telling myself that I had the money, that I deserved them, and that it was time to do what I wanted to do for a change. I took my time debating between red or black shoes, wishing I could simply buy both. I asked God what He thought, and He told me to give the money to a specific person who was working in ministry. I argued about how this would be my only chance to get these shoes, but God didn't change His mind. In my heart, I knew I wanted to obey God, so I gave the money to the person in the ministry He told me to, and as a result, the missionary was able to share the gospel.

A few months later, I was driving by a Nike outlet when suddenly God told me to stop and go inside, so I did. I eventually came to the back wall of the store, where they had shoes on clearance. To my surprise, they had one pair of the same special edition Air Jordans in black, marked way down in price, in my exact size! In my excitement, I asked the assistant if they had any more, and the result was that out of the back came the same pair in my size in red. The price on these was marked down as well. So now I had both pairs of shoes that I liked, and combined, they still cost less than the ones I had seen at the mall.

Now, I know my story may seem trivial, but for me, this was a little reminder of a much bigger truth regarding God's faithfulness, love, blessing, and mercies for me. God cares about the little things as well as the big things. When we hear and obey His voice, we will be blessed in a multitude of ways, thanks to Jesus.

The Curses for Not Hearing God

There are blessings to hearing and obeying the voice of God, but we see in Scripture that there are also curses for not listening to God's voice. How many times have we walked into a situation without hearing God when we should have and later regretted it? God loves us and cares for us; that's why He warns us throughout Scripture of the consequences of turning a deaf ear to the Shepherd's voice.

But it shall come to pass, if thou wilt not hearken unto the voice of the Lord thy God, to observe to do all his commandments and his statutes which I command thee this day; that all these curses shall come upon thee, and overtake thee.

Deuteronomy 28:15

The list of curses that follow this passage is significant. The promise was that the curses would overtake the Israelites completely, not just happen to them. That meant that there would be no outrunning them or hiding from them.

We see another account of the curses for not hearing God by Jeremiah, the weeping prophet, as he referred back to the time of the Exodus of the Jewish people from Egypt:

> *But this thing commanded I them, saying, Obey my voice, and I will be your God, and ye shall be my people: and walk ye in all the ways that I have commanded you, that it may be well unto you. But they hearkened not, nor inclined their ear, but walked in the counsels and in the imagination of their evil heart, and went backward, and not forward.*
>
> **Jeremiah 7:23–24**

When we do not listen and obey the voice of God, we can expect to be stagnant. The requirement for the Jewish people was to hear and obey the voice of God. The promise was that He would be their God and that they would be His people. The blessing was that life would go well for them. Yet, it did not go well because they did not hear or obey. The consequence for not listening to God's voice was not just stagnation but also regression. It was a physical regression as well as a spiritual one, which left them wandering backward in the desert.

Everything achieved; every bit of territory taken is chipped away and taken back by our own actions when we go backward by not hearing and obeying God. The robber doesn't even need to fight for ground because we end up giving it away in our stubbornness, ignorance, or pride. We often choose our will over God's. I know someone who has lived out his entire life under this curse. He has chosen to never permanently turn toward listening and obeying the voice of God, despite the many ways God has spoken to him. Instead, he follows his own desires in a perpetual circle, running after the same thing, trying the same methods, and expecting a different result. With each successive circle, he dwindles away time, energy, and money. He blames God but is never willing to surrender to God's will. Let's not take our last breath on earth having barely been saved by grace but never having walked into our purposes and callings because we chose to do everything our way.

We are called to run a race. That race cannot be finished by running backward when the finish line is in front of us. Jesus is on the other side of that finish line, cheering us on, calling to us with His voice. Do you hear Him? Will you follow Him? If you are still breathing, there is still time.

The Way God Speaks

And he said, Go forth, and stand upon the mount before the Lord. And, behold, the Lord passed by, and a great and strong wind rent the mountains, and brake in pieces the rocks before the Lord; but the Lord was not in the wind: and after the wind an earthquake; but the Lord was not in the earthquake: And after the earthquake a fire; but the Lord was not in the fire: and after the fire a still small voice.

1 Kings 19:11–12

This took place where God first made His covenant with Israel. The covenant started with a voice before it was written down in a contract. What I find interesting in this verse is the extremes that occur in nature are used in contrast with God's voice. The one who spoke all things into existence, the one who holds all things in His hand, the one who is more than capable of winning any shouting match speaks with a still, small, quiet voice. A voice like that requires attention and focus to hear. Elijah was called to hear it.

When looking at this passage, it is important to recognize that after hearing God's voice and being obedient to it, Elijah had a

154

radical redirection of his life and ministry. Are you in need of a radical redirection in your life? Have you tried listening for God's voice?

Jeremiah was also called to hear. God directed Jeremiah to meet Him in a specific location. Only by being obedient was he able to hear the complete message the Lord had for him.

> *The word which came to Jeremiah from the Lord, saying, Arise, and go down to the potter's house, and there I will cause thee to hear my words. ...O house of Israel, cannot I do with you as this potter? saith the Lord. Behold, as the clay is in the potter's hand, so are ye in mine hand, O house of Israel.*
>
> **Jeremiah 18:1–2, 6**

This chapter continues on, revealing the voice of the Lord giving Jeremiah a message to preach to God's people. But notice, before Jeremiah could deliver the message, he had to hear from the voice of God. I wonder how many pastors seek the Lord for a message to preach. On many occasions, I have heard three or more pastors I know, who live great distances from each other and have no contact with one another, preach on the same topic at the same time. How is this possible? It is possible because they do share one common contact: God. They seek His voice, and God directs in unity the body of Christ. How effective would the body be if we were all taking our orders from the same general? We are called to hear. "For as many as are led by the Spirit of God, they are the sons of God" (Romans 8:14).

Who does the leading? God does. How does He lead us? With His voice. The leading is an ongoing process, and the process only applies to the ones who choose to allow themselves to be led. Tell God that you choose to be led by His voice. Let Him be the Shepherd.

Jesus spoke of the importance of hearing God's voice many times throughout Scripture, particularly when He was speaking in parables. As He said many times in the Gospels, "If any man have ears to hear, let him hear" (Mark 4:23). Was Jesus talking about natural ears or spiritual ears? Presumably, everyone He was addressing had ears and, therefore, the ability to listen to Him. So why would Jesus emphasize this when talking in parables? Not everyone could understand His parables, but the Holy Spirit—the voice of God—could bring revelation and understanding of these parables, as He still does to this day.

In 2007, I had a dream from the Lord in which I saw about two hundred Christians from many denominations meeting on a hilltop that overlooked the Sacramento Valley. Everyone was gathered together to worship God and pray over the Sacramento Valley for the purpose of leading the lost to Jesus Christ. When I woke up, I could remember all the details clearly and was compelled to find the location of this hilltop. Having never been there before, I looked on satellite maps for geographical references I remembered from the dream. I was able to find what I thought would be the area, so I got in my car and drove there. When I reached the hilltop, everything was exactly like it was in my dream! I began walking the grounds and praying for the Lord to give me directions on what to do, but I heard nothing. I had enough details to force the situation to come together, but I knew if I did so, it would not be in God's timing. What was not in His timing would not be covered by His blessing.

Several years had gone by when I heard that an international evangelist was going to be coming to Sacramento with the goal of bringing all the churches together for a massive outreach. As the preliminary plans fell into place, I was asked to head up two prayer rallies for the purpose of covering the event in prayer. The purpose of the crusade was to reach the lost with the good news of Jesus Christ. I knew the first prayer meeting needed to be at the heart of Sacramento, where the crusade would eventually take place, but I was uncertain about where to have the second meeting. Then I heard God say, "Now is the time for the dream." We would place the seed of prayer in the heart of Sacramento, then cover it with prayer from the hilltop with the view of the entire valley. I obtained permission to use a park on the hilltop. Everything came together seamlessly, just as it had in my dream. It was a beautiful event that people continued to talk about months later. This event was set apart by God because I received a vision with instructions but waited for God's voice to know the timing.

This Is How Faith Comes

So then faith cometh by hearing, and hearing by the word of God.

Romans 10:17

Have you ever wondered why this verse doesn't say faith comes by reading the Bible? Faith comes by hearing God's voice. Sometimes that voice can direct us to a verse in Scripture when the Holy Spirit brings it to life with a powerful voice in one moment. Other times it comes as a still, small voice. Let's examine what we know so far:

1. God speaks
2. We hear
3. We respond
4. Faith comes

Let's break down some of the benefits that come from hearing and obeying the voice of God to build up our faith. The Prophet Isaiah was dependent on the voice of God for his calling. He also knew God's voice was trustworthy. He prioritized hearing and speaking God's voice in a world where it was not always welcomed.

The Lord God hath given me the tongue of the learned, that I should know how to speak a word in season to him that is weary: he wakeneth morning by morning, he wakeneth mine ear to hear as the learned. The Lord God hath opened mine ear, and I was not rebellious, neither turned away back. I gave my back to the smiters, and my cheeks to them that plucked off the hair: I hid not my face from shame and spitting. For the Lord God will help me; therefore shall I not be confounded: therefore have I set my face like a flint, and I know that I shall not be ashamed.

Isaiah 50:4–7

As a servant to God, Isaiah, just like Jesus, dedicated himself to hearing God speak every morning. He responded with obedience, and five things happened as a result:

1. He was given words of encouragement.
2. He received personal direction daily.
3. He developed obedience.
4. He received strength.
5. He developed determination.

As I will describe in this chapter's testimony on delaying my prayer for a woman's healing until God's timing, I heard God speak because I was listening. My response to receiving personal direction was to obey, no matter how ridiculous or illogical it seemed, because I had learned that blessing comes through obedience. Throughout the week of waiting, I received the strength to continue praying in anticipation. When the day came to pray for her healing from cancer, I was determined to go through with it because God is trustworthy. Everything happened according to God's direction so that when she was healed, my faith level soared. I had confirmation that I was hearing the voice of God; I witnessed that His promises are true. It is such an encouraging feeling to see God move when we walk in a supernatural level of faith, and a big key to living that is hearing the voice of God. We can expect to live a life that will be different from others when we hear God's voice and obey Him.

Now that we are aware of the reasons to listen for God's voice and of what it sounds like, in the next few sections, we will discuss some of the practical ways that we can learn to hear God's voice.

Preparing Our Hearts for God's Voice

Many people struggle to hear the voice of the Shepherd. If you find yourself struggling with this, do not be discouraged because you are not alone. It seems a very uncommon thing to find a Bible study or sermon that focuses on how to hear God, yet it is an essential key and mandate to Christian life. Even denominations that actively use the gifts related to hearing God's voice do not teach it often enough, in my opinion.

When Christians begin their first steps in listening for God's voice, many have preconceived ideas of what God's voice will sound like to them. The reality is that God speaks differently at different times. Sometimes it will be a deep feeling in the heart, and occasionally it may be an audible voice. There are so many other ways in which we can hear God's voice as well. Try to put your ideas aside and focus on letting God build His relationship with you in His way. In time, you will become familiar with His voice, and He will bring confirmation to build trust and fine-tune your ears. Ultimately, it is our hearts that will receive His voice. We know from Scripture that there are things we need to do to fine-tune our hearing and set ourselves in a position for receiving God's voice. Let's take a look at these together.

First, the most critical key to hearing God's voice is to have a hearing heart. To have a hearing heart, we must desire to hear God with our hearts. We must make the decision to believe and pursue Him with our entire hearts. When King Solomon, one of the wisest men to live, had a chance to ask God for anything, he asked Him for a hearing heart.

Give therefore thy servant an understanding heart to judge thy people, that I may discern between good and bad: for who is able to judge this thy so great a people? And the speech pleased the Lord, that Solomon had asked this thing.

1 King 3:9–10

The serious task of judging God's people led King Solomon to ask for a hearing heart: that is, a heart capable of receiving the voice of God with the intention to be obedient. King Solomon's dilemma was about being able to judge God's people rightly, and he knew the only one who could do so was God. So, to represent God's desire well, he realized he needed to clearly hear God's voice for direction.

We see that spiritual deafness comes with a hardened heart. The thirteenth chapter of Matthew speaks of the importance of hearing the voice of the Lord and points out that if we have a hardened heart (a heart unwilling to listen), we will not be able to hear God's voice. In the words of Jesus, we read,

And in them is fulfilled the prophecy of Esaias [known as Isaiah], which saith, By hearing ye shall hear, and shall not understand; and seeing ye shall see, and shall not perceive: For this people's heart is waxed gross, and their ears are dull of hearing, and their eyes they have closed; lest at any time they should see with their eyes, and hear with their ears, and should understand with their heart, and should be converted, and I should heal them.

Matthew 13:14–15

An unwilling heart will hear noises but have no understanding, and it will see but never comprehend. This is a setup for deception. The robber always has something to say, and a heart that is hardened in the flesh will agree with his deceptions. The only resolution to this is a soft, sensitive heart towards the Lord. A heart that can hear can lead us from wandering in the desert and guide us into His rest. As indicated in the chapter "Knowing the Will of God," we need a heart that hears so we will not wander in the desert of God's permissive will but will instead come into the promised land of His perfect will.

O come, let us worship and bow down: let us kneel before the Lord our maker. For he is our God; and we are the people of his pasture, and the sheep of his hand. To day if ye will hear his voice, Harden not your heart, as in the provocation, and as in the day of temptation in the wilderness: When your fathers tempted me, proved me, and saw my work. Forty years long was I grieved with this generation, and said, It is a people that do err in their heart, and they have not known my ways: Unto whom I sware in my wrath that they should not enter into my place of rest.

Psalm 95:6–11

Are you being robbed of peace, purpose, and direction because of a callous or hardened heart? Unresolved hurts like abuse, injustices, and loss can make a heart callous, and unforgiveness can turn a heart into stone. Is your heart in need of healing? Don't wait! Turn off the mute button and repent by turning away from that which is hurting you. Ask the Lord for healing so that you can hear God and respond to His voice. If you want to have a sensitive heart, then tell God something like this: "Dear God, I give You permission to do what You must to give me a sensitive, hearing heart that will respond to You. Let me grow in my relationship with You as my Lord and my heavenly Father. Amen."

How to Hear God's Voice

After our heart is ready to receive, we need to take action in positioning ourselves like a receiver to tune into the voice of God. We are constantly challenged by interference in the world we live in, so let us go over these five biblical steps for reception.

We need to:
1. Have an available heart.
2. Be humble.
3. Pay attention.
4. Be still and quiet.
5. Take time.

First, we need to have an available heart. Our heart not only needs to be hearing, but it also needs to be available to hear. The teacher in Proverbs advised anyone who sought wisdom: "Bow down thine ear, and hear the words of the wise, and apply thine heart unto my knowledge" (Proverbs 22:17). King Solomon was very dedicated to hearing the Lord for direction, and here he shared the wisdom he compiled regarding this. If we keep our heart unavailable because its bandwidth is consumed by other things, then there will be no room for receiving. Let's make sure to have a heart that is pure and available for God.

Next, we need to humble ourselves before God. We need to be willing to learn from what God has to say! If we have an attitude of arrogance and think we know it all, we will miss out on the depth of God's wisdom. Remember that pride comes before the fall (Proverbs 16:18). Remain teachable, and don't let God's voice pass over your ears unheard.

We also need to pay attention when God speaks. If we are attentive with open ears to His voice, we will receive godly wisdom. I think God speaks to us in a still, small voice most of the time because it forces us to listen very closely to what He is saying. He wants to train us not to miss out on the details. Everything God says is intentional, purposeful, and important. Be wise and pay attention.

Next, we need to be still, relax, and know that He is God. "Be still, and know that I am God: I will be exalted among the heathen, I will be exalted in the earth" (Psalm 46:10). To "know" is to recognize and understand that He knows everything, created everything, and holds all things in His hand. If we want to hear God's voice better, then we need to purge the clutter that consumes our bandwidth for hearing. We need to get rid of the things that occupy too much space in the air around us, which impede our ability to hear. When things are too loud, a still, small voice is drowned out.

To put this in perspective with an example, every time I drive by a school or college, I watch all the kids and young adults walking around so I can pray for them. Sadly, I notice that almost every single one of them has earbuds in the ears, zoned out and listening to music as they walk. We have a whole generation of people who are scared to death of quiet and stillness. The robber is just fine with that because as long as he is occupying their ears with noise, they will never hear the voice of God speak to them. But deep in their souls, they know there is a voice longing to have a conversation with them. The robber will do all he can to keep them from giving attention to it.

Finally, we need to take time to seek out and listen for God's voice.

Truly my soul waiteth upon God: from him cometh my salvation. ...My soul, wait thou only upon God; for my expectation is from him.

Psalm 62:1, 5

Waiting on God is an act of intentionally taking time to wait silently in submission to the Lord. It is often said that time is the one thing on earth money can't buy. But as priceless as time is, it is well worth the investment for the godly wisdom that comes from waiting on the Lord.

Even Jesus showed us the importance of being deliberate in taking time and finding a place of stillness and quiet to pray and listen for the Lord:

> *But thou, when thou prayest, enter into thy closet, and*
> *when thou hast shut thy door, pray to thy Father which is*
> *in secret; and thy Father which seeth in secret shall reward*
> *thee openly.*
>
> **Matthew 6:6**

Many Christians have the mindset that if we could just get rid of some things on the schedule or better manage others, we could have the time for God. Yet my experience indicates that this is deceptive thinking.

The robber knows that if he can get you focused on your schedule and make it the priority, the fleshly nature will never make time for God. We will always come to the conclusion that there is no time for God to fit into our schedules. The correct way of thinking according to biblical precedence is for our time with God to be the firstfruit of our day, and everything else in the schedule should be built off of Him as our foundation. Doing this puts trust in God and honors Him by putting Him first. Don't get robbed by the end of the day: Keep God first.

Confirmation for Hearing God's Voice

There are many counterfeits to God's voice in the world, and the robber will use them to distract humanity. We don't need to memorize what all of the counterfeits sound like; we need only to know God's voice. In the banking industry, employees are not trained to memorize what every kind of counterfeit bill looks like; they simply teach them to recognize the real thing.[57] A bank teller will become so familiar with a real bill—the feel, the look, even the smell—that when there is an imposter, it is instantly recognizable. This is how it should be for Christians when it comes to knowing the voice of the Shepherd, Jesus Christ. Knowing the tools we are given in Scripture to filter out any counterfeit signal is important. Here are four of the tools with which we can, over time, become so familiar with God's voice that it will be like the voice of a best friend:

1. God's voice always agrees with Scripture.
2. God's voice is often confirmed by proceeding events.
3. God's voice speaking to our hearts is attended by peace in our spirits.
4. God's voice is often confirmed to us through other believers.

First, God's voice will always speak in agreement with Scripture. This is an absolute guarantee. "All Scripture is given by inspiration of God, and is profitable for doctrine, for reproof, for correction, for instruction in righteousness" (2 Timothy 3:16). If you hear a voice coming from another person, from thin air, or even from your own heart, and it is in contradiction to Scripture, you can be sure that it is not the voice of God.

Beware of the counterfeit voice that will come in many different ways.

> *And when they shall say unto you, Seek unto them that have familiar spirits, and unto wizards that peep, and that mutter: should not a people seek unto their God? for the living to the dead? To the law and to the testimony: if they speak not according to this word, it is because there is no light in them.*
>
> **Isaiah 8:19–20**

The Word of God is the light, and the light comes from God. The two are inseparable. God's voice will always bring the light of God's Word.

King David loved God's laws and saw God's Word as a precious gift. He appreciated the ability of God's Word to guide him, saying,

"Thy word is a lamp unto my feet, and a light unto my path" (Psalm 119:105). Some Christians imagine walking around carrying the lantern illuminating wherever their flesh wants to go, but that is not how God's Word works. God is the one holding the lantern. The path it illuminates is true and trustworthy because God is carrying it. He can't separate Himself from it; He is the light, Himself. So, if we wander away from the light and follow another voice, we will lose sight of the path. Know the Word of God, and use it to filter out the cheap imitations.

The second way to discern God's voice is confirmation. God kindly gives us this confirmation of His voice so that we can build trust and recognition of Him. Confirmation comes to us through events around us. Examples of confirmation are found all throughout Scripture. One can be found in Jeremiah when God informed the prophet,

> *Behold, Hanameel the son of Shallum thine uncle shall come unto thee, saying, Buy thee my field that is in Anathoth: for the right of redemption is thine to buy it. So Hanameel mine uncle's son came to me in the court of the prison according to the word of the Lord, and said unto me, Buy my field, I pray thee, that is in Anathoth, which is in the country of Benjamin: for the right of inheritance is thine, and the redemption is thine; buy it for thyself. Then I knew that this was the word of the Lord.*
>
> **Jeremiah 32:7–8**

Jeremiah knew nothing about the land that he was purchasing, so he had to listen carefully to the voice of God for direction. Because of how this verse is written, it can be assumed he was not initially sure if the voice he heard was actually God. Yet confirmation came when the prophetic word of knowledge played out exactly how God said it would.

If you ever experience a situation where you are truly struggling with recognizing God's voice, be reassured that God is kind enough to give you what you need. Ask Him for confirmation. Sometimes people are afraid to ask the Lord for confirmation because they think it is rebellion. True rebellion is when you know you heard God but still choose not to obey. A healthy desire for confirmation comes from the will to do what is right. Asking God for confirmation when you are truly unsure of His voice is biblical.

The third thing to look for in hearing God's voice is that when we do, we can and will have the peace of the Lord in our hearts. "And let the peace of God rule in your hearts, to the which also ye are called in one body; and be ye thankful" (Colossians 3:15). The peace of God is the inner calm that comes to us when we walk with Him daily. Sometimes hearing God's voice can stir up all sorts of physical emotions, but at the very core level, there should always be an underlying peace. It is like a boat in the ocean, in the middle of rough, thrashing waters. The movement of the seas can be felt on the outside, but at the center, where the sleeping rooms are, rest can still be found.

Just as peace is confirmation, when there is no peace, we need to be cautious. Looking back on my life, I have never regretted walking away from an urgent decision for which I felt no peace. Sometimes, the lack of peace meant that it wasn't the right decision, and other times it was just the wrong timing. Either way, being patient often leads to the right choice. In fact, sometimes walking away even leads to better opportunities, accompanied by God's peace.

Finally, we can receive confirmation that we have heard God's voice through other believers. For example, God had a calling on Paul's life that He revealed directly to him. Paul was very aware of his calling and introduced himself in some of his letters as "Paul, an apostle, not of men, neither by man, but by Jesus Christ, and God the Father, who raised him from the dead" (Galatians 1:1). This calling was affirmed in a public confirmation by the leading of the Holy Spirit through Simeon, Lucius, and Manaen. In addition to all the other believers in attendance being put on notice of Paul's calling,

God Himself gave confirmation of His voice through the prophets and teachers.

> *Now there were in the church that was at Antioch certain prophets and teachers; as Barnabas, and Simeon that was called Niger, and Lucius of Cyrene, and Manaen, which had been brought up with Herod the tetrarch, and Saul. As they ministered to the Lord, and fasted, the Holy Ghost said, Separate me Barnabas and Saul for the work whereunto I have called them. And when they had fasted and prayed, and laid their hands on them, they sent them away.*
>
> **Acts 13:1–3**

God can always bring a random stranger to us for confirmation, but we need to be proactive in surrounding ourselves with mature, stable believers who live godly lives and who regularly listen to God's voice. This provides us with a network of people from whom we can seek out confirmation and wisdom when needed. The Holy Spirit's words, through them, can help build our faith and validate God's calling on our lives. God speaks to us through others sometimes because it requires us to rely on the community for counsel and wisdom instead of flying solo.

In my life, when I hear the voice of God, I may not necessarily always need confirmation. However, if He brings confirmation of His voice through another believer anyway, it is time to pay close attention. I might either be missing a detail in the word He gave, or I might be on the verge of passing by something that is time-sensitive. In fact, it was a similar case with this book. I heard God tell me to write it in 2010, but it was not my top priority until I received confirmation through a stranger in 2015. On that day, while I was doing ministry with a friend, a random stranger from Russia walked up to me, described this book in detail to me, calling it "The Owner's Manual" (my codename for the book), and told me that I needed to finish writing it. It was like a slap in the face from God. The moral of the story is, if you suddenly get confirmation on something you already knew you heard from God, it is time to stop and pay attention before you end up robbing yourself.

A Testimony of Listening

One Sunday after church, I was praying for people at the front of the room when a lovely couple came over for prayer for the wife's healing from terminal cancer. I quickly agreed, but I took a moment first to listen for God's voice for direction. To my surprise, I heard the Lord instructing me to pray for her husband first and have her come back next week for prayer. Immediately I start to rationalize things in my mind. She had only weeks or a few months at best to live, so there was no guarantee she could come back the next week. Her husband had not even asked for prayer. But I knew that I heard God, and I had no doubt I needed to obey. So I told them I wanted to pray for her husband first, and they both allowed me to do so. The Lord showed me that the husband had areas of hurt that needed healing and other areas that needed to be built up and strengthened.

After I was finished praying for him, I realized that the husband needed to pray for his wife out loud, with me encouraging and helping him through it. This was part of his healing process. After he was done, they both expected that it was my turn to pray. I continued to obey the Lord's voice and asked them to come back next week so I could pray for her. With a look of curiosity but some understanding, she agreed.

So as the week went by, I kept telling myself, "I hope I heard God. I hope I know what I am doing. I hope she makes it through the week and comes back." Toward the end of the week, when a church leadership meeting came up, I decided to talk with the prayer team about what happened and to ask them to be looking for her at the four services. Later in the meeting, one of the prayer team members brought up the subject of praying in tongues and claimed he didn't believe in it. Just as I was about to address it, I heard the Lord's voice say, "Wait; I have an appointed time to demonstrate this." So I kept silent.

That weekend, the wife came up to me after service for prayer. I like to make a habit of praying in teams of two or three, so I quickly grabbed two men to join me. One of them was the man who didn't believe in praying in tongues. I took a deep breath and checked in with the Lord. He instructed me to pray in tongues over her. I do believe in praying in tongues, but I do not often do it in public. Especially since I now knew that one of my prayer partners did not believe in it, I found the situation a bit uncomfortable. That's how God works sometimes. I made an excuse to God in my head that the woman would probably get offended if I prayed in tongues, but the Lord responded, "Ask her." When I did, she was excited about the idea. I gave in and stepped forward in obedience and faith. As soon as I started to pray for her, the presence of God showed up in a powerful way that was undeniable. The following week, she came back to church with before and after scans showing the exciting news that all the cancer in her neck and upper torso was totally gone. Thanks to God, she was instantly healed and is still cancer-free to this day!

Hearing God's voice and being obedient to His direction was critical in this situation. In fact, almost every time Scripture talks about healing, there is an emphasis on the need to hear God. There was a three-step process that needed to happen: to hear God, to obey His voice, and to declare in prayer the promises of God. When we prayed for the couple, the order of that process defied what our natural impulse would have been. In the natural, we would have just prayed for the most obviously pressing problem. But because I heard the Shepherd's voice and obeyed His direction, both husband and wife received healing, God was glorified, and God Himself demonstrated the power of praying in tongues to a doubter.

Hearing Will Happen

If you choose to listen to God's voice, the hearing will happen. Give it time, and don't be discouraged. Sometimes it's a process, and other times it's instant. Either way, He will reveal His voice to you. Take these tools you now have to verify His voice, and with them, you will also know the voice of God and reject the voice of the robber.

Don't let preconceived ideas about what you think your experience will be like distract you from noticing when God's voice reaches out. Have faith that God will speak to you in a way that you can understand. God will meet you where you are when you hearken to His voice.

Closing Prayer

Loving and merciful God, please lead us to a place where we can hear Your voice unimpaired. Grant to us the full measure of blessings that come from hearing and obeying Your voice. Give us strength and determination to begin each day in prayer and seek Your voice for direction. May we be so familiar with Your voice that the very breath that precedes the words of the counterfeit set off our alarm. May our hearts be sensitive and correctable. May our ears not be muffled with foolishness. And may our actions be pleasing to You. Amen.

CHAPTER 6:

Do Not Be Deceived

And the great dragon was cast out, that old serpent, called the Devil, and Satan, which deceiveth the whole world: he was cast out into the earth, and his angels were cast out with him.

Revelation 12:9

From the beginning of mankind, the robber has been using deception as a primary tool of thievery. He appears as something he isn't, he speaks with a crafty tongue and weaves lies around truths, and he tempts us with stimulants that appeal to our flesh and separate us from God. This is the nature of the one that personifies the blinding dark, the one who is cleverer than all but God, according to the accounts in Genesis 3. This cunning thief is the source of the lies that we are warned about throughout Scripture when we are told not to be deceived. Unfortunately, I have met many lifelong Christians who have never sought the tools God has made available to us to prevent deception from invading our lives and luring us away from God's perfect will. There are also Christians who know about the tools but never use them. This ignorance of the tools or unwillingness to use them allows many things to be stolen in the Christian life.

"Do not be deceived" is a recurring warning throughout the Old Testament. It is a priority for Christians to hear and obey God's voice. It behooves us to acknowledge the plethora of warnings from Jesus against being deceived. When Jesus Christ came in the flesh, He didn't abolish this warning but doubled down on it. This should be a foundational teaching for all Christians by pastors and teachers to the body of Christ, as it was for Jesus. This is a priority for all Christians! Deception is dangerous; it is a primary tool of the master of thievery. He steals dreams, friendships, gifts, callings, opportunities, provision, and even our minds through deception.

There are two Greek words that both translate into English as "word," but they both have two different meanings: *logos* and *rhema*. In this chapter, we will mostly be referring to the word *logos*, meaning God's total purpose, written and recorded (the Bible). The writers of the New Testament used *logos* more than 300 times, mostly with its basic meaning, but even this is arguably quite diversified. I believe a broader philosophical definition of *logos* is that it is a word often used in writing to persuade an audience using logical arguments and supportive evidence. God is a God of order, purpose, and design. These attributes are summed up in logic.

Some examples of *logos* are found in both the Old and New Testaments. King David observed, "For ever, O Lord, thy word is settled in heaven" (Psalm 119:89). This word can never change; it stands firm; it is eternal; it is unchangeable. We also see that Jesus, the living Word, is included as God's total purpose: "In the beginning was the Word, and the Word was with God, and the Word was God" (John 1:1).

In this chapter, we will also cover the tools God has put in place for us to utilize in building a safety system to combat deception. When these systems become a part of our Christian walk, we will have the ability to neutralize the robber and hold on to the things that are ours to keep. Some people already have a level of discernment built into their spiritual DNA because of their calling as prophets and apostles or because of the spiritual gift of discernment. If this is you, you may discover that you already use these tools to a degree but have never identified them specifically. By understanding and using all the tools God has made available to us, we can have security systems in place that will keep thievery at bay and take back ground that has been lost. Over time, your security system will become so proficient that you will even detect the robber intruding on the lives of others around you, giving you the opportunity to speak into their lives.

Be Grounded in Truth

To overcome deception, we need to be grounded in "the way, the truth and the life" (John 14:6). Jesus Christ is the truth, the bedrock of our faith, and the Bible is the anchor. The Bible is a physical thing capable of being held, but it isn't the physicality that makes it the anchor. It is the fact that it is the living, breathing Word of God that makes it an anchor. Every time we read it, we can discover new revelations in deepening layers as the Holy Spirit reveals them. "In the beginning was the Word, and the Word was with God and the Word was God," John 1:1 says, and Jesus Christ is the Word made flesh. The two are inseparable.

Imagine yourself as a ship, and the sea underneath you is life. There are times and seasons when the ocean is still and calm, and others when it is rough and choppy. For a ship to stay grounded in one location, the best place to lay an anchor is on bedrock that is hard, solid, and immovable. Jesus Christ is that rock. The Word of God is the anchor that tethers us to the immovable rock. The totality of Scripture is the perfect amount of rope that tethers the ship to the anchor so that whether the seas are calm or whether the winds blow and the seas rage, we will still remain centered on Him and will not sink. But the danger for Christians is that when we begin removing and discarding sections from the Bible, it stretches the tether, and we begin to float further and further away from where the anchor is set. Eventually, we can get to a point where so much has been removed from Scripture that our line is too slack, and the tether breaks, leaving us lost at sea.

Knowing this, the robber will do everything he can to deceive you into stretching your tether until it breaks from the anchor. Fortify your connection with unbreakable steel by knowing the truth. The world doesn't want us to know the truth. Instead, it wants us to believe in moral relativism. But there is absolute truth, and that truth is known as Jesus Christ.

What to Expect from Being Grounded

Because we read the Bible, we know that Jesus Christ is "the way, the truth, and the life: no man cometh unto the Father, but by [Him]" (John 14:6).

Because we read the Bible, when the world tells us that we evolved from prehistoric sludge, we know the truth is we were created in the image of God.

Because we read the Bible, when the world tells us we have no purpose and life is just random chance, we know the truth is God has a plan, a purpose, a calling for our life, and He determines every outcome.

Because we read the Bible, when the world tells us man is good and that it is our environment that makes us sin, we know the truth is that man is inherently sinful.

The world wants to tell us that everything we can see, touch, taste, and feel is real and to live in the here and now with no regard for the afterlife. The Bible tells us the things that are unseen are more real than what is seen; the decisions we make now have eternal consequences in the afterlife.

The world says we need to fight our battles in the flesh. The Bible tells us that we fight "not against flesh and blood, but against principalities, against powers, against the rulers of the darkness of this world, against spiritual wickedness in high places" (Ephesians 6:12).

Because we read the Bible, we know the promises of Scripture:

Promise 1: We will never be alone:

Go ye therefore, and teach all nations, baptizing them in

the name of the Father, and of the Son, and of the Holy Ghost: Teaching them to observe all things whatsoever I have commanded you: and, lo, I am with you alway, even unto the end of the world. Amen.

Matthew 28:19–20

Promise 2: We have nothing to fear:

And the Lord, he it is that doth go before thee; he will be with thee, he will not fail thee, neither forsake thee: fear not, neither be dismayed.

Deuteronomy 31:8

Peace I leave with you, my peace I give unto you: not as the world giveth, give I unto you. Let not your heart be troubled, neither let it be afraid.

John 14:27

Promise 3: There is no need to worry:

Therefore take no thought, saying, What shall we eat? or, What shall we drink? or, Wherewithal shall we be clothed? (For after all these things do the Gentiles seek:) for your heavenly Father knoweth that ye have need of all these things. But seek ye first the kingdom of God, and his righteousness; and all these things shall be added unto you. Take therefore no thought for the morrow: for the morrow shall take thought for the things of itself. Sufficient unto the day is the evil thereof.

Matthew 6:31–34

Promise 4: God can handle every circumstance in our life:

I will lift up mine eyes unto the hills, from whence cometh my help. My help cometh from the Lord, which made heaven and earth. He will not suffer thy foot to be moved: he that keepeth thee will not slumber.

Psalm 121:1–3

It is because of Scripture that we know of God's triunity, human depravity, the necessity of God's grace, the need for faith, Christ's virgin birth, His sinlessness, His deity and His humanity, His atoning death, His bodily resurrection, His bodily ascension, His intercession, and His second coming. We need to study the Word of God. Reading two hours of Scripture every Sunday at church isn't going to cut it; we need to take time to be in the Word of God daily.

Four Types of Hearers

Studying the Bible is important to our spiritual growth as followers of Jesus Christ. Jesus Himself compares reading the Bible with a seed planted in good soil. In the parable of the sower of the seed in Luke 8:5–8, Jesus used an example of a farmer spreading seed to grow crop and highlighted four different variables for how the seed would respond, depending on where it fell. He later went on to explain the meaning of the parable. Let's look at the following verses to see the four types of hearts Jesus illustrated when it came to receiving the truth of the Word of God.

Now the parable is this: The seed is the word of God. Those by the way side are they that hear; then cometh the devil, and taketh away the word out of their hearts, lest they should believe and be saved. They on the rock are they, which, when they hear, receive the word with joy; and these have no root, which for a while believe, and in time of temptation fall away. And that which fell among thorns are they, which, when they have heard, go forth, and are choked with cares and riches and pleasures of this life, and bring no fruit to perfection. But that on the good ground are they, which in an honest and good heart, having heard the word, keep it, and bring forth fruit with patience.

Luke 8:11–15

In this parable, we first see the ones by the wayside who have open ears to hear but also have open doors to thievery. Because of their choices, covenants, and lifestyles, the devil has legal permission to snatch away the truth from their hearts.

Second are the ones on the rocks, who have no roots to anchor them to the bedrock of Jesus Christ. They hear the Word and maybe even have a spiritual experience with supernatural joy and excitement. But when temptation comes, they fall away because they aren't grounded with the Word of God as their anchor.

Third are the ones who hear and believe, but when they go out into the world, they get lost to the things of this world. Their eyes are not fixed on Jesus, but they are instead distracted by the blinding dark. The Word of God is not the lantern at their feet lighting their path; the morning star of this world grabs their attention. It is my belief that at least part of the "prosperity gospel" is related to this concept because so much of it tends to focus on the material things of this temporary world. Verse 14 claims that those who represent the seed that fell in among the thorns are "choked with cares, riches, and pleasures of life, and bring no fruit to perfection." Other versions of this passage render the word "perfection" as "maturity;" notice that Scripture says there will be fruit from their efforts, but it will never come to maturity.

And last, we have the ones on good ground. These people with good, mature fruit have three qualities: First, they have noble hearts.

Second, they receive the Word and hold themselves anchored to the rock. Third, they have the patience to apply it.

Where do you find yourself in these four examples?

Three Voices

There are three types of voices that can speak to us. The first comes from the flesh, the second comes from the spiritual realm, and the third is God's voice. The thief will attack using many voices through both flesh and spirit, with the intent of planting his own seed in us.

He hopes we will water that seed so it will grow into a weed that will choke out God's voice. Through Scripture, we can learn about these different voices, and through the Word of God and the Holy Spirit, we can learn to discern between the voices.

The voice of flesh is our carnality. It is the voice that speaks from the knowledge of the things of this world. This voice can be good or bad, it can speak truth or lies, it can speak in love or deceit, and it can come from a friend or a foe. When our minds are renewed in Christ, and our judgment is sound with reasoning based on God's Word and His character, the truth will be spoken because our flesh is under submission to God's kingship. Using the tools to rightly discern and a mind renewed in Christ will overcome the natural rebellion of the flesh against God.

Second is the voice that comes from a spirit, which speaks from the realm of the unseen. Because these voices are multidimensional, their avenues for communication are numerous. Spiritual voices can range from messengers from heaven to demons from hell; they can give warnings to heed or can tempt us into a trap, and they can reveal themselves as they are or masquerade in deception.

Last is the voice of God. He speaks in many ways, from a still, small voice in the wind to a loud voice that shakes our spirits awake at night and leaves our bodies in wonder. He is always true because

He is truth. He always speaks in love because He is love, and He is always consistent because He never changes. He can speak as the Shepherd leading us by the Holy Spirit, or as sovereign Lord booming through the heavens like lighting, as He alone holds all things together in His hand. The robber desires to be like God, so he attempts to imitate God's voice. In fact, the book of Revelation tells us that Satan will pull out every trick he knows in the last days to do just that. But we can know the truth from the counterfeit.

God's Word Written through Man's Hand

There are many questions people ask about Scripture, questions such as: Why is Scripture trustworthy? Why would God deliver His written Word through flawed people? And hasn't the Bible been corrupted over the years? These questions and more are ones we as Christians can struggle with, too, if we do not know the Word of God. So let's fortify our tether to the rock by seeking answers, and let's build our faith in Scripture by discovering the supernatural qualities that prove its authenticity.

Why did God reveal His Word through man? This question is a valid one, but there is no clear answer. However, we need to be careful not to think that our ignorance of the answer diminishes the validity of the Word or the effectiveness of God's delivery method at all. Some of people's attempts to "justify" that the Word is truly from God are actually superfluous. Common questions I hear are, Why wouldn't He just give the message through a prophet? Why wouldn't He deliver the message in person? Why not make it appear miraculously? Why wouldn't it be written in the heavens? The answer to all of these is that God already has. These questions will only consume a Christian if he doesn't know the entirety of the Word of God. Don't neglect the Word of God. Take time to research the answers; they are there.

God chose a method of written communication to us through

the hands of flawed men. Scripture clearly lays out God's design for this, as He is the great architect for delivering the written Word of God to mankind.

The words of the Lord are pure words: as silver tried in a furnace of earthly clay, purified seven times.

Psalm 12:6

Earthly clay is the human vessel, and the fire is the refining fire of the Holy Spirit. The word "silver" in Hebrew (keceph) is also used for money and means "a resource of great wealth."[58] This silver is the message of God, purified seven times. The number seven in Scripture means perfection, completeness, and achievement. So we see, laid out for us in this verse, the blueprint God used to deliver His written Word to us. The words of direction and promise from God are pure words that are a bountiful resource of great wealth given to us, kept purified within Him by the Holy Spirit, and refined seven times to achieve perfection and completeness in written form. This is the supernatural, undeniable truth given to us.

The Sanctity and Authority of Scripture

The entirety of the Word of God is the anchor of faith that keeps us from wandering too far from the source of truth. The chain that tethers us to the anchor is a fixed length that keeps us from sinking and drowning when the waves of life rise up. Most Americans say they are fond of the Bible. Unfortunately, a recent study shows as little as ten percent have actually read the entire Bible once or more, and a whopping fifty-three percent have only read several passages or less![59] If we apply these numbers to the sixty-five percent of Americans that claim to be Christian, then at best, only fifteen and a half percent have read the entire Bible.[60] If most Christians don't know the Word of God, then the tether to the anchor will become so long that they can be swept far away from the truth—or, as we said earlier, their chain can even break. A Bible is physical and can be held onto, but that isn't the weight that grounds us; it is the weight of the words of truth and life within it that grounds us.

The weight of the words carries authority. The English word "authority" comes directly from the word "author." The author is the one who has all the authority: that is why we need to know the author of the Bible. He is the one who keeps us anchored in truth. Without access to the truth, we would be swallowed up by a world of deception and moral relativism.

Today there exists an all-out assault on the Bible. The agenda is to keep people separated from the anchor and permanently lost at sea. As long as truth exists in writing and in the hearts of Christians, the ruler of this world, Satan, cannot rob everyone, mold them into his image and streamline them into his plans. Deception is the robber's tool to convert hearts and rob the saints. As we have been discussing, a tool for combating deception is Scripture. The Word of God is truth, and the power of the blood and name of Jesus Christ is a sledgehammer that crushes the robber's deceit.

The multidimensional and trans-dimensional nature of the Word of God makes it a totally unique book apart from all other books, and it can be empirically proven as such. It tells us that the reality we cannot see, touch, or feel is more real than that which we can, and science has now revealed statements written thousands of years ago to be true. The archaeological and documentary discoveries that are constantly occurring continue to prove the Bible as accurate. It speaks of prophetic events that have happened and some that have yet to happen, proving its source comes from outside the confines of linear time. Its authentication comes from the one who "[declares] the end from the beginning, and from ancient times the things that are not yet done," according to Isaiah 46:10. Only God has this ability. God authenticates His Word through this attribute that is unique only to Him.

Paul wrote about how the vastness of Christ's love far exceeds our four dimensions in Ephesians 3:17–19. He referred to breadth, in Greek, *platos*, which can mean a great extent of time,[61] *mekos*, meaning length,[62] *bathos*, meaning depth,[63] and *hupsos*, which means height.[64] The Bible often refers to these dimensions as the things that can be seen. This is the physical reality our bodies interact with, but the Bible is also suggestive of six additional dimensions beyond the four Paul described. It used to be believed that space was an empty vacuum; the Bible has always indicated otherwise. These extra dimensions of space are what the Bible sometimes refers to as the things that are unseen. The Bible describes space as something that can be torn (Isaiah 64:1), worn out like a garment (Psalm 102:25), shaken (Hebrews 12:26), burnt up (2 Peter 3:12), rolled up like a scroll (Isaiah 34:4), and stretched (Isaiah 40:22). If these describe the different dimensions that we do not see, then that is a total of ten dimensions altogether, four knowable and six unseens. The prevailing assumptions of string theory, a theoretical explanation of the universe and all matter, just happen to involve ten dimensions.[65]

The dimensions that are seen consist of matter that is subjugated to the laws of entropy.[66] This means everything seen has an expiration date, but some subatomic particles are unseen and do not experience decay or death.[67] These truths have only recently been discovered by man, but they were revealed by God two thousand years ago, "for the things which are seen are temporal; but the things which are not seen are eternal," as recorded in 2 Corinthians 4:18.

We have sixty-six books, written by forty or more authors, spread over a wide geographical range, living over a period of two thousand years, with an integrated message that fits together like a complex puzzle. These facts combined suggest that the book can ultimately only have been written by one author. For example, the book of Revelation points to Daniel by using the same prophetic animal pictures to represent future empires, regardless of the 650 years separating the two books. Every book of the Bible is a key part of a linked and perfectly coordinated message, as every name, number, and detail exquisitely displays God's total sovereignty.

A Complex and Integrated Whole

For a further level of complexity, there are multiple layers of revelation behind the text, giving a four-dimensional property to Scripture. When I studied Scripture as a teen, I thought genealogical studies were boring, but now, that has changed. I have learned they are a fountain of revelation and a thumbprint of the author! The genealogy of Noah in Genesis chapter 5 is an excellent example of these deeper hidden messages. Hebrew meanings of names have much significance in the Bible and often contain a description of what is happening at the time of birth or a prophetic message of what is going to happen in a person's lifetime. When we take the meaning of each name from the Hebrew, we discover something amazing.

Adam: *adam* means "man, mankind."[68]

Seth: *sheth* means "substituted;"[69] Seth was appointed by God to be the "substitute" for Cain (Genesis 4:25), so the word is also used to mean "appointed."[70]

Enosh: *anash* means "mortal, frail, incurable, sick, desperately wicked."[71]

Kenan: comes from the root word *qiynah*, which means "sorrow, dirge, elegy, lamentation."[72]

Mahalalel: comes from two root words: *mahalal*, which means "the blessed, praise,"[73] and *El*, which means "God;"[74] complete meaning: "the blessed God."

Jared: *yaradh* means "to descend, to bring down, shall come down."[75]

185

Enoch: (who was raptured before the flood judgment): *chanak* means "initiate, discipline, train-up, dedicate, teaching."[76]

Methuselah: comes from two root words: *muwth*, which means "death, to die,"[77] and *shalach*, which means "sow, give, to bring, send forth;"[78] complete meaning: "his death shall bring."

Lamech: comes from two root words: *lemek*, whose meaning is "from an unused root of uncertain,"[79] and *nahah*, meaning: "groan, bewail, despairing."[80]

Noah: *nacham* means "console, to bring comfort, ease oneself, to sigh."[81]

So when the meanings of every name from the genealogy of Noah are placed in order of their birth, we read: Man (is) appointed mortal sorrow, (but) the blessed God shall come down teaching. His death shall bring the despairing comfort (and) relief. How incredible it is to see the entire redemptive plan of God to rescue all mankind from sin laid out in the first names mentioned in history! This is proof that the Christian gospel is found in the genealogy of the Jewish Torah. And that is only the beginning, as further studies will reveal that each name is a prophetic account of the happenings that were occurring within his lifetime. For example, Jared's name means "shall come down," and it is during his lifetime that we see the accounts of Genesis chapter 6 regarding the fallen angels (*bnei HaElohim*) coming down and taking the daughters of humans (*nashim HaAdam*). There is no way this could have been constructed by men, but only through the inspiration of the Holy Spirit.

We also see the extent of God's mercy and grace when judgment is involved. Methuselah's name means "his death shall bring." The impending flood judgment was preached on for four generations. Methuselah's father, Enoch, had a vision that as long as his son was alive, the judgment would be withheld. As we know, the year he died was the year of the flood. The Bible also tells us that Methuselah was the oldest man who ever lived; he was 969 years old when he died (Genesis 5:27). This demonstration, often overlooked in Scripture, shows how long God will wait—even until the last possible moment—to allow mankind every opportunity for repentance before His judgment. But that judgment must come, as both justice and mercy are needed for the ultimate expression of love.

Jared's and Methuselah's stories are just two small examples out of many complex demonstrations of the absolute integrity of design and origin. When we study the Bible in its entirety from Genesis to Revelation, we find that it all ties together. When we read the book of Revelation, we find that it is all in code; to decipher these codes, we must look back to every other book of the Bible. All of Scripture is one preplanned package delivered from outside the confines of linear time.

It can be proven many times over statistically, scientifically, archeologically, biologically, relationally, and prophetically that the Bible is true and that its information is sourced from outside the physical capabilities of man. The Word of God is living and breathing and has been made flesh in Jesus Christ. So if Scripture is not of this world, then the question is, "Who is the author? Does an author not sign his work?" Of course he does! The author is the one with all the authority. He has left His signature, the redemptive power of His blood, all through the Bible. So why should anyone think that the author is someone else? The author is God Himself. He is who He says He is. We are held accountable for what we know; it is God's revelation through His Word that provides knowledge for us to draw closer to Him in His perfect time. Be as sure of the Bible as you are sure by faith in Jesus Christ. The two are inseparable!

There are teachings that seek to diminish the Old Testament by claiming that it was made totally irrelevant by Jesus. On the other side, there are some who take the Old Testament laws too far by refusing to acknowledge how Jesus fulfilled its prophecies. The Old Testament is the New Testament concealed, and the New Testament is the Old Testament revealed. The truth is that they are inseparable because they are both one, as Jesus Christ is the Word made flesh. Jesus Himself said in John 10:35 that the Scriptures cannot be undone, annulled, discredited, or broken. The whole Scripture is one truth, so any removal from it breaks the reliability of the whole, making it untrue. We cannot pick and choose some passages and disregard others. It is all or nothing: truth is truth and cannot be true if modified in any way. Whenever we disregard things from Scripture, we stretch our tether from the anchor, risking damage, flooding, or even getting lost at sea.

Jesus Is the Word

It is important that we have correct and sound doctrine as a tool to fight deception. Salvation, growth, and spiritual maturity are all built on the sure foundation of the bedrock of Jesus Christ and the Word of God as our anchor. Because we depend so much on the truth of the Word, the robber comes to steal and destroy this foundation with false teachings about Jesus. He discredits the Word of God as a bundle of irrelevant stories, myths, or fables. God warns us many times in Scripture to be aware of false teaching, and we need to be able to recognize false teachers not only in the world but also in the church!

> *Take heed therefore unto yourselves, and to all the flock, over the which the Holy Ghost hath made you overseers, to feed the church of God, which he hath purchased with his own blood. For I know this, that after my departing shall grievous wolves enter in among you, not sparing the flock. Also of your own selves shall men arise, speaking perverse things, to draw away disciples after them.*

Acts 20:28–30

Not all false teachers are operating with the malicious intent to deceive, so we cannot judge false doctrine simply by a person's character. Many people will see a person's good intentions and accept his false teachings. This is one of the avenues by which demonic teaching easily enters the church. These teachings seek to separate the Word from the Word that was made flesh, Jesus. We must verify everyone's teachings against the Word of God.

There has been among some Christians for many years a growing movement to disregard the Old Testament; this same movement is now starting to chip away at parts of the New Testament as well. It teaches that Jesus has made parts of the New Testament, as well as the whole Old Testament, irrelevant. This teaching does not teach the Jesus of Scripture, but it teaches a Jesus the very Word of God warns us about. Scripture is one integrated message that came in the flesh through Jesus Christ. The robber seeks to remove the Word of God from Jesus because he knows that without the ability to know Jesus' identity through Scripture, a false Christ can more easily be accepted.

In Matthew chapter 3, we see that Jesus was baptized in the River Jordan by John, and the Holy Spirit descended like a dove and remained on Him. The use of the word "remained" is used very intentionally to notify us that from then on, the Holy Spirit never left Him. Jesus never said or did anything that caused the dove to fly away; He was perfect and without sin because He was (and is) God. As we continue with the story in Matthew chapter 4, we read that when Satan tempted Jesus, He responded to all three temptations of the devil with the written Word of God. Being filled with the Holy Spirit and as the Son of God, His tools for fighting back against Satan were endless. Yet His choice weapon came in the form of a double-edged sword, the Word of God.

And when the tempter came to him, he said, If thou be the Son of God, command that these stones be made bread. But he answered and said, It is written, Man shall not live by

189

bread alone, but by every word that proceedeth out of the mouth of God. Then the devil taketh him up into the holy city, and setteth him on a pinnacle of the temple, And saith unto him, If thou be the Son of God, cast thyself down: for it is written, He shall give his angels charge concerning thee: and in their hands they shall bear thee up, lest at any time thou dash thy foot against a stone. Jesus said unto him, It is written again, Thou shalt not tempt the Lord thy God. Again, the devil taketh him up into an exceeding high mountain, and sheweth him all the kingdoms of the world, and the glory of them; And saith unto him, All these things will I give thee, if thou wilt fall down and worship me. Then saith Jesus unto him, Get thee hence, Satan: for it is written, Thou shalt worship the Lord thy God, and him only shalt thou serve. Then the devil leaveth him, and, behold, angels came and ministered unto him.

Matthew 4:3–11

Notice that Satan had no answer to the Scripture: he simply moved on to the next subject. Neither Jesus nor the devil ever questioned the authority of Scripture. Unfortunately, fallen man can fall prey to sin and doubt that leads to disbelief and even to disobedience. A study of church history reveals that many pastors and theologians fall prey to the devil when he gets them to question Scripture, which ultimately draws them into false teaching or outright denial of that Scripture. Jesus' use of Scripture demonstrates its dependability, and the results of His use of it reveal its authoritative power.

Think not that I am come to destroy the law, or the prophets: I am not come to destroy, but to fulfil. For verily I say unto you, Till heaven and earth pass, one jot or one tittle shall in no wise pass from the law, till all be fulfilled.

Matthew 5:17–18

Here, Jesus was speaking about the written Word of God. He endorsed the complete written authority of God. Its expiration date is not to come until the fulfillment of all the prophecies written within it, the last prophecy in Scripture being the creation of the new heavens and new earth.

Later on in Jesus' ministry, the Sadducees came to Jesus asking a question concerning life after death. Jesus responded with ease, saying,

> *But as touching the resurrection of the dead, have ye not read that which was spoken unto you by God, saying, I am the God of Abraham, and the God of Isaac, and the God of Jacob? God is not the God of the dead, but of the living.*
>
> **Matthew 22:31–32**

These words were originally spoken by God to Moses approximately 1400 years earlier; Jesus applied them to the context of the here and now by saying, "Have you not read?" He could have explained this differently, but He chose to use His own words in the Word, demonstrating that Scripture never becomes obsolete and that the Word of God still speaks to us today.

Jesus' very life was the endorsement of the Old Testament, as His birth, life, death, and resurrection all took place so that the Word of God could be fulfilled. His endorsement of the New Testament can be found in the book of John, where Jesus spoke to His disciples who would become the future writers of the New Testament, saying,

> *These things have I spoken unto you, being yet present with you. But the Comforter, which is the Holy Ghost, whom the Father will send in my name, he shall teach you all things, and bring all things to your remembrance, whatsoever I have said unto you.*
>
> **John 14:25–26**

191

Jesus doubled down on it in chapter 16 verses 12–15:

I have yet many things to say unto you, but ye cannot bear them now. Howbeit when he, the Spirit of truth, is come, he will guide you into all truth: for he shall not speak of himself; but whatsoever he shall hear, that shall he speak: and he will shew you things to come. He shall glorify me: for he shall receive of mine, and shall shew it unto you. All things that the Father hath are mine: therefore said I, that he shall take of mine, and shall shew it unto you.

The Word of God is as alive as Jesus is. It is powerful, just as Jesus has the power to conquer death. Jesus and the Word are one and are the ultimate answer for man's salvation and purpose.

For the Word of God is quick, and powerful, and sharper than any twoedged sword, piercing even to the dividing asunder of soul and spirit, and of the joints and marrow, and is a discerner of the thoughts and intents of the heart.
Hebrews 4:12

Like any tool, a sword is as good as the person using it. Left alone, its purpose and function never change, but its advantages do not apply to a passerby until he picks it up and uses it. When I was in martial arts, I spent years practicing with Samurai swords. I have always appreciated swords and recognized their purpose by examining their design, just as I have accepted the Word of God as truth and recognized intentionality and purpose in its design. Because of my interest years ago, I studied the techniques of sword use and practiced cutting through targets in my yard. Similarly, I have studied the Word of God because of my passion for the truth, and I have put it into practice by living according to God's Word.

Using the Tool Correctly

The primary way to discern between the soul and the Spirit is the Word of God. It is the only thing sharp enough to determine what is of the flesh and what is of the Spirit.

For this cause also thank we God without ceasing, because, when ye received the word of God which ye heard of us, ye received it not as the word of men, but as it is in truth, the word of God, which effectually worketh also in you that believe.

1 Thessalonians 2:13

A condition of the effectiveness of the Word of God in us is that we believe it is authoritative.

Both a natural sword and the sword of the Scripture can be misused in the hands of an unbeliever or of someone who has never studied it. I am reminded of the seven sons of the priest in Acts chapter 19 who tried, using a religious formula, to do the same thing Paul did by faith, led by the Spirit, and knowing the Word.

Then certain of the vagabond Jews, exorcists, took upon them to call over them which had evil spirits the name of the Lord Jesus, saying, We adjure you by Jesus whom Paul preacheth. And there were seven sons of one Sceva, a Jew, and chief of the priests, which did so. And the evil spirit answered and said, Jesus I know, and Paul I know; but who are ye? And the man in whom the evil spirit was leaped on them, and overcame them, and prevailed against them, so that they fled out of that house naked and wounded.

Acts 19:13–16

There is a difference between moving in faith by the Spirit and the Word and using human reasoning or a religious formula in our ignorance. Our motivation can be tainted by our desires to get things done or to use our own power. In this example, the proper use of the sword by the Spirit would have divided demons from the flesh, but its misuse left the flesh running through the streets naked.

The truth is exceedingly valuable, and it is found in God's Word and through faith in our Lord and Savior, Jesus Christ. Peter opened his greeting to Christians in 2 Peter by expressing goodwill and peace that come through the knowledge of who Jesus is in the Word of God. He continued on to address the power available to us to live godly lives in 2 Peter 1:3–4:

> *According as his divine power hath given unto us all things that pertain unto life and godliness, through the knowledge of him that hath called us to glory and virtue: Whereby are given unto us exceeding great and precious promises: that by these ye might be partakers of the divine nature, having escaped the corruption that is in the world through lust.*

Where are the exceedingly great and precious things found? In the promises. Where are the promises found? In the written Word of God. Our provisions are found in the promises, our promises are in the Word of God, and Jesus is the Word made flesh. Just as John said, "the Word became flesh and dwelt among us" as Jesus, and "in the beginning was the Word, and the Word was with God, and the Word was God" (John 1:1). What can be more direct than that? If you neglect or discard the Bible, you are neglecting and discarding Jesus Christ! Don't ever neglect the Bible. It is the key to success, a record of promises, and a tool for discernment.

Expectations for Transformation

When the Word of God takes root in our lives, we can expect

to gain things that will equip us so we may not be deceived. These things will change us and lead us to be more Christ-like. The speed at which we can expect these changes to occur depends on the willingness of our hearts to allow God's refinement to happen. Some may say that the rate of change depends on how quickly God wants to change us, but this differs from God's perfect timing for answering prayers. God's warning is for us not to be deceived now! Looking at Scripture, the number eight represents resurrection and a new beginning, and there are eight primary expectations we can rightfully have in regards to transformation into Christ's image.

Let's look at these eight expectations that will refine us, sustain us, and move us forward from glory to glory.

1. We can expect to be fed by the Word of God.

As newborn babes, desire the sincere milk of the word, that ye may grow thereby.

1 Peter 2:2

Before a baby can eat solid foods, it must first grow on the foundation of milk. For a new Christian to grow, it is imperative to read the Word of God, the milk. It is foundational for good health and understanding. Our feelings and experiences can lead us into deception and heresy if our trust is not built upon the bedrock of the truth of the Word of God. We are called to use the written Word to judge the spoken *rhema* word, not the other way around. Like a ship at sea, if we do not anchor ourselves to Scripture, we will be fickle and unstable, moving with the tides.

For every one that useth milk is unskilful in the word of righteousness: for he is a babe. But strong meat belongeth to them that are of full age, even those who by reason of use have their senses exercised to discern both good and evil.

Hebrews 5:13–14

You can't strengthen a muscle without weight. For spiritual exercise, Scripture is that weight. In order to have good discernment, we are required to use the Word, for the use of the Word is the exercise that builds the muscle of discernment in us.

2. We can expect our faith to increase.

When we read Scripture, we have the opportunity to read God's prophecies, plans, and promises. The fulfillment of prophecy demonstrates His sovereignty, the playing out of His plans demonstrates He is in control, and the receipt of His promises demonstrates He is trustworthy. All of these will strengthen our hearts and build our faith in His written Word. If we do not know Scripture, then when we see these things come to pass, God receives no praise from us, and we miss out on the increase in our faith.

A pastor once said that when the judgment of God is poured out on the earth in Revelation 8:1, the reason the saints will be silent in Heaven is that most of the church will be stunned at what they see because they never read their Bibles. Whether or not this is true, the point is valid. We need to know what is in Scripture. We are constantly surrounded by the fulfillment of Scripture. "So then faith cometh by hearing, and hearing by the word of God" (Romans 10:17).

Don't grieve the heart of God by denying Him the glory He deserves and the opportunity we have to increase our faith by letting Him speak to us through His Word.

3. We can expect illumination of the mind.

The Word of God is "a lamp unto [our] feet" that lights our path, as David says (Psalm 119:105). Remember, God is the one holding the lantern. As long as we stay in the Word, our path stays illuminated. "The entrance of thy words giveth light; it giveth understanding unto the simple" (Psalm 119:130).

196

A comforting promise in this verse is that even gullible people with childlike minds will have understanding. When the Word of God is in our hearts, we will have an understanding of why things are the way they are, what God's desires are, and what is to come.

4. We can expect healing.

Fools because of their transgression, and because of their iniquities, are afflicted. Their soul abhorreth all manner of meat; and they draw near unto the gates of death. Then they cry unto the Lord in their trouble, and he saveth them out of their distresses. He sent his word, and healed them, and delivered them from their destructions.

Psalm 107:17–20

The first part of this passage states plainly that there is an affliction that can be avoided, but that because people choose disobedience to God and act out their sin, they bring pain and suffering upon themselves. However, as soon as they repent and pray to God, He brings them the Word of God followed by healing and deliverance.

Meditate on God's Word, listen to God's Word, and read God's Word, and it will bring health to you physically as well as spiritually and mentally. As Solomon urged in Proverbs 4:20–22,

My son, attend to my words; incline thine ear unto my sayings. Let them not depart from thine eyes; keep them in the midst of thine heart. For they are life unto those that find them, and health to all their flesh.

5. We can expect to be sanctified and cleansed.

Husbands, love your wives, even as Christ also loved the church, and gave himself for it; That he might sanctify and cleanse it with the washing of water by the word, That he

197

might present it to himself a glorious church, not having spot, or wrinkle, or any such thing; but that it should be holy and without blemish.

Ephesians 5:25–27

In this passage, we read that we are redeemed by the sacrificial blood of Jesus Christ and that we are sanctified by the washing of His Word. It is only by Christ and through Christ that we are made clean and presentable to Him, and not by any other means. The power of Christ's blood can cover any sin, and the water that flows from the throne never ends.

6. We can expect victory over sin and Satan.

Thy word have I hid in mine heart, that I might not sin against thee.

Psalm 119:11

We must study the Word of God so it can be engraved in our hearts that we will know it well enough to be convicted by it when we approach any act of sin. With the victory we have through Jesus, the Word made flesh, we can use the Word as Jesus did to rebuke the devil. The Word of God is priceless. A physical Bible can be stolen, seized, or destroyed, but when the Word of God is hidden in our hearts, it is safely stored in a place protected from thievery. We need to let the power of God's Word in our hearts continually fill us with His compassion.

7. We can expect to be looking into a spiritual mirror.

We are often reminded of the passage in Luke telling us to remove the beam from our own eye first before pointing out the mote (specks) in others' eyes (6:41–42). In order to see our beams, we must look into the mirror of spiritual truth.

For if any be a hearer of the word, and not a doer, he is like unto a man beholding his natural face in a glass: For he beholdeth himself, and goeth his way, and straightway forgetteth what manner of man he was. But whoso looketh into the perfect law of liberty, and continueth therein, he being not a forgetful hearer, but a doer of the work, this man shall be blessed in his deed.

James 1:23–25

Reading the Word of God will bring conviction to our lives. But that is more than okay; we need to face the things we see in the spiritual mirror. We need to be willing to change and exercise the discipline required to change. If we don't, we will get lost in pride and self-righteousness.

8. We can expect to become a new creation.

Of his own will begat he us with the word of truth, that we should be a kind of firstfruits of his creatures.

James 1:18

Jesus is the Word made flesh. It is because of His will that we can be born again according to His Word through Jesus Christ. Through this, we will be the prime example of His new creation, as we are called to be separate from the world, so Jesus can and will sanctify us and make us holy. He is our Lord and remolds us to His divine purposes.

Seeing ye have purified your souls in obeying the truth through the Spirit unto unfeigned love of the brethren, see that ye love one another with a pure heart fervently: Being born again, not of corruptible seed, but of incorruptible, by the word of God, which liveth and abideth for ever.

1 Peter 1:22–23

When we come to Christ, He purchases us and makes us His. We are reborn, spiritually transformed, renewed, and ready to be used for His glory. Release yourself into the Potter's hands, for He is the great artist, and we are His workmanship.

The Word Is a Sword that Separates Carnality from Truth

All scripture is given by inspiration of God, and is profitable for doctrine, for reproof, for correction, for instruction in righteousness: That the man of God may be perfect, thoroughly furnished unto all good works.

2 Timothy 3:16–17

This passage informs us of the divine origin of the Word. The words "given by the inspiration of God" translate more literally to mean "God-breathed by the Holy Spirit." The author of the Bible is the Holy Spirit, which means that when we challenge the Word of God on any level, we are challenging God the Holy Spirit and are taking issue with Jesus Christ.

Paul wrote in 2 Timothy 2:15, "Study to shew thyself approved unto God, a workman that needeth not to be ashamed, rightly dividing the word of truth." There is no shame in laboring over the Word of God so that we can become skillful with it. We need to present ourselves to God as dedicated workers who know Scripture and are not ashamed to talk about it or teach it accurately!

I have heard some Christians use the excuse that studying the Word of God is works-based and that we should avoid that in order to be more Spirit-led. This is the equivalent of a refusal to wear a seatbelt while riding as a passenger in a car because it requires work. The purpose of the work in putting our seatbelts on is to secure us in place for the ride ahead. It will keep us safe from potential injury or premature death when we are confronted by sudden changes in the car's movements. The Word of God is one of the ways He protects us and keeps us in place. It helps us to discern what is real and what is counterfeit. If you ever have a pastor or teacher tell you that you don't have to study the Bible because studying is works-based, run away! Anyone preaching such a doctrine focusing only on being Spirit-led positions himself to have no accountability to God and is simply living out of the desires of his flesh. We must read Scripture.

The robber is a master counterfeiter. He knows how to make lies look good, and he packages them so well when he presents them. The robber seeks to keep Christians so familiar with a counterfeit that when the real thing comes along, they will not recognize it as God.

This concept of counterfeits can be illustrated by two pairs of sunglasses, one pair an original the other a cheap knockoff. At first glance, they both look the same and feel the same on your face. The difference between the two is that the real one actually protects your eyes with all its fancy coatings for ultraviolet rays, blue light, black light, and polarization to reduce glare, while the counterfeit just has cheap dark lenses. The counterfeit will actually damage your vision because the darker lenses cause your pupils to open, allowing more of the damaging rays into your eyes. In contrast, real glasses enhance your ability to see clearly and protect your eyes. So just as with the sunglasses, when we partake in the robber's counterfeit, our lives are damaged, and our ability to discern is affected. But when we partake in the real things of God, we obtain protection and clarity of sight to see the counterfeit when it comes. We need to focus on the Word of God.

As a Christian living life in these times, not having a working knowledge and understanding of Bible prophecy is the equivalent to walking through a minefield blindfolded. One of the least-preached books in Scripture is the book of Revelation. It is not a coincidence that the Revelation of Jesus Christ, full of warnings and directions on future events, is the book that the robber seeks to keep hidden from Christians the most. Do not be robbed of the richness that awaits you by neglecting your "sword," the Word of God.

> *Quench not the Spirit. Despise not prophesyings. Prove all*
> *things; hold fast that which is good. Abstain from all appearance*
> *of evil. And the very God of peace sanctify you wholly; and I*
> *pray God your whole spirit and soul and body be preserved*
> *blameless unto the coming of our Lord Jesus Christ.*
>
> **1 Thessalonians 5:19–23**

God tells us not to reject spoken prophecies that give revelation, instruction, exhortation, or warnings but instead to test them all to see if they are from God. We test them with the sword, God's Word. When we know His Word, we can recognize truth and hold firmly to it. This is why the Word is foundational to Christian living. This chapter goes on to say we must stay away from every form of evil and allow the Holy Spirit to move.

The promise for knowing God's Word, using it to discern, rejecting wickedness, and allowing the Holy Spirit to move is that God Himself will sanctify us entirely, making us pure, whole, and spiritually sound. This is what it looks like to be thoroughly equipped in the Christian walk.

The Word says we will perish for lack of knowledge. It is not knowledge of Scripture we should run away from. We need the Word of God for discernment. The world says ignorance is bliss, but the Bible says ignorance can get us killed. Do not be ignorant of Scripture. We need to be thoroughly equipped to keep from being robbed.

The Details of Deception

Scripture is full of warnings concerning deception. Scripture itself is not the only tool, but it is the primary one for discernment. The Word of God is physical and can be picked up by anyone to read, and because it is truth, it keeps us grounded like an anchor to God, who is truth. It is the two-edged sword capable of dividing the carnality of the flesh from the spiritual things that are of God.

Colossians 2:8 warns,

Beware lest any man spoil you through philosophy and vain deceit, after the tradition of men, after the rudiments of the world, and not after Christ.

Simply put, this verse tells us not to get robbed of our faith in Jesus Christ through deception. We are not to blindly follow after human traditions and the world's way of doing things without using discernment. We must check all things even if they have a "Christian" label to see if they are sanctioned by Scripture, the character of Jesus Christ, and guidance of His voice.

According to 2 Timothy 3:13, "evil men and seducers shall wax worse and worse, deceiving, and being deceived." Another more accurate translation for the word "seducers" is the word "imposters!" In other words, evil people, including false teachers, will go from bad to worse. They will mislead people, but Scripture also says that they themselves will also be deceived. Avoid the deception with discernment to recognize false teaching.

Throughout the New Testament, there are multiple warnings to us as Christians not to be deceived, and most of those warnings have to do with the last days. In Matthew 24, when people asked Jesus what would be the signs of the last days, Jesus responded in verses 4–5 by telling them to be careful not to let anyone deceive them. He continued on with a claim that many people would come using His name with the intent to deceive many people.

Jesus continued in verses 24–25:

For there shall arise false Christs, and false prophets, and shall shew great signs and wonders; insomuch that, if it were possible, they shall deceive the very elect. Behold, I have told you before.

We cannot base the truth of a message solely on supernatural signs and wonders. It surprises me how many Christians are so readily willing to accept new doctrines based solely on signs and wonders when Jesus Christ Himself said that this alone is not the litmus test for truth. In fact, Jesus implied that deception in the last days would be so inevitable and dangerous that He closes by saying, *Listen,* meaning "pay attention," *I am warning you about this before it happens; the deception will be so believable that even God's elect could be deceived if it were possible.* That is a high level of deception.

Our warning is not to be deceived, either by the world or by teachings cloaked with the appearance of Christianity. In Romans 16:17–18, Paul urged brothers and sisters in Christ to keep watch for people teaching deceptive doctrines that would create division which would ultimately result in the falling away from the faith. We are told to stay away from them because they are not serving Jesus Christ but are instead feeding their own desires. Paul went on to warn us that these servants of flesh would sneak deception into the church body by seeking out ignorant and uninformed people to speak and teach doctrine that would sound spiritual so that the less spiritually mature and scripturally ignorant would buy into the lies. Anyone who is ignorant of Scripture will be easily deceived, especially if they have not exposed themselves to enough sound teaching as well.

Deception is rampant in the church partly because the majority of professing Christians are ignorant of Scripture; many pastors and teachers preach watered-down sermons that function as the milk that keeps believers in infancy. These pastors neglect to distribute the spiritual meat needed for their congregations to mature into responsible stewards. If you are reading this and you find yourself in a church feeding you milk when you are actually ready for solid foods, it is your responsibility to make the change. It is your responsibility to pick up your Bible and read it for yourself. If you don't want to be uninformed, if you don't want to be robbed, then pick up your tool for discernment and read your Bible!

Self-Deception

As Christians, we need to know now more than ever how to navigate the deceptions in the world. Satan seeks to blind minds from comprehending the truth, rendering them incapable of perceiving the fact that they are even deceived. Deception can weave itself deep into our carnality and perceptions.

One of the things that makes me cringe is when I hear Christians justify an unbiblical theology or doctrine based on something that isn't in the Bible. Another thing that concerns me is when people use popular tag phrases from catchy sermons or from social media posts that sound very spiritual yet appeal to the flesh and can easily be proven contrary to the Word of God. Let's take a look at some of these popular quotes and phrases that are not in or supported by Scripture:

"It's funny because he said it is finished, but I act like I'm still in a war."

Yes, Christ's work on the Cross is a finished work, but we are called to be soldiers for Christ according to 2 Timothy 2:3. We are in a war against unseen forces in spiritual realms, as described in Ephesians 6:12. And we are in a war against our flesh and sin, as Paul says in Romans 7:14–25.

"God helps those who help themselves."

This is a massive lie from the robber because we can never help our way into salvation. Romans 10:9–10 says,

That if thou shalt confess with thy mouth the Lord Jesus, and shalt believe in thine heart that God hath raised him from the dead, thou shalt be saved. For with the heart man believeth unto righteousness; and with the mouth confession is made unto salvation. It is only belief in Christ and confession of that belief that saves us.

"God will never give you more than you can handle."

The truth is that God will never allow you more than He can handle. One of the reasons why we may come face to face with a situation we can't handle is that we might learn to depend on God because He is God, and we are not. This keeps us grounded on the reality that we need a Savior. He wants to show us that through His power, we can have the strength to overcome, and by His works, miracles can happen when needed. Then we might have greater spiritual understanding and grow closer to God.

"This too shall pass."

This quote is often used to discard hardships as if they are abnormal for Christians, but James 1:2–4 exhorts us to rejoice in trials, as they will lead to endurance and sanctification. Trials and temptation will never end as long as we are in our mortal bodies, but our victory is in Jesus Christ, and our sanctification happens in the refining fire.

"The lion shall lie down with the lamb."

Scripture actually says, "the wolf will dwell with the lamb," according to Isaiah 11:6.

So how does this happen? How do quotes and phrases that are not in the Bible or based on Scripture become so universally known as Christian theology? The answer is a simple one: scriptural ignorance. Regretfully, as mentioned earlier in this chapter, only fifteen and a half percent of Christians have read the entirety of Scripture one time or more. With a statistic like this, it is no wonder that deception is rampant in the church. When we are not thoroughly equipped with the Word of God, we cannot use the sword to cut away deception.

When we are so ill-equipped, the robber tries to infiltrate our souls with deception, and he encounters little, if any, resistance along the way. We need to be on guard for his attacks.

We can be deceived in three primary ways:
1. We can be deceived through our eyes,
2. We can be deceived through our ears, and
3. We can deceive ourselves.

If we want to walk in the fullness of blessings and be grounded on bedrock, all three of these points of attack must be well covered.

Pitfalls to Avoid

We are all subject to deception, and the person most vulnerable to deception is the one who lives life under the assumption that he is not vulnerable to it at all. It's easy to be lulled into that false sense of security when we have been Christians all our lives or to believe that we cannot be deceived if we are surrounded by friends who are Christians, but these are dangerous assumptions. For example, I have found that it is entirely possible to go to church your entire life and never be taught the fundamental biblical tools for discernment. I also notice in Scripture that the robber can work through the lives of Christians by giving them over to a tormenting spirit, or Christians can be held captive to do his will legally because of unforgiveness in their lives, as seen in Matthew 18:35 and 2 Timothy 2:25–26. It is ultimately our responsibility as Christians to exercise our tools for discerning.

These are some red flags that indicate our vulnerability to deception. As you review them, ask the Lord to reveal the places of vulnerability in your life and seek reinforcement for your areas of weakness.

You will be more vulnerable if:

1. You do not know Jesus Christ personally.

2. You are ignorant of Scripture.
3. You are not familiar with the Holy Spirit.
4. You rely only or too much on your feelings.
5. You believe supernatural signs and wonders guarantee truth.
6. You rely only on human leaders.
7. You are guided by flattery.

Now let's examine the two most common causes I have seen that lead people to self-deception. The first is the idea that because we are Spirit-led, we cannot sin, and we cannot be deceived. The second is the oldest in the book: pride.

What some call "hyper-spiritualism" has become popular today, especially among the youth. It focuses mainly on the spiritual things of God, which, if not thoroughly grounded in the bedrock of God's Word, can lead to an experience-based doctrine that may go unchecked and may become prone to deception. By accepting any revelation or words of knowledge given as long as they are presented in a spiritual way, this knowledge is never filtered through the tools of discernment to see if it is truly from God. The Holy Spirit is alive and active, and I believe it is biblically accurate to say the gifts of the Spirit are for today, but it greatly concerns me that this is happening—especially because this tactic is focused on the youth who are God's next chosen generation.

I have seen great misuse of truth and damage done both intentionally and out of ignorance. Many of these doctrines give a false sense of security, assuming that charisma alone restrains deception from infiltrating into teaching. This gives the robber a wide-open door to infiltrate us with deception. Paul himself, when talking to the most charismatic church of his day, warned them of deception:

> *But I fear, lest by any means, as the serpent beguiled Eve through his subtilty, so your minds should be corrupted from the simplicity that is in Christ. For if he that cometh preacheth another Jesus, whom we have not preached, or*

if ye receive another spirit, which ye have not received, or another gospel, which ye have not accepted, ye might well bear with him.

2 Corinthians 11:3–4

Despite their sincere and pure charismatic devotion to Christ, the subtleties of the robber's ways could still deceive them! We also see that teachings that present a false Christ will most likely be accompanied by a spirit that is not the Holy Spirit. If we think we have it made just because we are a "spirit-led church," but we don't know the Bible, we are in major trouble.

Another place within us that is vulnerable to deception is pride. Lucifer himself was the most beautiful and wise of all the angels, but his pride made him turn from God and enter the business of deception and thievery. Pride is such an open door to the thief that every other religion founded on the doctrine of demons teaches the same pride-attracting promise: the lie that you can be like God. It was the first lie and arguably the last in Scripture. The devil may package it with different wrapping paper, but it is all the same at the core.

In stark contrast, we read in 1 Corinthians 1:26–29 that God's intention is to eliminate pride and that He has chosen to use "the foolish things," "the weak things," "the despised things," and the things considered to be nothing. We can never say God chooses us because we have something that He doesn't. He chooses us because He loves us, and He has a plan, a purpose, and a calling.

The next time the robber tries to bring you down by telling you that you are all those low things, rejoice! Rejoice because it means you meet the qualifications to be chosen and used by God mightily for His glory. In my own life, the more I get involved in ministry and the closer I get to God, the more I realize I'm totally insufficient for His use. When I am most dependent on Him is when I see the greatest miracles take place.

The Tools to Stop Deception

We find ourselves in a world riddled with problems, guided by a constantly-beating drum of ever-changing cultural values, steeped in moral relativism, a world that teaches that there is no absolute truth and that truth is merely based on our personal feelings and experiences. At its root, this preaching comes from the pulpit of the thief himself, Satan. It flies in direct defiance against the Word of God and the identity of Jesus Christ. Moral relativism is anti-Christ theology. This theology is a corruption of truth and will always ultimately fail because it places trust in humanity, which is carnal, sinful, fallen, and unstable in all its ways. The truth is the opposite of all that. In fact, the truth is founded on the one who ultimately redeems His creation and has humanity's best interest in mind. The truth is grounded with the unchanging promises of God that are immovable and irrevocable. The truth is absolute, and it does not lie!

God is not a man, that he should lie; neither the son of man, that he should repent: hath he said, and shall he not do it? or hath he spoken, and shall he not make it good?
Numbers 23:19

The problem is that society's standard for truth changes over time. Standards change as cultures change. Truth in the eyes of the world is a historically unstable thing. But God is not like people. He is not like humans because He tells no lies, and He does not change His mind; in other words, He does not repent. When God says He will do something, He will always do it, according to His nature as the truth. The difference between the real truth and anti-Christ teaching is that real truth is unchangeable, while counterfeit is changeable. In order to avoid deception, we must be able to recognize what is truth.

There are three points of absolute truth that are our tools for discernment. They are the standard against which we must compare all things in order for us to determine truth. They are the Bible (God's Word), the Holy Spirit (the Helper), and Jesus Christ (God).

The first and primary tool is the Bible. I say it is the primary tool because it is physical and tangible, capable of being picked up and read by anyone. It is different from the others in that both Jesus and the Holy Spirit require a relationship, a process that takes time and direction. The Word of God is true and unchanging and has been preserved from man's ever-changing ideals of truth throughout time. In the words of Jesus, we read, "Sanctify them through thy truth: thy word is truth" (John 17:17).

Secondly, we have the Holy Spirit, Who reveals the truth. In John's account, we see that it is the Holy Spirit who also gives witness to the truth of who Jesus Christ is:

This is he that came by water and blood, even Jesus Christ; not by water only, but by water and blood. And it is the Spirit that beareth witness, because the Spirit is truth.
1 John 5:6

And last, because He is the first and the last, is Jesus Christ the Word made flesh. According to John, "Jesus saith unto him, I am the way, the truth, and the life: no man cometh unto the Father, but by me" (14:6). Jesus encompasses the three qualities vital to our salvation. He is the way to everlasting life, and He is truth!

Any claim within the truth must and will comply with all three standards: the Bible, the Holy Spirit, and Jesus Christ. The robber will sprinkle elements of truth into lies to cook up his deceptions, so only the totality of truth will expose the deception. Sometimes, deception can linger subtly, while other times, the deception will be the elephant in the room that nobody wants to acknowledge. Sometimes deception introduced by people comes with malicious intent, and other times it manifests through sincere ignorance. We may find that some blatant attempts at deception can be exposed only by the Word of God. Here are some personal examples in my own life where the need for all three was evident.

The Bible as a Tool:

Recently I heard about an outreach that was thirty miles out of town and decided to check it out. As soon as I arrived, I could feel a very heavy spirit of witchcraft at work, so my discernment tools were immediately triggered. This meeting was being held in a large tent in a field. The atmosphere was supercharged with spiritual passion and strong feelings. Signs and wonders and miracles were even being demonstrated on the stage. But when it came time for the teaching, it wasn't biblical. Let me tell you, if a word doesn't line up with Scripture, it is not of God, period. It doesn't matter how many miracles are thrown into the proceeding. As I discovered later, many of the people who were paraded up on stage and told they were receiving a miracle had in fact not been healed; when they questioned their healing, they were told that they had been healed but had lost their healing through unbelief. This is sick teaching. It is deceitful, destructive, and rebellious, just as the spirit of witchcraft is rebellious. Signs and wonders alone are not confirmation of truth, but God's Word is.

The Holy Spirit as a Resource:

The opposite of the above situation can be true as well. I have visited churches where the pastor was teaching from every word of the Bible, but the church itself was dead. The preaching gave little to no life to the congregation. When I asked people about their personal growth and walk with Jesus, they admitted they experienced very little or none. How can people remain so stagnant in a church that only preaches the Word of God? Well, I often find that these churches are the ones that deny the Holy Spirit works and gives the gifts today. These churches pride themselves on their scriptural piety but hold themselves to an unbiblical and untrue teaching. As a result, there is no spirit or life in the words from the pulpit. It is all just dead teaching without the Holy Spirit. By denying the Holy Spirit, these churches resist personal encounters with Him, and their relationship with God remains distant.

And Last, Jesus Christ for Verifying Truth:

I was sitting in a coffee shop one day when I overheard some young men speaking about Jesus and was impressed by the use of spiritual words. Once I had an opportunity to sit down and ask them about the Jesus they were talking about, it quickly became apparent that the Jesus they spoke of was not the same Jesus of Scripture! Throughout my life, I have encountered many such people who talk about Jesus but who, when asked who Jesus is to them, give so many different feelings-based answers. For example, there is the "Buddhist" or "New Age" Jesus, who was a great man and a good teacher but not God; the "liberal" Jesus, who never spoke of sin or judgment but proclaimed that all roads lead to heaven; and finally, the "Liberation Socialism Marxism" Jesus, who said that we are all "entitled" to have the same earthly things and do what we feel is right. These are examples of false Christs and counterfeit Christianity. Only the true Jesus Christ of Scripture is truth. Amen.

So when we are confronted with the need to discern spiritual things, we need to ask ourselves:

1. Is it true to the Bible?
2. Does the Holy Spirit bear witness to it?
3. Does it line up with the character of the true Jesus Christ?

Putting the Tools to the Test

When we know the three tools identified to fight deception, it is time to put them to use. Think of these as tools like the ones used for a surgical procedure. They are expeditious and effective as long as the surgeon is willing to and capable of using them. Skillfulness requires practice, and implementation requires action. With time, discerning truth and lies will become second nature to you, just as a master surgeon is well-trained to carefully cut away infected tissue from healthy tissue. Let's review the exercises and attitudes that will build up our skillfulness with these tools.

The best teacher we can ever have is God, but there is an enrollment fee into all the heavenly classes to be fully educated on the tools from heaven. The price for admittance is humility and fear of the Lord. Psalm 25:8–9 declares,

> *Good and upright is the Lord: therefore will He teach sinners in the way. The meek will He guide in judgment: and the meek will He teach His way.*

Verse 12 goes on to say, "What man is he that feareth the Lord? Him shall he teach in the way he shall choose."

True wisdom and knowledge always begin with humility, and true humility will always result in respect, a righteous fear of the Lord. Throughout Scripture, we see that the majority of the promises of God are in some way attached to the fear of the Lord. So now it is time to take account of your life. Are you humble enough to be instructed by the Lord, and do you have a reverential fear out of respect for who He is? If you are unsure, ask for revelation, ask for forgiveness, and repent. Start by giving Him permission in your heart to do whatever is required to place you exactly where you need to be relationally with Him.

We have access to the tools of discernment because of God's mercy, and His mercy is the thing that allows us freedom from deception. By His mercy, we judge with the tools He has given so that we may reach godly conclusions even about things not specifically addressed by God. An example of this can be found in 1 Corinthians, where Paul answered the Corinthians' question concerning an issue for which he didn't have a direct commandment from the Lord:

Now concerning virgins I have no commandment of the Lord: yet I give my judgment, as one that hath obtained mercy of the Lord to be faithful

1 Corinthians 7:25

Because of God's mercy, Paul had the freedom within God's permissive will to utilize the tools given to him for discerning what would be right and honoring to God.

Practice makes perfect, and practice takes time. Patience and discipline are important in the Christian walk. Take time to exercise your discernment. Hebrews 5:12–14 talks about the need for us to grow up as Christians, to switch from the milk of seeker-sensitive teachings to the meaty teaching of the uncompromising truth of the Word! This eating of meat takes discipline and time to refine our senses with the tools to discern good and evil. We need to practice. We need to learn to discern.

The love and desire for truth is a mandate for Christians. This love is the fuel that will keep us charged for patience, fueled for practice, and driven to discern. Do you have a love for the truth? Second Thessalonians 2:9–10 warns us that without the love for truth, the ability to discern, truth is compromised. The robber has many tools at his disposal. If you have no love of the truth, then you will be deceived. There is no middle ground. A love for the truth does not mean being tolerant of the truth, nor does it mean letting others find the truth for you. It means searching for and seeking the truth because you are driven by love for the truth and know that truth is also a man. He is Jesus Christ, the only Son of the living God, "the Way, the Truth and the Life!" If you are lacking love for the truth, then I encourage you to take time now and ask the Lord to help you find that love for it.

The Need to Discern Prophecy

215

The same tools for discernment also apply to testing the authenticity of a prophetic word of knowledge or prophecy from God given by man too. The perpetrators of deception depend on the ignorance of Scripture. The first and primary tool is comparison to the entirety of Scripture, along with the second tool of the character of who Jesus Christ of Scripture is, and finally, the confirmation of the Holy Spirit. Longstanding Christian doctrine says that God will never speak a word that contradicts either His written Word or His character, so there is a built-in safeguard against misinterpretation and deception. Yet, the obvious danger is for those who are not familiar with Scripture to be deceived. They can misinterpret, misunderstand, or be intentionally deceived by what they perceive is spiritually from God. All feelings and experiences must come under the truth of God's Word, which keeps us from deception.

Prophecy and words of knowledge are powerful and amazing things. Scripturally, God gives prophecy for many reasons, and it is His character to do so according to Amos 3:7–8. Some examples of why God gives prophecies are to warn the lost and encourage them to repent and turn to Him (Genesis chapters 6, 8, 19), to give us time to prepare for trouble (Genesis chapter 41), and to prove He is God (Isaiah chapters 44–46). Even though God moves in these ways, the robber is always looking for a door to break in and steal or to disrupt God's messages. Let's look at both sides of dealing with deception in prophecy, first for the Christian who delivers it and then for the Christian on the receiving end of it.

First, as Christians with a calling or desire for the gift of prophecy, we are living in a time unlike any other in church history where it has become popular for people to pay money to go to a school that teaches them how to be prophets. There they are educated on how to be prophetic, they are told to practice on people to get better at it, and they are taught how to activate their own gifts. They graduate with a certificate saying they are now prophets. This is so far from God's plan laid out in Scripture that it demonstrates just how many Christians are totally ignorant of what the Bible says of prophecy.

The calling of a prophet is given by God. It is who He has made a person to be, as discussed in the chapter on the five callings. The gift of prophecy is given by God and is not earned through works. Second Peter 1:21 points out that man can't speak prophecy by his own will, but only holy people chosen by God and moved by the Holy Spirit will speak prophecy. The Holy Spirit gets to choose when, where, and how to speak. He will work through submitted holy people. In Scripture, there is a personal price to pay for the gift and the burden that comes with it, but that price is not a monetary one.

The standards and responsibilities set by Scripture for prophesying are very high, so much so that false prophets were stoned to death in the Old Testament. I have attended classes at one of these prophecy schools, and I have also spoken with graduates as well, and I found that these accountabilities were neglected in their teaching. What concerns me is their lack of seriousness for being God's prophetic mouthpiece. Their instruction to "practice prophesying over people" in order for students to get better at their gift becomes a potentially dangerous scenario if they do not pursue holiness, don't know the voice of God, and lack spiritual maturity. If we speak "prophecy from God" that is not true, we make God out to be a liar, which flies in the face of Scripture. This is why we must be careful with the presentation of our words. I would argue the egregiousness of the sin of speaking false prophecy is even greater than murder because we end up speaking as if we are God and taking His name in vain, breaking the first two commandments of God!

The people who are practiced upon often end up getting hurt in some way. I have had to do follow-up ministry with many who have been affected by this. If someone were truly versed in the Word of God with a reverential fear of Him, there would be a lot more respect and honor for the gift and the calling. It is my experience through biblical counseling that most people with a calling of prophecy run from it rather than chasing it like a shiny new toy to have fun with.

This explosion of focusing on prophetic gifts more than on the Word of God has caused words of knowledge to be thrown around more often than the gospel of Jesus Christ in some circles. I am not trying to discourage seeking the spiritual gift of prophecy, just as many people will point out that Joel 2:28 and Acts 2:17 declare that sons and daughters will prophesy in the last days. Prophecy does exist, and God does work through the spiritual gifts of prophecy, but the robber has a counterfeit prepared for the prideful and ignorant. When false "prophecy" is given through the will of man by immaturity and carnality, God is discredited, and Satan wins a battle. The robber will mask his voice to try to sound like God's, and he will lead us astray at every opportunity.

Basing everything on Scripture is foundational. As Christians, it is dangerous to go to a "prophet" to receive a word if we are not already living on the scriptural foundation. There is a reason why this is: We can live the Christian life solely on God's Word, but we cannot live the Christian life solely on spoken prophecy. We need the Word of God to judge the prophecy.

If you don't have a close relationship with Jesus Christ, spend time in His Word, and develop the maturity that comes with time in His presence, then you can be deceived by the counterfeit voice. Many of the people who attend schools of prophecy are young believers in the faith. Instead of being grounded deep into the Word of God first, many will run after supernatural things like prophecy and words of knowledge. They are given an unwieldy sword, and if they are not called to prophecy by God and are not grounded in the Word, they can go out into the world, unintentionally hurting people and misrepresenting God.

A Testimony of Deception

Now I have been blessed to both receive and give words of knowledge and prophecy in my life, so I know that it is a very real thing, just as Scripture says. However, I have also had to deal with the aftermath of false and misguided prophets. Some words of knowledge that have gone astray have caused Christians to turn away from faith because they were so disillusioned by the words of these people. I myself have received words from these "prophets" on two different occasions.

The first time this happened, I was approached by a graduate of one of the schools of prophecy. He came up to me after I preached at a rural outreach and asked if he could give me a "word from the Lord," and I agreed. He assumed I was wealthy and proceeded to tell me that the Lord wanted me to give more money away because I wasn't generous enough and that he saw me in his vision at a gas station being selfish with someone. He claimed that I needed to pay attention to those in need.

When he told me this, I was at a point in my life where I had already sold and given everything away to do ministry. My only possessions at the time were my clothes, my bed, a television, and a nineteen-year-old Ford Explorer that a wonderful lady had given me for ministry. I had no bank account and lived off of random donations from people who supported my ministry.

Even aside from this, little did this man know that earlier that same day, I had encountered a young homeless man at a gas station who was tormented by demons and in need of help. There I had asked him for his life story, and he had shared it with me. I had then told him about Jesus and prayed for him, which had resulted in his being delivered. And on top of that, I had given him all the money I had in my pocket, not knowing the next time I would have money myself. So you see, not only was this man's prophetic word wrong, but even more, it was a direct and specific attack from the robber intended to discourage me and take me out. He saw something by a spirit, maybe even the Holy Spirit, but He interpreted it in his carnal flesh and delivered an inaccurate word that misrepresented God.

The second time this happened, I was prophesied over by someone from this same prophecy school. She told me she had a vision in which I was in the front yard of a house enclosed by a chain-link fence with strippers. I asked her if I was ministering to

219

them, but she adamantly denied it and claimed I was having fun doing other things with them. Once again, little did she know that I was then in the midst of editing a testimony video I had shot for a friend who used to be a stripper but who had come to Jesus and had received salvation and healing from Him. I worked hard all that week putting the video together so that she could hand-deliver gift bags with her testimony to other women who were still in that business. Again, I was receiving a word that directly opposed the truth concerning what God was actually doing through me at the time.

I'm sure both of these people had good intentions, but what they saw was too specific to be chance. Even though they were Christians, they could only see in part, and their interpretations were distorted by flesh and immaturity. Thankfully, I had the tools for discernment and the maturity to use them, but there are many others who are not prepared with the tools to judge a prophetic word. Words like these can be piercing to the heart, and they have the potential to cause deep emotional wounding. So let's look at how we as Christians are commanded to handle prophetic words.

Wisdom, Not Fear

When it comes to revelation from God, it is our own personal responsibility to determine if what someone or something tells us is a true word from God or not. So there are no excuses, no passing the buck. With prophecy, the buck stops with us!

Also, words of prophecy should come with confirmation from another person. Confirmation may or may not come at the time the word is delivered. I had had times when confirmation came from three different people at three different locations and times, sometimes years apart. Let me emphasize: if God ever confirms something to you in an obvious way, pay close attention and don't forget the word! In fact, write it down!

"*Let the prophets speak two or three, and let the other judge*" (*1 Corinthians 14:29*).

The Word tells us two or three people should give confirmation of a word from God, and we who receive it are responsible for determining if what each person says is right or wrong. Next, in addition to it being our responsibility to judge a word, it's our job to use the tools given to test the word. After using the tools of discernment, we are to discard what is not true and only hold onto what passes the test. "Quench not the Spirit. Despise not prophesyings. Prove all things; hold fast that which is good" (1 Thessalonians 5:19–21).

This verse starts by telling us that we should not shut down what the Spirit of God is doing and should never despise spiritual manifestations from God. Our fear of being deceived cannot rule us when it comes to allowing the Holy Spirit to manifest in our churches. I have been in many churches that, instead of operating out of discernment, operate out of fear and suppress the works of the Holy Spirit. When this happens with you or those around you, remember the biblical steps:

1. Don't quench the Holy Spirit.
2. Don't despise spiritual manifestations.
3. Test the words.
4. Hold onto what is good.
5. Look for confirmations.

If someone prophesying is not willing to have his words judged, then he should not prophesy. There have been times when I have heard someone who prophesied tell me, "Don't judge my word, or God will judge you." If you hear something to that effect, then you can be confident that if you *don't* judge that person's word, God will judge you! Never let prophecy terrorize you or dictate to you.

And when they shall say unto you, Seek unto them that have familiar spirits, and unto wizards that peep, and that mutter: should not a people seek unto their God? for the living to the dead? To the law and to the testimony: if they speak not according to this word, it is because there is no light in them.

Isaiah 8:19–20

We are called to judge prophets by the Word of God. If their prophecies do not pass our tests for verification, then the light of God is not at work within them. Be careful, though. When you have a great hunger to hear a prophetic word from someone, but you have no hunger to read the Word of God, then deception will be ready to test your mind. Don't ever accept Satan's plan for your life by letting him speak to you through a false prophet. To avoid this, let's look at some examples of how we can get misled in prophecy.

Having then gifts differing according to the grace that is given to us, whether prophecy, let us prophesy according to the proportion of faith.

Romans 12:6

When we add to or go beyond what we already have through the Word, whether we are receiving it or giving it, we wander into the murky depths of deception. When prophecy goes beyond our level of faith and maturity in Christ, we are tempted to add to the word of prophecy we hear. In my own life, there have been times when God has shown me things to share that have seemed incomplete. My natural tendency is to try to piece things together to build what I think would be a more complete picture. I had learned to deliver a word or vision exactly as given because I had seen enough times when God had worked things out in His time, even when the words did not make sense at first.

Remember also that just because a statement is true, that doesn't guarantee it is from God. We must apply all three of our tools because the robber mixes truth with lies to lure us to take the bait. This can be seen in the Bible, as Paul met one of these truth-tellers with dubious intentions himself:

> *And it came to pass, as we went to prayer, a certain damsel possessed with a spirit of divination met us, which brought her masters much gain by soothsaying: The same followed Paul and us, and cried, saying, These men are the servants of the most high God, which shew unto us the way of salvation.*
>
> **Acts 16:16–17**

What's interesting in this account is that the soothsayer was the first person in the city to know who they were. Every word she said was true, but the spirit speaking through her was not of God. Paul confronted her and cast the unclean spirit out of her, which dispelled her gifts as well. Fortunetelling is demonic, and sometimes elements of truth are intertwined with the lies, but it is that truth that hooks us to swallow the lie.

All true prophecy will point back to Jesus and exalt Him. Any spirit that seeks to detract glory from Him is not of Him. In contrast, for example, John's revelation was from God because the one who showed it to him gave glory to God:

> *And I fell at his feet to worship him. And he said unto me, See thou do it not: I am thy fellowservant, and of thy brethren that have the testimony of Jesus: worship God: for the testimony of Jesus is the spirit of prophecy.*
>
> **Revelations 19:10**

The character of Jesus is infused in true prophecy. If the Spirit of Jesus isn't in the prophecy, it is deception. A word from God not delivered in the Spirit of God is not from God. Whose voice is speaking to you, the flesh, a spirit, or God? Does it line up with the totality of Scripture? Is it within the character of Jesus Christ? Does the Holy Spirit give witness and confirmation? Do not be deceived!

Closing Prayer

Thank You, Lord, for Your mercy and love, by which You have given us the tools for discernment to combat the robber who seeks destruction. Help us to have a love for the truth and a reverential fear for You as humble students of Your teaching. Help us to discern carnality from Your Spirit and truth from deception.

I pray blessings over us, that we will be fully equipped Christians with the maturity of discernment, who stand up for the truth, in truth, and through truth. In Jesus' name, amen.

CHAPTER 7:

The Holy Spirit

And grieve not the Holy Spirit of God, whereby ye are sealed unto the day of redemption.

Ephesians 4:30

When I was a kid, I used to wake up every morning saying, "Good morning, God; good morning, Jesus; good morning, Holy Spirit." I had a basic understanding of the trinity: God the Father, limitless overall; the Holy Spirit, the Great Helper who dwells among us; and the Son, Jesus Christ, the Word made flesh. Telling God alone good morning felt incomplete. There was something inside of me that wanted to make sure all three were welcomed to be a part of my day. I know this may sound silly to some or even legalistic to others, but it is important to live life in relationship with God's triune being. He desires to have a relationship with us in His fullness.

God has given us the greatest gift, His Son Jesus Christ, and He has given us the greatest Helper, the Holy Spirit. The robber will do all he can to keep people in ignorance or denial about the Holy Spirit so that they will go through life helpless. Many denominations exist today because of the devil's efforts to segregate and fracture the unity of the body of Christ. Many of these fractures have occurred because of disagreements about the Holy Spirit, making Him a theology instead of the person of God given to provide help to His people. It is not a coincidence that the Holy Spirit came at Pentecost when the entire church body was all together in one place and in total agreement. Satan knows this, so the robber's strategy against the Holy Spirit is to keep the church segregated and compartmentalized, inhibiting the works of the Holy Spirit in believers. If he can't steal your salvation, then he will do his best to rob you of the Holy Spirit by leading you into the false belief that His gifts and help are no longer for today.

When most people think of the gifts of the Holy Spirit, the first that usually comes to mind is speaking in tongues. This gift is probably the most controversial among Christians. This may be partly due to the abuses, misuses, and hurt that have been caused by false teachings concerning tongues. Some of these teachings include that if you do not speak in tongues, you are not saved or are not filled with the Holy Spirit. Misunderstandings about the gift have caused many to simply give up on the gift altogether. It is important to know that such teachings are unbiblical and can be rooted in pride. When Paul wrote about this gift in 1 Corinthians, he was clearly addressing Christians, as he reminded his readers: "Now ye are the body of Christ, and members in particular" (12:27). He also asked a few sentences later, "Have all the gifts of healing? do all speak with tongues? do all interpret?" (verse 30). Salvation and being filled with the Holy Spirit are not contingent on whether someone speaks in tongues because not all the Christians to whom Paul wrote had ever spoken in tongues, though Paul encouraged them to desire it.

Just as the robber always works against God with a contrary agenda, he also brings confusion with his own counterfeits. These counterfeits are intended to discredit genuine works of the Holy Spirit. I'll be the first to admit that there have been times when the counterfeits have been so outlandish and blatantly unbiblical that I have found myself shying away from the spiritual gifts myself because I do not want to be associated with charlatans. But that is only part of the robber's goal. Fight the thief by using the tools discussed in the chapter "Do Not Be Deceived" to judge spiritual things. The Holy Spirit is a gentleman, and any operation in the spiritual gifts should always be orderly and respectful and should proceed in a decent manner, giving all glory to God. As Jesus said in Matthew 6:5,

Thou shalt not be as the hypocrites *are*: for they love to pray standing in the synagogues and in the corners of the streets, that they may be seen of men. Verily I say unto you, they have their reward.

Do you or does someone you know ever feel helpless? The answer to helplessness is the Great Helper, the Holy Spirit. Some well-meaning Christians do not believe the workings or the gifts of the Holy Spirit are for today, and others feel that the Holy Spirit is only for some Christians but not for them. If either of those is you, then you are being robbed. These ideas are lies from the robber in an attempt to steal away the great help God has for you. If you believe in your heart and confess with your mouth that Jesus Christ is your Lord and Savior, that Jesus was born of the Virgin Mary, that He lived a sinless life, died on the cross, overcame death and the grave, and is now seated at the right hand of the Father, continuously interceding for you, then I tell you, with certainty, the Holy Spirit is for you! And if God is for you, then who can be against you? Jesus Christ made it clear that when He left, He would be sending the Holy Spirit to help us. And if His help were only going to be for the twelve apostles, then wouldn't you think that Jesus would have shared that detail rather than encouraging us to live a life full of the Holy Spirit's help and power? And not only Jesus but Paul encouraged us toward the Holy Spirit as well, as we will study in this chapter.

I once heard Dr. Chuck Missler, the founder of Koinonia Institute, say at a conference in 2010, "There are two common errors concerning the gifts of the Holy Spirit: the denial that they are for today, and the other extreme, the over-emphasis of both the gifts and experiences, which substitutes aspiration for inspiration." Scripture calls us to aspire to walk in these gifts for the benefit of the body and the glory of God, but they are not our source for inspiration. I believe in the gifts and have experienced the continuation of all the gifts of the Holy Spirit, as revealed in Scripture, and know firsthand the blessing of being baptized in the Holy Spirit. I am not ashamed to say that I am in need of help in my life; even now, as I write this, I am in need of help, and I am so glad that I have the Helper to depend on, the Holy Spirit. Anything in me and anything of value that is done by me is because of Him. All glory and honor and praise belong to God forever! So let us reject the lies of the thief and hold onto the promises of Scripture.

The Ascension

Before we can look at the day of Pentecost when the Holy Spirit came, we need to look at the day of ascension that preceded it. Ascension Day, also known as Holy Thursday, is the anniversary of the bodily ascension of Jesus Christ into heaven and is one of the feasts celebrated by many Christian churches. This feast day is also associated with the feasts of the Passion, Resurrection Sunday, and Pentecost. Ascension Day is traditionally celebrated on a Thursday, the fortieth day after Resurrection Sunday, following the accounts given in Mark 16:19, Luke 24:51, and Acts 1:2.

The former treatise have I made, O Theophilus, of all that Jesus began both to do and teach, Until the day in which he was taken up, after that he through the Holy Ghost had given commandments unto the apostles whom he had chosen: To whom also he shewed himself alive after his passion by many infallible proofs, being seen of them forty days, and speaking of the things pertaining to the kingdom of God: And, being assembled together with them, commanded them that they should not depart from Jerusalem, but wait for the promise of the Father, which, saith he, ye have heard of me. For John truly baptized with water; but ye shall be baptized with the Holy Ghost not many days hence.

Acts 1:1–5

The words "many proofs" used in this verse to describe the fact that Jesus was alive and did indeed conquer death are the Greek words *polus* and *tekmerion. Polus* means "abundant,"[82] and *tekmerion* means "infallible and unquestionable."[83] So Jesus was never failing in demonstrating large quantities of proof that He was alive again.

Next in this passage, Jesus said that there was a day coming soon when the people would be baptized with the Holy Spirit. The word "with" used between baptized and the Holy Spirit is the Greek word *en,* meaning "to be united or made one with."[84] The Greek word for Holy Spirit, *hagios pneuma,* in Greek means "pure, blameless"[85] and "wind, breath, empowered."[86]

So the promise that Jesus described here was that we would be baptized and united with the pure and blameless one who would empower us. This baptism of the Holy Spirit is clearly separate from John's baptism, which was a baptism of repentance. John the Baptist said in Matthew 3:11,

I indeed baptize you with water unto repentance: but he that cometh after me is mightier than I, whose shoes I am not worthy to bear: he shall baptize you with the Holy Ghost, and with fire.

This is not a judgment fire but a refining fire. It gives us passion and moves us toward glory and sanctification, and its purpose is to transform us to be more like Christ with dynamite power.

But ye shall receive power, after that the Holy Ghost is come upon you: and ye shall be witnesses unto me both in Jerusalem, and in all Judaea, and in Samaria, and unto the uttermost part of the earth. And when he had spoken these things, while they beheld, he was taken up; and a cloud received him out of their sight.

Acts 1:8–9

Jesus told us that the primary purpose of the baptism of the Holy Spirit is for Christians to be witnesses for Him throughout the whole world. The main purpose of being filled with the Holy Spirit is to point people to salvation in Jesus Christ. Christ proved that He conquered death as He ministered for forty days, and then He ascended into heaven so that the Helper would come in a powerful way. It is exciting to know that just as one generation got to experience Jesus' ascension to heaven, another generation will get to see His glorious return.

We Need a Helper

The world is becoming more complex. The pace of life continues to increase exponentially, and technology distracts us from the reality around us. These distractions have kept many American Christians unaware of the record-setting global persecution toward Christians. According to *Open Doors' 2019 World Watch List*, an in-depth investigative report focusing on global Christian persecution, it has reached an all-time high in modern history and continues trending upward, a fulfillment of end-times prophecy. Ungodly laws are being passed under the premise of love, laws whose purpose is to socially reengineer the standards of morality and to direct younger generations toward perversion. This, too, is mentioned in biblical prophecy. Transhumanists are manipulating genetic codes in a quest to make man like God. With biology, science, and fossil records continuing to mount up evidence that evolution is untrue, a new agenda is rapidly gaining ground. This agenda says we were seeded here on earth by aliens, an idea put forth by many scientists, including Richard Dawkins, a modern-day leading advocate for evolution, in the 2008 documentary film *Expelled*.[87] This is becoming the new substitution to the biblical truth of the origin of man. We are living in what Scripture calls the last days, and I am confident that we are living in the last of the last days before Jesus returns. The incredible increase in deception, oppression, propaganda, and programming going on demonstrates that our need for spiritual help to combat these deceptions and to share the truth of Jesus Christ is at an all-time high!

In the Old Testament, it was the death of Methuselah, whose name meant "his death shall bring," that was the sign for the season of the judgment flood (Genesis). Throughout the New Testament, the rebirth of Israel as a nation is one of many signs of Christ's coming very soon. Before the great flood, Enoch was caught up to be with God (Genesis), just as the church will be caught up before God's judgment wrath during the great tribulation (Revelation). Before the great flood, Noah and his family entered the ark, where God enclosed them and sealed the door to protect them from His wrath (Genesis). In Revelation, we see the 144,000 sealed by God to protect them during the great tribulation.

The book of Matthew tells us that just before Christ's return, it will be like it was in the days of Noah, and we are living in similar times today (24:37–39). Sorcery, child sacrifice, perversion of mankind, a drive toward a one-world order with a global bank, the erosion of sovereign nations and their borders, along with changes to the foundations of religion to bring about one global unifying belief, are growing and rising up. These things were all predicted to happen in the last days. It is time to stop "playing church" and start moving in the Holy Spirit! It is "not by might, nor by power, but by [His] Spirit" (Zechariah 4:6) that we receive help and the ability to tell the lost about salvation through Jesus Christ, and by which we are equipped as soldiers for Christ in the last days.

Another barometer of the times we live in is in the area of technology. Our secular understanding of reality and the building blocks of the universe has increased so quickly in such a short amount of time that mankind has become a cocky and vain steward of the earth. Yet without spiritual understanding and godly principles, mankind is actually more ignorant and foolish. This foolishness is rooted in the earliest sinful seed planted in the mind of man, the idea that we can be like God. Most people are unaware that humanity is now dabbling in areas that God has strictly forbidden. We have moved from simply observing the genetic code toward manipulating our genes, replacing some of them with those of beasts.[88] It is my conjecture that technology had also advanced in this direction before the great flood of Noah, and God's forbiddance of this was part of the reason that global judgment was enacted, to prevent it from advancing any further. God will not allow these kind of changes to occur that will move mankind beyond the point of redemption. Jesus died to redeem His creation, not genetic perversions of man or Satan that no longer represent His design and image. Jesus gave us a clear warning of what it would be like before His triumphant return in Luke 17:26: "And as it was in the days of Noah, so shall it be also in the days of the Son of man." The first global judgment was by water, and the book of Revelation explains to us that the next time will include fire. We live in a time when Jesus' return for His church can happen any time, and assuming there will not be a major catastrophic event that will curb the advances in these dark technologies, that time will be soon.

My passion for apologetics and eschatology led me into theoretical physics in 2007. Ever since then, I have kept a close eye on technologies that resemble what I call pre-flood angelic mischief. Three areas of potential dark technology that concern me most are transhumanism,[89] quantum computing,[90] and particle accelerator colliders being developed, particularly at CERN.[91] I mention this because there are many supernatural events on the horizon that will shake most Christians and challenge their faith. Without the Holy Spirit's help, many will be seduced and will fall away in the last days, as the Bible prophesies. This is the time when being led by, strengthened by, and filled with the Holy Spirit is critical!

The Holy Spirit is for You

I have met some Christians who have told me that the Holy Spirit is not for them or that the gifts of the Spirit are not for them but for others because they are excluded for one reason or another. Thoughts like these are untrue and are not supported by Scripture at all. Let's look at the account of the upper room.

> *And when the day of Pentecost was fully come, they were all with one accord in one place. And suddenly there came a sound from heaven as of a rushing mighty wind, and it filled all the house where they were sitting. And there appeared unto them cloven tongues like as of fire, and it sat upon each of them. And they were all filled with the Holy Ghost, and began to speak with other tongues, as the Spirit gave them utterance.*
>
> **Acts 2:1–4**

The Holy Spirit did not come until all the believers were together and everyone was in unity, and it was the Holy Spirit Who empowered them. Did the richest person in the room get left out? No. Did the poorest person in the room get left out? No. Was the shortest or the tallest person excluded? No. The precedent God clearly set was that no one was left out and that everyone was present.

The Holy Spirit was so important to Jesus that He put a lot of importance and value on Him. Jesus spoke intensely about the Holy Spirit! One example is found in John 14:16–17:

> *And I will pray the Father, and he shall give you another Comforter, that he may abide with you for ever; Even the Spirit of truth; whom the world cannot receive, because it seeth him not, neither knoweth him: but ye know him; for he dwelleth with you, and shall be in you.*

Jesus made two points about the Holy Spirit here: One was that the Holy Spirit was already real, and the second was that the Holy Spirit was about to come. At the time when Jesus was speaking, the Holy Spirit dwelled with the disciples, but the Holy Spirit was not in them. If the Spirit of God was so important to the life of Jesus, how much more so for our lives today?

The baptism of the Holy Spirit is not for a lucky few Christians, and receiving Him is not like trying to win the lottery. God loves everyone, and He is generous to all of His children. In the Scripture above, everyone in the room received the Holy Spirit, and *all* means *all*. God didn't play favorites here. All the known languages of the time were also represented at that moment, displaying God's character that He desires all to be saved and all to receive His Holy Spirit.

Now, if you are a Christian and you believe the indwelling of the Holy Spirit and the gifts are only for some Christians and not for you, ask yourself: "Do I believe in my heart and confess with my mouth that Jesus Christ is Lord and Savior?" If the answer is yes, then the Holy Spirit is for you!

There is no doubt that in the church, a life filled with the Holy Spirit should be the norm. The filling of the Holy Spirit was even a requirement for serving in the church. The body of Christ needs a Helper, and without living a life full of the Holy Spirit, it is impossible to build the body of Christ. Without Him, we end up limiting God's work in our lives. The gospel stripped of an emphasis on the Holy Spirit becomes anemic. We read many times in the New Testament that whenever there is a special manifestation of God, those involved are filled with the Holy Spirit.

For example, John the Baptist was full of the Spirit from the beginning of his time in his mother's womb:

For he shall be great in the sight of the Lord, and shall drink neither wine nor strong drink; and he shall be filled with the Holy Ghost, even from his mother's womb.

Luke 1:15

During this time of pregnancy, Elizabeth was filled with the Spirit when Mary greeted her:

And it came to pass, that, when Elisabeth heard the salutation of Mary, the babe leaped in her womb; and Elisabeth was filled with the Holy Ghost.

Luke 1:41

Zechariah, the father of John the Baptist, was filled with the Holy Spirit when he prophesied (Luke 1:67). Finally, Jesus was filled and led by the Holy Spirit into the desert: "And Jesus being full of the Holy Ghost returned from Jordan, and was led by the Spirit into the wilderness" (Luke 4:1).

After Jesus' ascension, everyone was filled with the Holy Spirit in the upper room, and Peter was also filled with the Spirit when he preached on the day of Pentecost in Acts 2:14–36. The young Stephen is another example:

But he, being full of the Holy Ghost, looked up stedfastly into heaven, and saw the glory of God, and Jesus standing on the right hand of God.

Acts 7:55

Paul, being inspired by the Holy Spirit, rebuked a sorcerer:

But Elymas the sorcerer (for so is his name by interpretation) withstood them, seeking to turn away the deputy from the faith. Then Saul, (who also is called Paul,) filled with the Holy Ghost, set his eyes on him, And said, O full of all subtilty and all mischief, thou child of the devil, thou enemy of all righteousness, wilt thou not cease to pervert the right ways of the Lord? And now, behold, the hand of the Lord is upon thee, and thou shalt be blind, not seeing the sun for a season. And immediately there fell on him a mist and a darkness; and he went about seeking some to lead him by the hand.

Acts 13:8–11

Our need for a Helper comes down to our dependency on God. He sent the Holy Spirit so that we could live a blessed, fulfilling, purposeful life in relationship with Him. Don't be robbed. Give praise to God for the great gifts He gives. Jesus skillfully expressed the essence of this experience:

If ye then, being evil, know how to give good gifts unto your children: how much more shall your heavenly Father give the Holy Spirit to them that ask him?

Luke 11:13

Who and Where Is the Holy Spirit?

Everything physical that is considered to be solid in this world is actually made up mostly of empty space. If you were able to look at an atomic level, you would see that there is far more space between particles than there are particles. Things merely feel solid because of opposing forces. This space in between is where the invisible person who holds all things together dwells. He is in this space because He cannot touch anything tainted by death without changing it permanently. The whole physical world is tainted by death. Where there is sin, there is death, and where there is God, there is life. Whatever God touches turns to life, as Jesus Himself said: "The thief cometh not, but for to steal, and to kill, and to destroy: I am come that they might have life, and that they might have it more abundantly" (John 10:10). So the Holy Spirit interacts with His creation in this in-between space. It is where He can dwell as the restrainer. In this way, He can be within us, empowering us, convicting us, and speaking to us, but yet still be separated from the sin of the world and the sin of our flesh. When I reach out to hold my wife's hand, no matter how hard I squeeze it, there will always be space in between us where God can be closer to us than we could ever be to each other.

God may be invisible, perhaps, but He is very real. I believe the Holy Spirit is the least understood person of the trinity. After hearing Christians describe the Holy Spirit as a ghost (in the traditional secular sense), a secondary replacement of God, or a mysterious force that binds the galaxy together, it is clear to me that they are lacking a relationship with Him. After all, how can you have a relationship with someone you are clueless about? Instead of believing that the Holy Spirit performs marvelous works that manifest in reality as the Bible describes, people often think that He is equivalent to the manifestations themselves. Some believe that the Holy Spirit appears by chance or moves in response to some kind of conjuring. Beliefs like these couldn't be further from the truth. It is explicitly communicated throughout Scripture that God is one supreme being who is triune.

God's triune nature explains how we are born again, and the Holy Spirit lives in us when we receive Jesus Christ into our lives through faith. An illustration of the triunity of God can be seen in water (H_2O). Depending on environmental conditions, water can be in three different forms. In a lukewarm environment, water is a liquid; under hot conditions, water is steam; and when the temperature dips below freezing, water becomes ice. Whatever form it may take, though, it is still water. The Holy Spirit is a triune individual within God's being, and it is vital for the church to know Him, relate to Him, and understand how He manifests.

The Holy Spirit is an important figure throughout Scripture. From the beginning of Scripture to the end, the Holy Spirit has been active: "the Spirit of God moved upon the face of the waters" in Genesis 1:2 and "the Spirit and the bride say, Come," in Revelation 22:17. In the beginning, He creates, and at the end, He tends to us. He helps us, guides us, reminds us, teaches us, counsels us, intercedes for us, and comforts us. Who doesn't need help like this in life? The Holy Spirit will help in all these ways and more!

Some people think that the Holy Spirit is a secondary person acting in the gap for God because He operates on His creation "hands-off." Others think the Holy Spirit is an "it" or some kind of a mystical governing energy field put into motion like in *Star Wars*. In actuality, the Holy Spirit is a person, part of the triune being of God. Even calling the Holy Spirit a person is still a totally inadequate word to describe Him, but it is the best we have in our limited vernacular.

As a person, the Holy Spirit has feelings. He can become angry, as seen in Isaiah 63:10: "But they rebelled, and vexed his holy Spirit: therefore he was turned to be their enemy, and he fought against them." Or He can be sad, as we read in Ephesians 4:30: "And grieve not the holy Spirit of God, whereby ye are sealed unto the day of redemption." He can be blasphemed:

> *Wherefore I say unto you, All manner of sin and blasphemy shall be forgiven unto men: but the blasphemy against the Holy Ghost shall not be forgiven unto men.*
>
> **Matthew 12:31**

And He can be insulted: "Ye stiffnecked and uncircumcised in heart and ears, ye do always resist the Holy Ghost: as your fathers did, so do ye" (Acts 7:51).

The interaction and presence of the Holy Spirit have changed throughout the different dispensations. In the Old Testament, the Holy Spirit came to certain people and was very location-specific. After the ascension of Jesus Christ, the Holy Spirit has come in a

238

new way as a restrainer of evil on the earth and as one who can dwell within every Christian.

During Jesus' life on earth, the Holy Spirit was present at each stage of His life. When the angel appeared to Mary, the mother of Jesus, he declared,

> *The Holy Ghost shall come upon thee, and the power of the Highest shall overshadow thee: therefore also that holy thing which shall be born of thee shall be called the Son of God.*
>
> **Luke 1:35**

Later on, at Jesus' baptism, which marked the beginning of His public ministry, the Holy Spirit was present and could even be seen in material form:

> *And Jesus, when he was baptized, went up straightway out of the water: and, lo, the heavens were opened unto him, and he saw the Spirit of God descending like a dove, and lighting upon him.*
>
> **Matthew 3:16**

During His ministry, Jesus taught about the Holy Spirit and had a relationship with Him. Furthermore, He urged His disciples to receive Him into their lives.

Jesus pointed out that the disciples were not to "know the times or the seasons" in Acts 1:7, but in verse 8, He emphasized the primary concern at hand: that they would "receive power" from the Holy Spirit. The receipt of this power depended on the Holy Spirit's coming into them. The idea of receiving this power must have caught their attention. Until that point, the Holy Spirit would only minister to people and come upon them but did not constantly live inside them. Jesus' relationship with the Holy Spirit was different, as He and the Father were one, and the indwelling of the Spirit never left Him. While He lived on this earth, He depended on the power of the Holy Spirit to enable Him to do ministry. This demonstrated to us an important pattern: our need for the Holy Spirit to live within us so that His power can work through us. For over three years, these men had been witnesses of the continual manifestation of God's abiding power through Jesus, and now the doors were being opened for them to access this continuous power that they had so admired.

In order to receive the Holy Spirit's power, one does not need a religious formula but rather a relationship with Him. Notice Christ's encouragement to give the Holy Spirit permission to come in and to develop a relationship. The promise was not something that had already existed but something that was coming. The Holy Spirit would live not only in the Jews but in the Gentiles too.

The Holy Spirit came at Pentecost, and ever since then, He has been placing every believer into the body of Christ and has remained in him or her. He places Gentiles and Jews together as equals (Galatians 3:28). He is the proof that we belong to God. If we are His, then the question is, how much of your life do you allow Him to occupy and have access to?

To describe the relationship with the Holy Spirit, I like to use the analogy of a farmer growing crops. The farmer depends on the crops to bear fruit for provision and nourishment and to sustain life. It takes a lot of time and energy to tend to the crops, somewhat like building a relationship. The plants need time, dedication, and understanding of how they produce. The farmer needs to invest by sowing, watering, and taking care of the crops, even as he is still waiting for the fruit. His expectation is that as he steps out in faith and does what is required of him, a harvest will come. The disciples also desired the fruit of the Holy Spirit, but for that, it was necessary for them to relate to Him as a person and to receive His baptism. By stepping out in faith under His leading, a harvest came, and good fruit was produced.

The Mark of the Holy Spirit

When I ask Christians how they can tell if someone is full of the Holy Spirit, most of them give me one of two answers: They can tell either by their love or by whether they speak in tongues. Neither of these answers is correct. The book of Acts clearly communicates how we can recognize someone who is full of the Holy Spirit. The primary indication, despite what some denominations may say, is much greater than love or tongues: It is being a witness of Jesus Christ! In the words of Jesus Christ Himself,

> *But ye shall receive power, after that the Holy Ghost is come upon you: and ye shall be witnesses unto me both in Jerusalem, and in all Judaea, and in Samaria, and unto the uttermost part of the earth.*
>
> **Acts 1:8**

There is so much emphasis on love in the church today, but unfortunately, culture has redefined love from God's perfect love to a deceptive love based on carnality. Even many people in the church have substituted the true love of God with this worldly carnal love. This perverted love enables people all the way to hell. The love of God doesn't coddle sin. It corrects and defeats sin. God's real love comes from holiness because He is holy. It leads to sanctification because His greatest act of love was the sacrifice of His Son Jesus Christ. God's love leads people to salvation, not to eternal damnation.

Love is a distinguishing mark of being a disciple of Jesus Christ (John 13:35), but being a witness for Jesus Christ distinguishes those who are full of the Holy Spirit. It doesn't matter how many supernatural experiences someone may have; whoever does not testify of Christ does not show evidence of being filled with the Holy Spirit.

In Paul's letter to the Galatians, he called them out for being superficial and thoughtless in their thoughts and actions (3:1). In regards to the Holy Spirit, Paul asked them, "This only would I learn of you, Received ye the Spirit by the works of the law, or by the hearing of faith?" (Galatians 3:2). This is a rhetorical question, as no one receives the Holy Spirit based on works. We don't receive the Holy Spirit by obeying the requirements of the Law or as a result of hearing the message of salvation and believing it. We experience salvation freely, and there is no reason to relate to God differently when it comes to our experience with the Holy Spirit. It is a grace-based experience, much in the same way that we receive Jesus Christ without doubting whether He will enter our lives or not. Don't be robbed: Receive the Holy Spirit by faith and believe that He will respond to your request.

What the Holy Spirit Does

The Holy Spirit is active in our world today. The book of Acts, which is more accurately called "The Acts of the Holy Spirit through the Apostles," attests that the Holy Spirit continues to do His works in the world and in the lives of followers of Jesus Christ. Being part of the trinity of God, the Holy Spirit is both limitless and busy at work. There are four areas where the Holy Spirit is at work that I want to mention. First, there are the things that the Holy Spirit does for us; then, there is what the Holy Spirit does in the lives of unbelievers; next, there are gifts the Holy Spirit gives; and last, there is the fruit of the Holy Spirit.

Everything the Holy Spirit does is important and intentional. Who He is and what He does are fundamental and critical to the Christian life, and without the Holy Spirit, we will live a life robbed of the fullness that God intends. What He accomplishes can tell us much about His character and personality, and what He does is always in our best interest. Let's start by looking at fifteen things the Scripture tells us that the Holy Spirit does for us.

1. The Holy Spirit is our Helper.

But the Comforter, which is the Holy Ghost, whom the Father will send in my name, he shall teach you all things, and bring all things to your remembrance, whatsoever I have said unto you.

John 14:26

Are you overwhelmed in your Christian walk? Has life handed you more than you can handle? Are you called to accomplish more than you are able to? These are the times when God wants to show us His faithfulness and get our attention focused on the fact that we need Him as a Helper. The Holy Spirit is available and dependable, ready to help. As we follow the voice of the Lord in our daily Christian walk, the Holy Spirit is always there to help us through any situation. There is no situation where the Holy Spirit can't assist us and even, if necessary, intervene. From bringing Scripture to mind as we witness about Jesus Christ to the casting out of demons, the Helper is there for you to experience the true fullness of the Christian life. What a pleasure and comfort it is to know that we do not have to labor through life alone because the Holy Spirit is our constant Helper, and our victory is secure in Him!

2. The Holy Spirit indwells us and seals us.

In whom ye also trusted, after that ye heard the word of truth, the gospel of your salvation: in whom also after that ye believed, ye were sealed with that holy Spirit of promise.

Ephesians 1:13

The Holy Spirit is God's seal on the hearts of Christians. It is His claim on us as His very own. The Greek word *arrhabon* means "a pledge:" that is, a part of a purchase given in advance, like a security deposit.[92] The gift of the Spirit to believers is a down payment on our heavenly inheritance, which Christ has promised us and secured for us at the cross. It is the sealing of the Holy Spirit that assures us of our salvation. No one can break God's seal. The Holy Spirit is the first installment of our full inheritance as children of God who will be fully delivered in the future. The Holy Spirit confirms that we belong to God, and His Spirit is a gift, just like grace and faith are gifts.

3. The Holy Spirit intercedes and assists us in prayer.

But ye, beloved, building up yourselves on your most holy faith, praying in the Holy Ghost.

Jude 1:20

The Holy Spirit prays for us because God's knowledge is perfect. God always knows what the Spirit is thinking, so when the Holy Spirit prays for us with groans that cannot be expressed in words (Romans 8:26), God knows and understands the prayers of the Holy Spirit. The Holy Spirit knows God's thoughts, and God knows the thoughts of the Holy Spirit because the two are always in full agreement. First Corinthians 2:11 says,

For what man knoweth the things of a man, save the spirit of man which is in him? even so the things of God knoweth no man, but the Spirit of God.

We do not have God's unlimited intellect, and even if we did, human language itself would still be extremely limiting to the vastness of God. This is why the Bible has to come alive by the Holy Spirit translating God's thoughts to us from the words, as in 1 Corinthians 2:13:

Which things also we speak, not in the words which man's wisdom teacheth, but which the Holy Ghost teacheth; comparing spiritual things with spiritual.

Knowing that God's thoughts have been revealed to us by the Holy Spirit in the written Word of God, we can have great confidence that the words the Holy Spirit prays through us on our behalf to God the Father are always perfect in accordance with Scripture, prayed in perfect faith and without interference from our flesh.

Likewise the Spirit also helpeth our infirmities: for we know not what we should pray for as we ought: but the Spirit itself maketh intercession for us with groanings which cannot be uttered. And he that searcheth the hearts knoweth what is the mind of the Spirit, because he maketh intercession for the saints according to the will of God.

Romans 8:26–27

The Holy Spirit prays for us because of our weakness. He comes to our assistance and rescues us, makes our prayers acceptable to God, and helps to shoulder our heavy burdens. This is a ministry of the Holy Spirit in our physical human weakness. Physical, emotional, and spiritual weaknesses reveal our need for the Holy Spirit. Even the sinless Son of God, Jesus Christ, experienced physical human weakness so that He could relate to our weaknesses and rely on the Holy Spirit.

The Holy Spirit prays for us because we can be ignorant and can sometimes not know what to pray or how to pray. In our ignorance, it is wise to ask the Holy Spirit to teach us how to pray. In the book of Matthew, the sons of Zebedee came to Jesus with their mother to demand a position of leadership. Jesus responded, "Ye know not what ye ask" (20:22). The Holy Spirit prays for us because our knowledge is incomplete.

4. The Holy Spirit regenerates and renews us.

Not by works of righteousness which we have done, but according to his mercy he saved us, by the washing of regeneration, and renewing of the Holy Ghost; Which he shed on us abundantly through Jesus Christ our Saviour.

Titus 3:5–6

Notice two key points in this verse: First, regeneration is directly tied to salvation in Jesus Christ. We are saved by God's grace and mercy, and when He saves us, a regenerative work by the Holy Spirit takes place within us. Second, this regenerative work is done directly by the Holy Spirit Himself. When we are weak and feeling down, it is the Holy Spirit who gives us new breath in our lungs and new strength in our bones. The Holy Spirit can give us living water in the desert to accomplish the calling and purpose that God has for our lives.

5. The Holy Spirit baptizes us into the body of Christ.

Know ye not, that so many of us as were baptized into Jesus Christ were baptized into his death?

Romans 6:3

The Greek word used here for "baptized" is *baptizo*, which means "to submerge something in liquid."[93] Metaphorically, Jesus Christ is the liquid, and it is by the power of the Holy Spirit that everyone saved through Jesus Christ is baptized into Him forever and benefits from His finished work on the cross! This means that we will also experience His resurrection unless we are alive when He returns so that we will instead experience a physical transformation. Even now, this baptism gives us a kind of resurrection as we walk in the newness of life and in relationship with God and other believers.

I indeed baptize you with water unto repentance: but he that cometh after me is mightier than I, whose shoes I am not worthy to bear: he shall baptize you with the Holy Ghost, and with fire.

Matthew 3:11

The baptism of the Spirit is an infilling of the Spirit. When we are baptized with the Holy Spirit, we receive strength, power, and boldness from God to accomplish His work and overcome sin in our lives. To know when you have experienced the baptism of the Holy Spirit, just look at the disciples at Pentecost. The experience can be expressed in many ways, but when it happens, our lives are changed. The Holy Spirit's power can pass into the believer's body like electricity, filling him or her with joy and happiness. The disciples were so filled with joy speaking in other tongues that the people thought they were all drunk with new wine. Baptism of the Holy Spirit can come immediately after repentance, sometimes accompanied by the gift of tongues, but this is not often the case.

6. Believers receive the new birth by the power of the Holy Spirit.

Jesus answered and said unto him, Verily, verily, I say unto thee, Except a man be born again, he cannot see the kingdom of God.

John 3:3

The result of the regenerative work done by the Holy Spirit at the moment of our salvation through the Lord is that our human spirit is immediately born again. Jesus Himself tells us exactly what it means to be born again in John 3:5–7:

Verily, verily, I say unto thee, Except a man be born of water and of the Spirit, he cannot enter into the kingdom of God. That which is born of the flesh is flesh; and that which is born of the Spirit is spirit. Marvel not that I said unto thee, Ye must be born again.

There is a difference between receiving the Holy Spirit and being filled with the Holy Spirit. We receive the Holy Spirit when we give our heart to Jesus Christ and accept Him as Lord and Savior. We are filled with the Holy Spirit when we surrender ourselves to His control and allow Him to enter our lives.

7. The Holy Spirit comforts us with fellowship, hope, and joy.

Now the God of hope fill you with all joy and peace in believing, that ye may abound in hope, through the power of the Holy Ghost.

Romans 15:13

The grace of the Lord Jesus Christ, and the love of God, and the communion of the Holy Ghost, be with you all. Amen.

2 Corinthians 13:14

The Holy Spirit is a vital force in a Christian's soul. The work of the Holy Spirit as Comforter occurs when He links believers in Jesus Christ with Him. The Holy Spirit testifies of Christ, glorifies Christ, and brings to remembrance the words of Christ. He feeds the soul with the truth of Christ. The Holy Spirit will show believers the things of Christ as He does the will of Christ with the personality of Christ. Not only does He come to put a new nature in the soul, but He also comes to manifest the very presence of Christ in the soul. His work in us can make Christ as real to us as if He were physically walking by our side. That is the level of comfort, fellowship, hope, and joy He can bring.

8. The Holy Spirit sets Himself against the desires of the flesh and leads us into righteousness.

This I say then, Walk in the Spirit, and ye shall not fulfil the lust of the flesh. For the flesh lusteth against the Spirit, and the Spirit against the flesh: and these are contrary the one to the other: so that ye cannot do the things that ye would. But if ye be led of the Spirit, ye are not under the law.

Galatians 5:16–18

When we "walk in the Spirit," we are not controlled by sinful desires that come from our flesh. The flesh produces one kind of desire, and the Holy Spirit produces another kind, and they are always opposed to each other. Walking by the Spirit is what we do when we choose the desires produced by the Holy Spirit because we are led to be submissive to God. The renewing of our mind means that we no longer desire what is produced by the flesh. So, "walking by the Spirit" is not something we do in order to get the Spirit's help, but rather it is something we do by the enablement of the Holy Spirit. Ultimately, all the good desires that we have are given by the Holy Spirit because apart from our spirit and His Spirit, we are just sinful flesh.

9. Works of the flesh become less evident, and the fruit of the Spirit becomes more evident.

Now the works of the flesh are manifest, which are these; Adultery, fornication, uncleanness, lasciviousness, Idolatry, witchcraft, hatred, variance, emulations, wrath, strife, seditions, heresies, Envyings, murders, drunkenness, revellings, and such like: of the which I tell you before, as I have also told you in time past, that they which do such things shall not inherit the kingdom of God. But the fruit of the Spirit is love, joy, peace, longsuffering, gentleness, goodness, faith, Meekness, temperance: against such there is no law. And they that are Christ's have crucified the flesh with the affections and lusts. If we live in the Spirit, let us also walk in the Spirit. Let us not be desirous of vain glory, provoking one another, envying one another.

Galatians 5:19–26

The fruit of the Holy Spirit is the visible growth of a Christian in Jesus Christ. It is a biblical term that sums up the nine visible attributes of a true Christian life. These are not individual fruits from which we pick and choose, but rather, the fruit of the Holy Spirit as a whole characterizes all who truly walk in the Holy Spirit. All of these characteristics should be produced in a Christian's life in Jesus Christ. The fruit of the Holy Spirit is a physical manifestation of a Christian's transformed life. As we mature as believers, there should be a progression of increased quality and abundance of the fruit in our Christian walk for others to see and experience.

10. Believers are commanded to *be filled with the Spirit.*

And be not drunk with wine, wherein is excess; but be filled with the Spirit.

Ephesians 5:18

Christians often neglect their spiritual maintenance, and for those who are filled with the Holy Spirit, there are times when refilling is needed. We need to be continually filled with the Holy Spirit—we will all run out of gas at times. It is the power of the Holy Spirit that recharges our lives. In the original Greek, the phrase "be filled" is a present-tense verb of the word *pleroo,* which literally means "to cram full."[94] Paul didn't use the past tense or the future tense of the word but instead chose the present tense. He was specifying that the filling of the Holy Spirit is not a one-time thing but a continual experience with the Holy Spirit.

Being filled with the Holy Spirit gives great joy in God, and "the joy of the Lord is your strength" (Nehemiah 8:10). There is power in this joy for overcoming evil and boldness to witness for Jesus Christ. To be filled with the Holy Spirit means to partake in the joy, to flow in love for God the Father and God the Son Jesus Christ, with the very love with which they love us.

The Holy Spirit is God. He is one in essence with the Father and the Son, but He is also a distinct person and has all the attributes of a person. That is why we refer to the Holy Spirit as the third person of the trinity. Like a person, the Holy Spirit helps, searches, and guides. He knows, He feels, and He wills. The Holy Spirit has a mind, gives instruction, and loves. Someone who is filled with the Spirit is driven by the Holy Spirit, and He motivates us in a gentle, loving way. A Holy Spirit-driven person will allow Him to direct and guide every decision, plan, and activity in his or her life. The natural state of the fallen world doesn't operate this way and is actually very opposed to this lifestyle. This is why we must be filled and renewed continually.

11. The Holy Spirit is a giver of gifts.

Now there are diversities of gifts, but the same Spirit.
1 Corinthians 12:4

The gifts of the Holy Spirit are special abilities provided by the Holy Spirit to Christians for the purpose of building up the body of Christ. The gifts of the Holy Spirit are the tools that complete everything we need to fulfill His purposes and callings for our lives. We can easily get caught up with what spiritual gifts we have and focus only on those areas of our ministry, but that is not how it should work. We are called to serve Christ, and He will equip us with whatever gifts of the Holy Spirit we need to accomplish our callings and purposes. Yes, God calls some to be teachers and gives them the gift of teaching, for example, but that is not an excuse not to serve God in other ways as well.

The Apostle Paul explained in 1 Corinthians 12 that the gifts of the Holy Spirit are all valid, but their value is determined by their worth to the church. He used the analogy of the human body. All members of the body have functions, but some are more important than others. The service of each Christian should be in proportion to the gifts that he has. All believers are members of the body of Christ, and all body parts are needed to be fully functional. The full potential of the church will never be realized until all of the gifts of the Holy Spirit are working together in unity. The gifts of the Holy Spirit are gifts of grace given in grace, so their use must be controlled by the rule of love, which is over all the gifts of the Holy Spirit. "But all these worketh that one and the selfsame Spirit, dividing to every man severally as he will." (1 Corinthians 12:11).

Scripture explicitly states that the gifts of the Holy Spirit that believers possess are given to them by Him as He determines in His wisdom. They are not given by a man or in man's wisdom, nor does any man have some extra Holy Spirit of his own to give out. Unfortunately, I know there are Christians who chase after other Christians because they believe or have been taught that they can get their spiritual gifts imparted to them. The gifts of the Holy Spirit are not man's to give. God can and does use us in ministry as He wills when giving gifts, but ultimately it is Jesus Christ who is the baptizer, and it is the Holy Spirit who gives the gifts in His wisdom.

12. The Holy Spirit restrains sin and fights the power of lawlessness in the world.

And now ye know what withholdeth that he might be revealed in his time. For the mystery of iniquity doth already work: only he who now letteth will let, until he be taken out of the way. And then shall that Wicked be revealed, whom the Lord shall consume with the spirit of his mouth, and shall destroy with the brightness of his coming: Even him, whose coming is after the working of Satan with all power and signs and lying wonders, And with all deceivableness of unrighteousness in them that perish; because they received not the love of the truth, that they might be saved.

2 Thessalonians 2:6–10

The world is not as evil as it could be for one reason: The Holy Spirit restrains evil. The Holy Spirit works to make us holy as He is holy, and for now, He also restrains evil in the world. It is this work of the Holy Spirit that keeps the rise of the Antichrist at bay. There is great wickedness and evil in this world, such as murder, sex trafficking, perversion, immorality, war, and slavery. If you think it's an evil world now, just imagine what it will be like when the Holy Spirit leaves the world. The Holy Spirit is in the world, convicting it of sin, righteousness, and judgment. By doing so, He restrains evil from being worse than it would be. The Holy Spirit is also at work convicting believers of sin so that we will confess our sins and repent.

13. The Holy Spirit gives us wisdom by which we can understand God's communication with us.

But God hath revealed them unto us by his Spirit: for the Spirit searcheth all things, yea, the deep things of God. For what man knoweth the things of a man, save the spirit of man which is in him? even so the things of God knoweth no man, but the Spirit of God.

1 Corinthians 2:10–11

Only the Bible contains writings from the Holy Spirit rather than from man's wisdom. Only the Bible reveals what "eye hath not seen, nor ear heard, neither have entered into the heart of man, the things which God hath prepared for them that love him" (1 Corinthians 2:9). The Bible is unique because it reveals the things of the Spirit of God that we cannot find out on our own. These things are usually opposed to our natural way of thinking, which is why we need spiritual wisdom to understand. Even though God's Word appears in human language to communicate actual thoughts, it differs from thought in its revelatory nature. Because of this, it is possible for the unbeliever to mentally grasp the logical meaning of its content, but without the Holy Spirit, he cannot understand God's Word in the fullest sense. The spiritual implications of biblical truth, especially the life-changing elements in relation to the unbeliever, remain a mystery to him. Without the Holy Spirit, we cannot truly understand the things of God.

14. The Holy Spirit teaches us things that can't be replaced by human knowledge.

Now we have received, not the spirit of the world, but the spirit which is of God; that we might know the things that are freely given to us of God. Which things also we speak, not in the words which man's wisdom teacheth, but which the Holy Ghost teacheth; comparing spiritual things with spiritual.

1 Corinthians 2:12–13

There are always lessons to learn in life, and we have been given the most amazing teacher in the Holy Spirit. Not only can the Holy Spirit teach us wisdom and knowledge, but He will also bring Scripture verses to memory. He can give us His words of knowledge and wisdom, along with anything else we may need to be taught. This is why the Holy Spirit is also called the Helper, but He cannot help us unless He is able to speak His words of knowledge and wisdom as we will need them. We need to be good students of God's Word and allow Him to guide us into a lifestyle of learning from Him for His glory and our good.

Receiving teaching from the Holy Spirit is as simple as submitting our lives to Him each day and making time to listen to Him and to study the Word of God. God will use pastors, theologians, or scholars to teach Scripture, but the Holy Spirit as Teacher is the most necessary of these. The Holy Spirit will teach us as He did the disciples. He will teach us how Scripture applies to our lives and will guide us into the way of truth. We must take time to study Scripture, but it is equally important to do so with the Holy Spirit instead of apart from Him. The Bible is a supernatural book that will impact the lives of all who read it under the supernatural teaching of the Holy Spirit.

15. The Holy Spirit brings conviction of sin.

And when he is come, he will reprove the world of sin, and of righteousness, and of judgment.

John 16:8

The word used here translated as "reprove" in Greek is the word *elegcho*, meaning "to confute, convict, rebuke, reprove, and to tell a fault."[95] Jesus used this word in order to highlight that even if man can point out an error, it is the Holy Spirit who brings conviction of sin. He reveals the foolishness of sin, shows the offense, points out the consequences, and leads the sinner to repentance. He is the church's greatest ally in evangelism. Without the help and the presence of the Holy Spirit, the evangelistic task of the church would fail.

The Holy Spirit convicts people of sin for the purpose of reconciling them to God. The robber brings condemnation for the purpose of shaming people away from God. A person can be in sin, and because of the Holy Spirit, he can understand that he is in sin yet still fail to grasp the real eternal consequences of what that means. I have seen people come to a church service where they hear about sin, and they acknowledge that the sermon is true and that they are sinners, yet they leave church and continue living the same lifestyle they did before getting there. Something different begins to happen when the Holy Spirit begins to work in a person's soul. The Holy Spirit lovingly points out faults in that person until finally, the Holy Spirit brings him to a place of truth. It is at this point that the scales start to fall from his eyes so that he can truly see for the first time his unrighteousness and the sin of unbelief in Jesus Christ. Only the Holy Spirit can reveal these truths.

There is a difference between godly sorrow and worldly sorrow. People can be sorry for what they did, but sometimes they are only sorry because they got caught. This is what distinguishes worldly sorrow from godly sorrow. Some people have made a wreck of their lives by making chains of bad decisions, and they are sorrowful about the personal inconveniences that result from it, but that also is not godly sorrow. Godly sorrow will make you think about the others you affected, and not just yourself. Godly sorrow will lead to repentance, and that repentance will lead to salvation with no regrets.

> *If ye love me, keep my commandments. And I will pray the Father, and he shall give you another Comforter, that he may abide with you for ever; Even the Spirit of truth; whom the world cannot receive, because it seeth him not, neither knoweth him: but ye know him; for he dwelleth with you, and shall be in you.*
>
> **John 14:15–17**

The Helper, Counselor, Advocate, Intercessor, and Strengthener is here for us, but how much access do we allow Him to have in our lives? We need to know that sin and the things of the flesh can stop the flow of the Holy Spirit in us. Sometimes we can also be so cluttered with busyness and distractions that we don't allow room for the Holy Spirit to move in our lives. I think of the many people I know who have garages that are meant for cars but are full of stuff that hasn't seen the light of day for years. Their cars, which are usually their second most costly possessions and will most likely out of necessity be used for survival, are kicked to the curb, where they are left out in the elements to deteriorate faster and are exposed to thievery. This makes no sense. The Holy Spirit is your greatest asset, so don't leave Him out on the curb when He should be parked in the garage!

The Conviction of the Holy Spirit

As a Christian, knowing what the Holy Spirit does among the

unbelievers is a key to successful strategic evangelism. The ministry that the Holy Spirit accomplishes in our lives and the lives of others before we become saved is very important. Whenever we try to win souls in our own flesh instead of walking in the Holy Spirit's agenda, we walk in foolishness. Scripture speaks about the work of the Holy Spirit among the unsaved, and we need to understand what the Holy Spirit seeks to accomplish in the lives of unbelievers so that we can walk in line with His agenda and be used by Him in their lives.

The Holy Spirit convicts people of sin with the purpose of reconciling them to God; the devil brings condemnation with the purpose of shaming people into running away from God. In the book of John chapter 16, Jesus taught that the Holy Spirit brings conviction to unbelievers in three specific areas. Knowledge of these three areas of the Holy Spirit's work and role in relation to unbelievers will help us as Christians to effectively and strategically be used by Him in evangelism. Knowing His work regarding sin, righteousness, and judgment helps us walk in step with Him as we evangelize because that is exactly the work the Holy Spirit is doing in unbelievers.

> *Nevertheless I tell you the truth; It is expedient for you that I go away: for if I go not away, the Comforter will not come unto you; but if I depart, I will send him unto you. And when he is come, he will reprove the world of sin, and of righteousness, and of judgment: Of sin, because they believe not on me; Of righteousness, because I go to my Father, and ye see me no more; Of judgment, because the prince of this world is judged. I have yet many things to say unto you, but ye cannot bear them now. Howbeit when he, the Spirit of truth, is come, he will guide you into all truth: for he shall not speak of himself; but whatsoever he shall hear, that shall he speak: and he will shew you things to come. He shall glorify me: for he shall receive of mine, and shall shew it unto you.*
>
> **John 16:7–14**

The blueprint for effective evangelism was laid out by Jesus Christ in this passage. It was here in His upper room discourse to His disciples that Christ addressed the many truths related to the Holy Spirit's activity and purposeful work in the lives of the unsaved. Jesus Christ introduced this topic by saying, "Nevertheless I tell you the truth." Jesus has always spoken the truth because He is "the way, the truth, and the life" (John 14:6), so whenever Christ began a subject by saying, "I'm telling you the truth," He was emphasizing that what followed was something extra important. In the subsequent verses, Jesus expounded on exactly what He meant by the Holy Spirit's conviction of unbelievers in three areas: sin, righteousness, and judgment. Let's look at each of these individually.

First, Concerning Sin:

The word for sin used in John 16:9 is singular, and this singular sin Jesus was talking about in the rest of the verse was the sin of unbelief in Him, as Jesus said, "Because they believe not on me" (verse 9). The failure to believe in Jesus Christ is the one sin that sends the unbeliever into an eternity without Jesus Christ.

> *He that believeth on the Son hath everlasting life: and he that believeth not the Son shall not see life; but the wrath of God abideth on him.*
>
> **John 3:36**

The Holy Spirit strives to bring this to the unbeliever's attention by convicting him of the sin of failing to believe in Jesus Christ rather than seeking to reform him morally. Such sanctification only transpires after an unbeliever becomes born again in Christ. This explains why the Holy Spirit's priority is convicting the unbeliever of the specific sin of unbelief. It is God's desire that all be saved, and the process of being molded in the Potter's hands comes after we have given our lives over to His possession. In other words, instead of primarily convicting unbelievers of drug abuse, sexual immorality, or greed, the Holy Spirit seeks first to convict them of unbelief in Jesus Christ. This is why Jesus said, "And if any man hear my words, and believe not, I judge him not: for I came not to judge the world, but to save the world" (John 12:47). There is an appointed time when everyone will be judged, but right now, the Holy Spirit is working to save unbelievers.

There is only one condition that must be met for someone to become a Christian: belief in Jesus Christ, the one true Son of God.

For God so loved the world, that he gave his only begotten Son, that whosoever believeth in him should not perish, but have everlasting life.

John 3:16

The Holy Spirit's conviction of sin will always point back to Jesus' work on the cross.

Second, Concerning Righteousness:

When Jesus Christ spoke to His disciples about the Holy Spirit's coming, He knew He would be returning to the Father soon and that we would no longer have a tangible representation of Christ's righteousness on earth. The representation in Christ's absence would be the Holy Spirit's work in the hearts of unbelievers for the purpose of convicting them of their lack of true righteousness and their inability to achieve it by their own works. The Holy Spirit wants the unbeliever to understand how he falls short of God's perfect moral standards so that he may realize his dependency on Christ to be made righteous.

But now the righteousness of God without the law is manifested, being witnessed by the law and the prophets; Even the righteousness of God which is by faith of Jesus Christ unto all and upon all them that believe: for there is

> *no difference: For all have sinned, and come short of the*
> *glory of God; Being justified freely by his grace through*
> *the redemption that is in Christ Jesus: Whom God hath*
> *set forth to be a propitiation through faith in his blood, to*
> *declare his righteousness for the remission of sins that are*
> *past, through the forbearance of God.*
>
> **Romans 3:21–25**

Third, Concerning Judgment:

Jesus Christ explained the Holy Spirit's conviction of judgment in unbelievers was "because the prince of this world is judged." The robber is judged, it is finished, his sentence is the lake of fire, and house arrest on earth is his temporary sentence from God. From the moment of Jesus Christ's crucifixion, God assured Satan's total and utter defeat, finalizing his judgment in an instant. From the very first prophecy in Genesis 3:15 to the final sentencing in Revelation 20:2–3, Scripture tells us that Satan is now in this moment defeated, without any hope or chance of changing his outcome. It is a fixed point in the spacetime continuum. When John was recording the accounts in his book of Revelation, he wasn't watching a play or looking at some abstract painting on a wall; he was watching actual events from the future by God's sovereign will.

The warning from the Holy Spirit is that everyone who aligns himself with Satan rather than Jesus Christ is destined to share in Satan's ultimate defeat and sentencing at trial. Hell was originally created for Satan and his fallen angels, not for human beings, but those who do not believe in Jesus Christ will experience Satan's eternal judgment there, as described in Matthew:

> *Then shall he say also unto them on the left hand, Depart*
> *from me, ye cursed, into everlasting fire, prepared for the*
> *devil and his angels.*
>
> **Matthew 25:41**

This is why the Holy Spirit seeks to convict unbelievers of the reality of hell so that they can change their eternal destiny. When someone believes in Jesus Christ, trusting in Christ's salvation by grace through faith, he is no longer destined to participate in Satan's defeat and instead joins Jesus Christ on the winning side of history. This opportunity to change our destination is the reality that the Holy Spirit works to make clear to every unbeliever.

The Recent Trend of Evangelism

What a blessing it is that the Holy Spirit ministers both inside and outside the body of Christ! He even ministered to us before we became Christians, just as He convicts unbelievers now of the sin of unbelief in Jesus Christ, of righteousness, and of judgment. So important is the Holy Spirit's work that without Him, no one would be saved. This is why it greatly concerns me to see an ever-increasing number of churches moving away from the Holy Spirit's agenda clearly laid out by Christ regarding evangelism and instead adopting a worldly and powerless model for reaching the unsaved. Even some "Spirit-filled" churches are guilty of abandoning the Holy Spirit's work in unbelievers.

The so-called "old school model" of evangelism that includes preaching about sin, hell, and righteousness is being left for a new fresh marketing approach called the "seeker-sensitive model." This discourages all talk about what Jesus Christ Himself emphasized, that the Holy Spirit comes to convict the unbelievers of sin, righteousness, and judgment! The very words "sin, hell, and judgment" are no longer permissible speech because they might offend someone. I have friends who have been in these churches for many years and have never heard a message on sin. My mother, who is a tender, soft-spoken woman, was even chastised by a singles pastor at one church for telling someone that pornography is a sin.

This seeker-sensitive model instead wants to focus on worldly love, experiential encounters, and positive affirmation. It is a worldly love because true love walked among us, Jesus Christ, and He talked more about hell than He did about heaven for an important reason: He loves us so much that He doesn't want us going there. There is also an emphasis on experiential encounters that appeal to the flesh and substitute real life-changing encounters with God for the happy feelings you can get from a concert. Without biblical discernment, this kind of atmosphere is an invitation for the counterfeit to come, and along with it, judgment. Lastly, positive affirmations without a discussion about sin are counterintuitive to righteousness. This church model is man-inspired and is total foolishness. It is prideful to think that we know better than God.

The avoidance of difficult discussions is not the way to partner with the Holy Spirit in evangelism. Although it may bring larger numbers to a building, there are multitudes of people in the church whose lives haven't been changed into a new creation. In the words of Jesus Christ, "Wherefore by their fruits ye shall know them" (Matthew 7:20). Many also continue to follow the pattern of the world, even though we are called out of the world. This is why the Holy Spirit works to lovingly bring an unbeliever to a place where he finally sees his sin for himself. Every unbeliever has a choice: to stay in sin or to repent and turn toward God. Helping the unbeliever reach the point of making this eternal decision is the purpose of the Holy Spirit's ministry of conviction in his life, and creating an environment contrary to that work is not only counterproductive but also combats the work of the Holy Spirit.

The conviction of the Holy Spirit will not continue indefinitely. The Holy Spirit's convicting ministry didn't last forever back in Noah's day: "And the Lord said, My spirit shall not always strive with man, for that he also is flesh" (Genesis 6:3).

Just as the Holy Spirit's convicting ministry came to an end just before the flood, His convicting ministry will similarly terminate once more before the appearing of the Antichrist and the return of Jesus Christ according to 2 Thessalonians 2:7. We cannot assume that the Holy Spirit will indefinitely convict unbelievers, so the time to partner with the Holy Spirit in effective life-changing evangelism is now.

For he saith, I have heard thee in a time accepted, and in the day of salvation have I succoured thee: behold, now is the accepted time; behold, now is the day of salvation.

2 Corinthians 6:2

The Fruit of the Holy Spirit

The fruit of the Holy Spirit is probably the most known and talked-about aspect of His work in the Christian church. I'm going to provide a different perspective on the fruit than I have heard taught in hopes that the Holy Spirit will speak to you in a fresh way that will enlighten you.

There are many teachings about how we are not to judge people. In spite of the controversy surrounding the topic, we as Christians must believe the words of Jesus Christ when He assigned to us to judge whether people are wolves or whether they are about God's business. We do this by the fruit that is produced in their lives. This call for us to judge isn't about someone's salvation. Only God can judge that. It is, however, a call to judge whether someone is being used by God (whether he or she is a Christian or not) or being used by the robber as a wolf in the guise of a sheep.

Beware of false prophets, which come to you in sheep's clothing, but inwardly they are ravening wolves. Ye shall know them by their fruits. Do men gather grapes of thorns, or figs of thistles? Even so every good tree bringeth forth good fruit; but a corrupt tree bringeth forth evil fruit. A good tree cannot bring forth evil fruit, neither can a corrupt tree bring forth good fruit. Every tree that bringeth not forth good fruit is hewn down, and cast into the fire. Wherefore by their fruits ye shall know them. Not every one that saith unto me, Lord, Lord, shall enter into the kingdom of heaven; but he that doeth the will of my Father which is in heaven.

Matthew 7:15–21

So the issue of the fruit of the Holy Spirit is important, and it has many layers to it: It is part of our testimony, it is part of our identification as Christians, and it is part of our blessing to give out generously into the lives of others. When the Holy Spirit is alive in your life, the fruit will be bountiful because the water source is a river that will never run dry.

This I say then, Walk in the Spirit, and ye shall not fulfill the lust of the flesh. For the flesh lusteth against the Spirit, and the Spirit against the flesh: and these are contrary the one to the other: so that ye cannot do the things that ye would. But if ye be led of the Spirit, ye are not under the law.

Galatians 5:16–18

A fruitless tree standing beside a trail has nothing to offer others who walk by. A tree that has bad fruit may fill someone's belly, but it will eventually bring sickness and death. Only a tree with good fruit provides nourishment and strength for others to continue on their life's journeys.

Using Jesus' analogy of fruit and trees, I would like you to think of yourself as a tree while reviewing the individual fruits of the Holy Spirit. Ask yourself how much of each fruit is on your branches? How many of the different fruits are on your tree? Are any of the fruits available for others to pluck, or do you keep them to yourself? If they are available for others, are they all within reach to pluck, or do you make sure to keep some out of reach from certain people?

Be thinking about these questions as you read the list of the fruit of the Holy Spirit.

> *But the fruit of the Spirit is love, joy, peace, longsuffering, gentleness, goodness, faith, Meekness, temperance: against such there is no law.*
>
> **Galatians 5:22–23**

1. Love

The Greek word for love used here is *agape*, meaning "affection or benevolence, love, goodwill," and is also a "feast of charity and a dear love."[96] It is "the expression of seeking the highest good of others."[97] A detailed description of this kind of love is also found in 1 John:

> *Beloved, let us love one another: for love is of God; and every one that loveth is born of God, and knoweth God. He that loveth not knoweth not God; for God is love. In this was manifested the love of God toward us, because that God sent his only begotten Son into the world, that we might live through him. Herein is love, not that we loved God, but that he loved us, and sent his Son to be the propitiation for our sins. Beloved, if God so loved us, we ought also to love one another. No man hath seen God at any time. If we love one another, God dwelleth in us, and his love is perfected in us.*
>
> **1 John 4:7–12**

This type of love is not based on emotions or feelings, though it does involve them; it is the purposeful decision to be committed to the wellbeing of others without any conditions or circumstances. This is the love God has for us, and His Spirit pours this into us so that we can also love others in the same way.

2. Joy

The Greek word used here for joy is *chara*, meaning "cheerfulness, calm delight, gladness, to be exceeding joyful."[98] It is a gladness that is not based on circumstances. In a letter, Peter described this kind of joy:

> *Wherein ye greatly rejoice, though now for a season, if need be, ye are in heaviness through manifold temptations: That the trial of your faith, being much more precious than of gold that perisheth, though it be tried with fire, might be found unto praise and honour and glory at the appearing of Jesus Christ: Whom having not seen, ye love; in whom, though now ye see him not, yet believing, ye rejoice with joy unspeakable and full of glory: Receiving the end of your faith, even the salvation of your souls.*
>
> **1 Peter 1:6–9**

Even though the people Peter addressed in this letter did not see Jesus and experienced many trials of their faith, they still had joy that was supernatural, a joy that challenged every human understanding of the emotion. A joy unspeakable is a joy that is incapable of being described with human words. This joy is more than happiness and is not based on physical possessions or circumstances; this joy is found in knowing God's promises are true! Spirit-filled joy is found in God's perfect will, receiving His forgiveness, participating in fellowship with other believers, ministering to others, and sharing the good news of Jesus Christ. It is in active relationship with the Holy Spirit where the source of this joy is found. If the robber has stolen your joy away, take it back by tapping into the vine and partnering with the Holy Spirit to do something! Fill up on joy and give the joy of the Lord to others as good fruit.

3. Peace

The Greek word for peace is *eirene*, which means "to join peace both literary or figuratively, implying prosperity, quietness, rest."[99] It is contentment and unity between people. Because this peace is supernaturally given, it is part of the relational unity with the Holy Spirit also.

> *Be anxious for nothing; but in every thing by prayer and supplication with thanksgiving let your requests be made known unto God. And the peace of God, which passeth all understanding, shall keep your hearts and minds through Christ Jesus.*
>
> **Philippians 4:6–7**

This supernatural peace is living in a state of assurance and total contentment. It is the fellowship of harmony and unity between people and the deliverance from worry and fear. Because this is something that the robber depends on to gain control in areas of our lives, it is a battlefield that he will not surrender easily. But by the power of the Holy Spirit, we can submit whatever lack of peace we have to God. God did not create us to be like the Atlas of the Greek myths, with the weight of the world bearing down on our shoulders; we were created to let God carry our burdens.[100] If you are starting to feel anxious about anything, take it to God in prayer, with thanksgiving. Ask the Holy Spirit to deal with it so that you walk in peace and so that you can also be an extension of God's peace as you minister to others around you.

4. Longsuffering

Some English Bible translations will use the word patience instead of longsuffering, but the Greek word used is *makrothumia*, meaning "longanimity, forbearance, fortitude, longsuffering, patience."[101] Patience is the ability to wait, but longsuffering is how we act during the waiting. Part of that demeanor is being slow to speak and slow to anger.

> *Be longsuffering therefore, brethren, unto the coming of the Lord. Behold, the husbandman waiteth for the precious fruit of the earth, and hath long patience for it, until he receive the early and latter rain. Be ye also patient; stablish your hearts: for the coming of the Lord draweth nigh. Grudge not one against another, brethren, lest ye be condemned: behold, the judge standeth before the door.*
>
> **James 5:7–9**

Longsuffering is the exercise of personal discipline and restraint that prevents us from speaking or acting hastily in the face of disagreement, opposition, or persecution. It is the work of the Holy Spirit that gives us this ability, as it is contrary to our fleshly nature. Longsuffering is the act of patiently enduring pain or problems without complaining. Longsuffering also does not make avenging wrongs a priority because those who have developed it understand that God is in control and that He is our defender.

5. Kindness

The word for kindness in Greek is *chrestotes*, which means "usefulness, excellence in character or demeanor, gentleness, goodness, kindness."[102] It is the act of being merciful, sweet, and tender.

> *A gracious woman retaineth honour: and strong men retain riches. The merciful man doeth good to his own soul: but he that is cruel troubleth his own flesh.*
>
> **Proverbs 11:16–17**

Someone with the fruit of kindness will have an eagerness to put others at ease and will seek to make them comfortable. A person who practices kindness develops a peaceful and attractive temperament that shows friendliness towards others. In a strongly divided and bitter world, kindness is like a beacon in the dark that draws people to its source. Let them see that the source is not of us but of the Holy Spirit in us.

6. Goodness

The Greek word used here is *agathosune*, meaning "goodness, virtue or beneficence."[103] It is the act of being generous and openhearted, with an emphasis on others' best interests.

> *And let us not be weary in well doing: for in due season we shall reap, if we faint not. As we have therefore opportunity, let us do good unto all men, especially unto them who are of the household of faith.*
>
> **Galatians 6:9–10**

This spiritual fruit is a reflection of Jesus Christ because it goes beyond what others deserve, just as Jesus Christ shows undeserved goodness to us. Do you struggle to do good beyond what others deserve? If so, pray and ask for the Holy Spirit's help because when you do act in goodness on others' behalf, they will see Christ in you.

7. Faithfulness

In Greek, the word for faithfulness here is *pistis*. This means "assurance, belief, faith, fidelity."[104] It is based on truth, God, the great Teacher. It is reliance upon Jesus Christ for salvation. He is faithful; He is dependable, loyal, and full of trustworthiness because that is who He is. Jesus said in His revelation to John:

> *Fear none of those things which thou shalt suffer: behold,*
> *the devil shall cast some of you into prison, that ye may*
> *be tried; and ye shall have tribulation ten days: be thou*
> *faithful unto death, and I will give thee a crown of life.*
>
> **Revelation 2:10**

Faithfulness is absolute devotion to God despite anything, even the threat of death. This is part of our testimony that witnesses to the unbeliever. It is shown in our loyalty to friends and or dependability to carry out our responsibilities. The supernatural fruit of faith is the conviction that even now, God is working and acting on our behalf. Remaining faithful to God is a requirement unto death made possible by the Holy Spirit.

8. Gentleness

In Greek, the word used for gentleness here is *praotes*, which means "gentleness and implied humility, meekness."[105] Gentleness will manifest as humble, calm, non-threatening behavior.

> *But sanctify the Lord God in your hearts: and be ready*
> *always to give an answer to every man that asketh you a*
> *reason of the hope that is in you with meekness and fear.*
>
> **1 Peter 3:15**

Gentleness creates a humble and nonthreatening demeanor that derives from a position of strength and authority, according to the original meaning of the word. It is not a weak or passive quality because it is contrary to the fleshly carnal nature and draws on the Holy Spirit for His strength. This is the position from which we should always defend our faith. Proverbs also says, "A soft answer turneth away wrath: but grievous words stir up anger" (15:1). This means that gentleness from the Holy Spirit even has the power of calming another's anger. Do you deal with anger issues? If so, change the source from which you draw strength and ask the Holy Spirit for help.

9. Self-control

The Greek word for this is *egkrateia*, meaning "self-control, temperance, and especially continence."[106] It is the act of being disciplined and behaving well.

> *For the grace of God that bringeth salvation hath appeared to all men, Teaching us that, denying ungodliness and worldly lusts, we should live soberly, righteously, and godly, in this present world.*
>
> **Titus 2:11–12**

Self-control is the restraint of our own carnal emotions, actions, and desires. It is living in harmony with the perfect will of God and His nature. Self-control is the act of living God's perfect will, not ours. Self-control can be seen when our spirit, instead of our carnal nature, is in control of our body. We let the robber steal from us when we allow him to convince us that our body is ruler. If this is a struggle for you, speak out loud and believe in your heart that despite what your flesh may think, you choose for your spirit to be in control and that you choose to submit to the perfect will of God. Ask the Holy Spirit to bring the healthy fruit of self-control into your life.

This is the fruit of the Holy Spirit that characterizes the life of a Christian. If an unbeliever were to walk by you on any given day of your life, what kind of fruit could he or she pick from you? Would it be fruit good for life or for death? As Christians, we are the branches grafted into the tree that is rooted in Jesus Christ. For a graft to thrive and produce fruit, maintenance is required.

> *And if some of the branches be broken off, and thou, being*

271

a wild olive tree, wert grafted in among them, and with them partakest of the root and fatness of the olive tree.

Romans 11:17

For a grafted branch to reach its full potential, two things are needed: pruning and water. Pruning is necessary because it assures that all the available recourses go toward the health and productivity of the branch. When unhealthy things come into our lives, they steal away our resources of time, money, health, and relationships. The robber will come to tempt us with these opportunities that only lead to thievery. Their ultimate purpose is to rob us of God's best for our lives and keep us from bearing fruit. This is why it is important to let God prune us. Some of the things in our lives that need pruning can be obvious, like habitual sin, but others can be less obvious. This is why we need God to identify what needs pruning. What are the dead things you need to let Him cut off in your life?

The second thing a grafted branch needs to reach its full potential is water, and it is the Holy Spirit Who does the watering. With the Holy Spirit, we have access to water twenty-four hours a day, seven days a week. With that kind of availability, how often do you water yourself? A healthy garden needs to be watered every day, yet most Christians will only water themselves once a week.

Not long ago, we had a drought where I lived, and I could only water the lawn once a week. It didn't take long before it turned brown and looked dead. I noticed that a nearby house was still beautiful with lush green grass. This home was not on public utilities but on well water. How many people do you think ever drove by my house attracted to my lawn when my neighbor down the street had lush green grass? Yet many of us are living life being fed water through public utilities on Sunday, and we think that people will be attracted to our fruit. But we have access to a well that will never go dry! We have access to water that flows from the river of the Holy Spirit, and its source is the throne room of God. Stay in the flow of the unlimited water source.

272

Then I will give you rain in due season, and the land shall yield her increase, and the trees of the field shall yield their fruit.

Leviticus 26:4

The Gifts of the Holy Spirit

With the complexities, deceptions, and increasing fulfillment of biblical prophecy, I believe that today, we as Christians need the gifts of the Holy Spirit more than ever. God knew that this would be the case, and He promised that in the last days, He would pour out His Spirit on all flesh. When God empowers us with the gifts of the Holy Spirit, it is for the benefit of the body, to bring the church to maturity, and to give glory to Him.

But the manifestation of the Spirit is given to every man to profit withal. For to one is given by the Spirit the word of wisdom; to another the word of knowledge by the same Spirit; To another faith by the same Spirit; to another the gifts of healing by the same Spirit; To another the working of miracles; to another prophecy; to another discerning of spirits; to another divers kinds of tongues; to another the interpretation of tongues: But all these worketh that one and the selfsame Spirit, dividing to every man severally as he will.

1 Corinthians 12:7–11

These verses list all nine gifts of the Holy Spirit. The Holy Spirit is the exclusive giver of the gifts in His timing and for His purposes. We read that Paul had all nine listed gifts of the Holy Spirit:

1. Words of wisdom (2 Peter 3:15)
2. Words of knowledge (Acts 13:9–11)
3. Faith (1 Corinthians 13:2)

4. Healing (Acts 14:8–10)
5. Working of miracles (Acts 20:9–12)
6. Prophecy (1 Corinthians 14:6)
7. Discerning of spirits (Acts 16:16–18)
8. Different kinds of tongues (1 Corinthians 14:18)
9. Interpretation of tongues (1 Corinthians 14:13)

The robber can't control the gifts, but he can keep you from receiving them if he can convince you that they don't exist or they are not for today. A thorough study of Scripture finds no support for those lies. If the gifts didn't exist, then there would be no purpose for the robber to create some of the counterfeits we can see today, such as demonic tongues, fortune-telling, lying signs, and wonders. For a counterfeit to exist, an original must exist!

In 1 Corinthians 12:31, we are encouraged to desire all the gifts and to pray for them, so we should ask the Holy Spirit for all the gifts, just as Paul had all of them. We only need to be willing to submit to the Holy Spirit and be refined by Him so that we can be mature and responsible with the gifts. Let's look at each of the gifts in a little more detail.

The nine gifts of the Holy Spirit can be grouped into three categories:

1. Revelation gifts
2. Vocal gifts
3. Power gifts.

1. Revelation Gifts

The revelation gifts are words of wisdom, words of knowledge, and discerning of spirits. They are called the gifts of revelation because they reveal something. The gift of words of wisdom is the supernatural application of the Word of God into a particular situation. Wisdom itself is not a gift of the Holy Spirit because even unbelievers can gain human wisdom. The gift of words of wisdom is a supernatural gift available specifically to Christians. It is God's wisdom pertaining to the future or to events otherwise unknown to the believer. The gift can be applied either to the one who hears it or to others who need it. The Holy Spirit may give a word of wisdom to guide or help someone make a decision or to give warnings.

For this gift to operate, the Word of God must be in our lives, and we must also know the Lord personally:

> *That the God of our Lord Jesus Christ, the Father of glory, may give unto you the spirit of wisdom and revelation in the knowledge of him.*
>
> **Ephesians 1:17**

This gift is also the prerequisite for us to be able to receive all of the other gifts. Jesus provided a very clear example of how this gift is used in Matthew 4:3–7, where He spoke the Word of God to shut down Satan. Two more examples are found in Acts 21, where Paul received a word of wisdom from Agabus concerning what would happen when he went to Jerusalem (verses 10–14), and in chapter 23, where Peter used the Word of God to turn the Pharisees and Sadducees against each other (verses 6–10).

The gift of words of knowledge is specific information given by the Holy Spirit concerning a need or problem. Like wisdom, knowledge unto itself is not a gift of the Holy Spirit, but when knowledge is given supernaturally by the Holy Spirit to a believer, it becomes a gift of a word of knowledge. Jesus operated under a word of knowledge in John 4, when He told the Samaritan woman at the well that she had five husbands, and the man that she was currently living with was not her husband. Remember, Jesus was anointed with the Holy Spirit when He was baptized in water by John. We also are anointed with the Holy Spirit and with power (Acts 1:8), and we can do the same works that Jesus did. This gift operates by the witness of the Spirit: "The Spirit itself beareth witness with our spirit, that we are the children of God" (Romans 8:16). These words are given by God as an impression, an inner witness, and a vision, as Hosea wrote about his gift: "I have also spoken by the prophets, and I have multiplied visions, and used similitudes, by the ministry of the prophets" (12:10). Another example of this gift in use is found in Acts 5, when Peter knew Ananias and Sapphire stole from God (verses 1–6).

Discerning of spirits is the supernatural ability to detect or perceive the source of manifestations. This can include their intent and their spiritual authority. Discerning spirits is not the same as discernment. Anyone can develop discernment to some degree on his or her own, but the gift of discerning spirits is to discern the spirit in operation behind a person or on a location. When the Holy Spirit gives knowledge of the spirit realm, the gift for discerning spirits is in operation. Some examples of this gift in use include Peter's discernment of spirits in Simon in Acts 8:18–23 and Paul's discernment about the spirit on the female servant in Acts 16:16–19. In the latter, the servant was speaking truthful things, but the source of the power in her was demonic. This reminds us that truth alone is not sufficient proof that God is in someone, which is why we need this gift of the Holy Spirit.

2. Vocal Gifts

The vocal gifts include tongues, interpretation of tongues, and prophecy. These are called vocal gifts because they say something. The gift of tongues is a supernatural utterance in an unknown tongue. There are three different kinds of tongues: one is a sign to the unbeliever, one is a personal language from the Holy Spirit, and one is used in public to be interpreted for the church. The gift of tongues works with the gift of interpretation. God speaks through a person in a heavenly language, and this is followed by an interpretation of what was said for the body of Christ. This does not mean that someone's personal prayer in tongues needs to be or even should be interpreted, but if a person were to stand up and publicly speak in tongues, an interpretation should follow for the congregation. When the gift of tongues functions as a sign for unbelievers, an unknown language is spoken and understood by the culture of that tongue.

An example of the use of tongues as a sign to unbelievers is found in 1 Corinthians 14:22:

Wherefore tongues are for a sign, not to them that believe, but to them that believe not: but prophesying serveth not for them that believe not, but for them which believe.

The most famous of all the examples for this gift is probably Acts 2, when the early church was filled with the Holy Spirit and began speaking in all the known languages of the world at the time (verses 4–6). Personal prayer language that is known only to God is also explained in Scripture in 1 Corinthians 14:2:

For he that speaketh in an unknown tongue speaketh not unto men, but unto God: for no man understandeth him; howbeit in the spirit he speaketh mysteries.

God's Word speaks clearly about the public use of tongues in a church for interpretation equal to prophecy for the edification of the body. In 1 Corinthians 14, Paul wrote:

How is it then, brethren? when ye come together, every one of you hath a psalm, hath a doctrine, hath a tongue, hath a revelation, hath an interpretation. Let all things be done unto edifying. If any man speak in an unknown tongue, let it be by two, or at the most by three, and that by course; and let one interpret. But if there be no interpreter, let him keep silence in the church; and let him speak to himself, and to God.
1 Corinthians 14:26–28

Speaking in tongues corporately must be accompanied by

interpretation, and if there is no interpretation, then tongues are only beneficial as a private communication with God.

Interpretation of tongues is a gift of the Holy Spirit that is for those who already have the gift of tongues. This is why people with this gift are encouraged to pray for the gift of interpretation: "Wherefore let him that speaketh in an unknown tongue pray that he may interpret" (1 Corinthians 14:13). This chapter also says in verse 3 that the gifts of tongues and the interpretation of tongues together are equal to the gift of prophecy. Paul wrote in 1 Corinthians 14:5, "For greater is he that prophesieth than he that speaketh with tongues, except he interpret, that the church may receive edifying." There is a difference between an interpretation of tongues and a translation of tongues. Sometimes you may wonder why the interpretation of what was said is longer or shorter than the length of the tongue given. The reason is that it is an interpretation, not a direct translation.

Prophecy is a gift of the Holy Spirit for the purposes of edification to build up, exhortation to stir up, and comfort to give peace to the body of Christ. The *rhema* word is a spoken word, here and now, and many times God will give a *rhema* word to His people through the gift of prophecy. To have a good understanding of the other vocal gifts of the Holy Spirit, we should first understand the gift of prophecy. Most people think prophecy is just a gift to foretell future events, but prophecy is foundationally a supernatural utterance in a known tongue. Have you ever been speaking to a person when suddenly, encouragements and Scripture began rushing from your mouth? You could have actually been operating in the gift of prophecy, with the Holy Spirit speaking through you. This is something we cannot just conjure up, but if we have faith and are available to the Holy Spirit, we can certainly be used by God in this way.

Prophecy can and should be judged. First Corinthians 14:29 says, "Let the prophets speak two or three, and let the other judge." It is important to understand that God thinks of this gift so highly that He desires that all His people should prophesy. This is found to be true in both the Old and New Testaments. In Numbers 11:29, Moses said to Joshua, "Enviest thou for my sake? would God that all the Lord's people were prophets, and that the Lord would put his spirit upon them!" Paul also exhorted all Christians, "Follow after charity, and desire spiritual gifts, but rather that ye may prophesy" (1 Corinthians 14:1). In Scripture, it is demonstrated that this gift is given sometime after the baptism of the Holy Spirit:

> *And it shall come to pass in the last days, saith God, I will pour out of my Spirit upon all flesh: and your sons and your daughters shall prophesy, and your young men shall see visions, and your old men shall dream dreams.*
>
> **Acts 2:17**

3. Power Gifts

The power gifts are faith, healing, and miracles. These are called gifts of power because they actively do something. Faith is the God-given ability to believe God for the impossible. The gift of faith through the Holy Spirit comes for a reason and a season through prayer and hearing God. This is not the same as the faith that develops through growth. It is important to understand that there is a difference between worldly faith that anyone can muster and the gift of faith from the Holy Spirit. Gifts are given as the Holy Spirit desires and in His timing, not ours. We can say we exercise our faith in God and His Word, believing for a miracle, but the gift of faith is God's supernatural faith on a believer by the Holy Spirit for a time so that he or she can receive a supernatural miracle. The Holy Spirit's gift of faith will evaporate all doubt and unbelief in a second and replace it with the pure faith of God, as Romans 10:17 says: "So then faith cometh by hearing, and hearing by the word of God." This amazing faith brings into operation the miraculous power of God through the truth and the absolute dependability of His Word.

> *And he said unto them, Go ye into all the world, and*

preach the gospel to every creature. He that believeth and is baptized shall be saved; but he that believeth not shall be damned. And these signs shall follow them that believe; In my name shall they cast out devils; they shall speak with new tongues; They shall take up serpents; and if they drink any deadly thing, it shall not hurt them; they shall lay hands on the sick, and they shall recover.

Mark 16:15–18

Healing is the gift of the Holy Spirit that is the mark of the great commission, according to Jesus. The Holy Spirit's gift of healing is the supernatural ability to heal other people by the power and the working of the Holy Spirit through us for God's glory. It is unclear why in 1 Corinthians 12, it is referred to as the gifts, rather than the gift, of healing. Some Christians think that it is because some people are specially used by God for specific types of sicknesses. The reason behind the wording is probably not vitally important to our faith, but the bottom line is that not all divine healing is done through the gifts of healing. The Word of God describes itself as health to our bodies. In Scripture, there are four different applications of the spiritual gifts of healing. First is immediate healing, as seen when Jesus touched the man with leprosy, who instantly became clean in Matthew 8:3. Second, there is gradual healing, as Jesus healed the government official's son of fever in Capernaum in John 4:52. The third type of healing comes through speaking the Word of God, as seen in the confession of the centurion to Jesus in Matthew 8:8. Fourth is healing with the anointing of oil seen in James 5:14, when elders of the church were called to pray for the sick to be healed.

The working of miracles is simply the gift of the Holy Spirit that supersedes the governing laws of our reality and defies the laws of physics, a supernatural intervention by God. We can all receive a miracle through prayer and by faith in God's Word, but the spiritual gift of working miracles is more than just the answering of our prayers—it is evangelistic in nature. If this gift is given to you, you will experience the supernatural at work in your home, in your business, and on the streets. This gift is used to give witness to the Lord, as Acts 4:33 says: "And with great power gave the apostles witness of the resurrection of the Lord Jesus: and great grace was upon them all." This gift defeats every obstacle of the robber because miracles of the Holy Spirit are another testament to the living power of Jesus Christ.

My prayer is that you will not be robbed of experiencing any of these gifts of the Holy Spirit. Operating in these gifts is a blessing to others but also to ourselves because of the fellowship we have with God when we are operating in them. May we be transparent enough that when these gifts are at work through us, others can see Christ in us, and God can receive all the glory that is His to receive.

A Testimony of Tongues

I want to share a testimony concerning speaking in other tongues because whenever the gifts of the Holy Spirit or the baptism of the Holy Spirit are mentioned, the first thing people usually think of is the gift of tongues, especially in other languages.

To illustrate this, here is the story of my visit to a Russian-speaking church that an old friend of mine had invited me to attend one evening. This was my first time attending a church like this. As we entered, we were offered headphones to listen to an English translation for those of us who didn't understand Russian. I grabbed a pair of headphones and sat down next to a young man who looked to be in his early twenties. The service started, and the worship was powerful. The presence of the Lord was really strong, and before the pastor preached, he got down on his knees and asked the congregation to pray for him. During the sermon, the young man sitting next to me was on his phone the entire time. I could tell his intention for being there was for something other than worship and a sermon.

As the service was coming to a close, the pastor called the people who wanted to give their lives to Jesus to the front. Music started playing, people began to go to the altar, and the worship continued to intensify, but the young man just remained seated, playing with his phone. At this point, I felt the Holy Spirit prompting me to start worshiping in tongues, and I knew it would not be disruptive to do so because everyone around me was worshiping in Russian anyway. As the Holy Spirit moved my lips, I watched as the young man next to me looked up at me, looked back down at his phone, and then stood up and walked to the altar to give his life to Jesus.

Near the end of the service, the young man approached me and said that because I had the headphones on during the service, he had assumed I didn't speak Russian. He was surprised when I admitted that I didn't. With confusion on his face, he told me that I had clearly spoken out his sins and told him that he needed to repent in Russian, and that was why he had gone forward for the altar call.

I have wondered at times what would have happened in that young man's life if I had not obeyed the leading of the Holy Spirit. It was the only time before or since that I have operated in the spiritual gift of speaking in another known tongue; most of the time, I speak in another kind of tongues. I count it a blessing and a privilege to have experienced all the different gifts of tongues, and I pray you may also have the gifts as well for the glory of God.

Why We Are Robbed

The robber wants nothing less than for us to live out our Christian walk totally in the limited strength and wisdom of our weak, foolish flesh. I believe that Satan especially hates the gift of tongues and prophecy above all others. Here are the reasons why I believe he attacks these gifts especially.

Tongues were the first of the gifts used at the upper room after the Holy Spirit came and everyone evangelized in the streets, speaking every known language. Praying in tongues also gives us the power to pray perfect prayers without the interference of doubt. Additionally, tongues can keep things hidden from the enemy because it is a personal prayer language to God.

Prophecy reminds the robber of his future. Prophecy can also call out the wolf in sheep's clothing. It will bring light to the dark and expose the hidden things. Prophecy reveals the devil's plans before they are acted upon. The person who has a calling of a prophet is a threat to thievery because his or her gift of discernment can see the lies clearly, and it is in his or her nature to want to expose them.

If the robber can keep us ignorant of what the Holy Spirit does and who He is, then he can be successful in diminishing our relationship with the Holy Spirit, or he can even convince us to totally neglect the Holy Spirit. If the robber can keep us ignorant of what the Holy Spirit does in the lives of unbelievers, then we are more likely to partner with the foolish ideas of man when evangelizing, such as a prosperity-focused gospel or seeker-sensitive gospel, instead of partnering with the work that the Holy Spirit is already doing. If the robber can cause us to doubt that the gifts of the Holy Spirit are for us, then he can keep us dependent on our own strength to fight spiritual battles. How, then, will the world know us by the fruit of the Holy Spirit in our lives?

Be Encouraged

Being led by the Holy Spirit is a choice we must make every day as Christians. Choosing the Holy Spirit over our flesh is the only option if we don't want to live a life robbed of the supernatural. Listening, following, and obeying as God leads us by His Spirit is the walk of a Christian.

Too many Christians are behaving as if the Holy Spirit is a prize for crossing the finish line at the end of the race. The Holy Spirit isn't for after the end of life; He is available right now to the born-again believer in Christ Jesus. He is there to give us the power to run our race victoriously, to cross the finish line, and to hear those glorious words, "Well done, thou good and faithful servant" (Matthew 25:21).

How much room have you given the Holy Spirit to move in your life? How is your relationship with the Holy Spirit? Do you believe the gifts are for today? You are made to be in need of a Helper, and that Helper is the Holy Spirit. Invite Him into your life, and I guarantee that you will never be the same again! When our tongues of flesh meet the fire of God, our mouths will be filled with words of power that are not of this world!

Closing Prayer

Thank You, Lord, for sending Your Holy Spirit to be our great Helper. Thank You for all You do in the lives of unbelievers and all You did in our lives before we came to faith in Jesus Christ. Thank You for the gifts of Your Spirit so that we may operate in the supernatural for Your glory and our privilege. Thank You for the fruit in our lives; may it be healthy and bountiful as a testimony to Your truth. Thank You for all that Your Spirit does. Thank You for being with us and for working inside of us from the moment we were born again. Thank You that we can have fellowship with You. Forgive us of any and all sins against You. Help lead us in fellowship with the Holy Spirit. Amen.

CHAPTER 8:

By the Blood and Our Testimony

And they overcame him by the blood of the Lamb, and by the word of their testimony; and they loved not their lives unto the death.

Revelation 12:11

This verse is often quoted in Christian circles, but many of us do not understand its significance. A powerful verse like this is rich in life, truth, and victory. The blood of Jesus is the only currency with the power to pay our debt to sin in full, yet when Christians are asked by nonbelievers to explain the necessity of Christ's blood, many are unable to articulate an explanation or share a testimony of its overcoming power. The unique properties of Christ's blood, the extreme sacrifice Christ made to offer its power to us, and the testimony of the blood at work along with the Word of God are at the center of the Christian life! This is why the robber works so hard to keep these truths from being heard and understood.

When we accept Jesus Christ as Lord and Savior, His blood becomes a payment that removes us from Satan's kingdom of darkness and places us in Christ's kingdom, as Colossians 1:13 declares: "Who hath delivered us from the power of darkness, and hath translated us into the kingdom of His dear Son." As Christians, our testimonies are also part of how we overcome the robber because they give glory and honor to God for all He has done for us and in us. Unfortunately, when asked about their testimony, I have heard many Christians respond with, "I don't have one" or "I don't know;" even worse, some of them might share testimonies that are all about themselves. Our testimonies only have the power to conquer the robber when they are not about us but about the power of the blood of Jesus Christ at work for us. Satan cannot defeat us if we confess our faith in Jesus Christ because of His finished work on the cross. The Bible does not guarantee that victory will come in the form of any measure of earthly success or physical prosperity—those are temporary things that will perish. Our victory is in the things that are eternal. These eternal things are spiritual and are more real than what we currently perceive as real. Our eternal victory is because of Christ's blood, whose power crushes death, rescuing us from the clutches of Satan. This is the root of our testimony!

The "they" referred to in the verse above are *us*, the saints of God, the followers of Jesus Christ, and more specifically, in the context of the passage, they are the tribulation martyrs. The "him" in the verse is the robber, Satan himself. When everything is stripped down to the fundamental basics, it is the blood of the Lamb and the word of our testimony that we saints are overcoming him with. Even the tribulation martyrs are conquerors by these two assurances. The "blood of the Lamb" is the perfect sacrificial blood of Jesus Christ that was shed on the cross. The "word of their testimony" is when we confess with our mouths what the Word of God says about the blood. I think this is why so many Christian testimonies today are powerless because it is impossible for us to testify to what the Word of God says about the blood if we have not read or are unfamiliar with the Word of God. This is an anemia that must be remedied by recognizing and fulfilling the essential requirement to read Scripture.

When the verse above says, "they loved not their lives unto the death," it means that despite the inherent human drive to stay alive, the saints did not prioritize preserving their physical bodies. They prioritized obedience and total commitment to God. We are called to be soldiers for Christ. There is no guarantee that we won't lose our mortal bodies in an earthly battle, but the covering of the blood guarantees us everlasting life and victory over death. As Paul wrote to the church, "For to me to live is Christ, and to die is gain" (Philippians 1:21). Our number one priority in life should be to follow the perfect will of God.

All of God's desires for us as Christians fall under His perfect will, and one of those desires is for us to walk in victory over the thief. There are three keys to overcoming Satan. First is being obedient to God. Obedience is following His perfect will and always resisting the devil. Second is when we personally testify to what the Word of God says, and third is what the blood of Jesus Christ does for us. This is why knowing the purpose and power of the blood of Christ and our testimony is a fundamental necessity for the Christian life.

Walking in ignorance toward the blood of Christ and toward our testimony is a disservice to God and leaves the front door open for Satan to rob us. With more churches making compromises in their reverence for the sovereignty of Scripture, along with incomplete teaching of Scripture due to the rising belief that some parts are outdated, many Christians are ignorant of the keys to victory. This has allowed mass thievery to take place. For this reason, we must address the anemia in the body of Christ. Let's start by focusing on the blood of the Lamb, and later in this chapter, we will look into the word of the testimony.

The Blood of The Lamb: The Ultimate Power

There is power in the blood of Jesus Christ. Just one drop of His blood has more power than the entire kingdom of darkness. His blood does something no other blood can do, and there is no other commodity that is more valuable or has more power in our universe. It truly is priceless. Understanding how and why the blood of Jesus is so different and so powerful will increase your faith, put things into perspective, breathe understanding into mysteries, and bring boldness to your testimony.

The first shedding of blood occurred after the fall of man when God sacrificed an animal to take its skins in order to cover the shame and nakedness of Adam and Eve. The sad irony of God's action was also an example of what it would take to redeem man from sin. Later, Abel's blood was spilled when his brother committed the first murder. Natural blood has always cried out for revenge, but Christ's supernatural blood cries out for forgiveness.

In the Old Testament, God's people were commanded to sacrifice a perfect animal every year, and its blood would only cover the sins of that year. It was only a temporary solution that lacked the supernatural power to cover a spiritual problem. The blood of Jesus Christ is the perfect answer to this issue. Its supernatural power comes from an eternal source and has no expiration date. This is how it can cover all sins to which it is applied at any point in time. When Jesus said, "It is finished" on the cross (John 19:30), that meant it is done, it is set in stone, and it will never change.

Here is the difference between when God makes a promise and when we make a promise. With you and me, if we make a promise to do something in the future, even if we have a sincere heart and have every intention to make it happen, there are always multiple factors outside of our control that may keep us from completing our commitment. It is not the same with God because God is completely outside of time. This gives Him the unique ability to do everything that He promises. He could even fulfill every promise with Jesus' death at all points in time, simultaneously. There are no interfering factors or constraints of time. His promises are true because they have already been done, and because they have already been done, they cannot be undone. We can have absolute confidence and faith in them! Even future promises we haven't received yet are already done and waiting for us to reach that moment in time.

Understanding how the blood of Jesus Christ contains this supernatural power to transcend time will help us be great witnesses when sharing our testimonies. On a few occasions, I have been able to witness to Muslims about Jesus Christ. When I do, I always bring up the issue of Christ's blood. Muslims believe that Jesus was a prophet, not the Son of God. They reject the notion that Christ's blood has any significance, but they do believe He was born of the

Virgin Mary. So when I bring to their attention the biological fact that it takes the seed of a man to determine the blood type of a child, they are faced with a conundrum that has only one explanation.[107]

Jesus Christ is the Son of God, and His blood is uniquely different from all other blood because His blood was determined by the Holy Spirit of God! His blood was natural enough to be sacrificed but supernatural enough to transcend all boundaries using a power that is not of this world! It is important that, as Christians, we understand this. Jesus Christ is the Son of God; when on Earth, His blood had the physical properties of a man with the supernatural properties of God. He did not come as an angel or any other kind of spiritual being. He came as a man to save man, and that is why His blood covers us but does not cover any other created being.

Jesus became the final sin offering when He gave up His life and poured out His blood on the cross at Calvary. The blood of Christ is precious, it is holy, and it is the only thing that can wash us white as snow. Because God sent His only Son to die for us, we no longer have to make yearly sacrifices for our sins. But imagine what it would be like if we still did. Imagine what would happen if we had to look for a perfect animal and then have to kill it with our own hands because of our own sins. Would we take sin a lot more seriously so that we could treat the gift of Christ's blood with a lot more reverence? "The world and its evil desires are passing away. But the person who does the will of God lives forever" (1 John 2:17).

In the chapter "Knowing the Will of God," we discussed how there is stability, peace, and strength when we walk in the perfect will of God. God's perfect will is always under the covering of the blood of Christ! When we do the will of God, the covering of Christ's blood is there to remind us that we will live forevermore and that our sins are forgiven. When we make our profession of Jesus Christ, we are making a declaration that is a formal, explicit statement and an announcement that is kept on record in the courtroom of God. The profession gives us legal access to Christ as our defender, and His blood is our payment in full for our transgressions.

Wherefore, holy brethren, partakers of the heavenly calling, consider the Apostle and High Priest of our profession, Christ Jesus.

Hebrews 3:1

The submission of our confessions of sin and our profession of Christ make it necessary for the words of our mouths to agree with the words of God. Jesus taught that our words are vitally important: "For by your words you will be acquitted, and by your words you will be condemned" (Matthew 12:37). God has given us a clear legal process that requires us to submit our plea with our hearts and our mouths. The blood of Christ is the only thing that makes possible our not guilty plea and crushes the plans of Satan.

The Application of the Blood

A common and true saying in the church is that the Old Testament is the New Testament concealed, and the New Testament is the Old Testament revealed. Keeping this in mind, let's look at the most well-known example of the application of blood for protection and deliverance in the Old Testament, the Passover.

Then Moses called for all the elders of Israel, and said unto them, Draw out and take you a lamb according to your families, and kill the passover. And ye shall take a bunch of hyssop, and dip it in the blood that is in the basin, and strike the lintel and the two side posts with the blood that is in the basin; and none of you shall go out at the door of his house until the morning. For the Lord will pass through to smite the Egyptians; and when he seeth the blood upon the lintel, and on the two side posts, the Lord will pass over the door, and will not suffer the destroyer to come in unto your houses to smite you.

Exodus 12:21–23

Notice here that the blood from an innocent lamb sacrificed was not enough to provide protection from God's judgment. This protection also required an action: the application of the blood using hyssop. Hyssop is a weed that is very common in the Middle East. Hyssop was and is readily available to everyone, making it valueless monetarily. No one had to work to earn it, but it did require an "action" to pick it up off the ground. If we compare this to salvation by Jesus' blood, we can say that becoming saved requires an action. Some people may say that this sounds like works-based salvation, but before we make that assumption, we need to look at the definitions of *work* and *act.*

A *work*, according to the dictionary, means "a mental or physical effort done in order to achieve a purpose or result." An *act*, according to the dictionary, means "a gesture (gratitude) or movement (adoption), a legal process."[108] Do you see the difference? The action of applying the blood is a legal action that takes place in the courtroom of God, where we become sons and daughters by adoption. We are totally incapable of achieving the power of the blood through any physical work or payment by our own means. It is only attainable by God, and that is why Jesus Christ is the only way to eternal life through salvation. Jesus paid the price so that the blood would be freely obtainable through the action of a legal process. The action now is no longer to use hyssop to spread the blood of an animal but to confess with our mouths and believe in our hearts that Jesus Christ is our Lord and Savior, the only Son of the living God.

So who is the ultimate judge? God is. For us as Christians, Who is our substitute before the judge in court? Jesus Christ is. What is the legal action and payment to obtain Jesus as our substitute? The application of the blood of Christ.

The last step of the Passover was that the Jews had to be obedient to the Lord by staying inside their houses after the blood was applied in order to remain under its covering and protection. Some may consider this no longer relevant because it is in the Old Testament, but let's look at a greeting in the New Testament from Peter to God's chosen people who are temporary residents in the world.

> *Elect according to the foreknowledge of God the Father, through sanctification of the Spirit, unto obedience and sprinkling of the blood of Jesus Christ: Grace unto you, and peace, be multiplied.*
>
> **1 Peter 1:2**

It is with the Holy Spirit's help that we can be obedient to Christ, and obedience to Christ precedes the covering of the blood. The blood did not cover the disobedient during the first Passover, and those who were disobedient and went outside the door would not be safe.

The Passover in the Old Testament was merely a glimpse of what was yet to come in the fulfillment of the sacrificial death of Jesus Christ on the cross. Paul alluded to this in 1 Corinthians:

> *Purge out therefore the old leaven, that ye may be a new lump, as ye are unleavened. For even Christ our passover is sacrificed for us.*
>
> **1 Corinthians 5:7**

The blood of the Passover lamb was a temporary fix for the moment, but the blood of Jesus Christ assures us of the finished work of eternal redemption.

What the Blood Does for Us

There are many prophecies in the Old Testament concerning Jesus Christ. One aspect of these prophecies deals with the shedding of His blood seven times to permanently supersede God's law from the book of Leviticus, which prescribed the sprinkling of blood seven times for the cleansing of sin. Jesus bled seven times to fulfill the Law of God. When He prayed in the Garden of Gethsemane, He bled. When Jesus was taken to the home of the high priest, He was hit with rods across His face, and He bled. When they pulled chunks of hair from His beard, Jesus bled. When Jesus was beaten by the Romans with whips and rods, He bled. When they placed a crown of thorns on His head, He bled. When Jesus was nailed to the cross, He bled, and when His side was pierced by the spear, He bled. These are the ways Jesus Christ bled for you and me, and just as He bled for us seven different ways, there are seven different ways His blood works for us.

Have you taken action to come under the covering of the blood of Jesus? If so, do you allow the power of Christ's blood to work for you? As we review these seven blessings, ask the Lord to reveal to you any areas of their application over your life that you are not walking in fully because of thievery. There is absolute assuredness of their promises. Lies and deception from the enemy can cloud our perception of the blood, and we can perceive that we are being robbed of something that cannot actually be stolen. Let's look at what the price of Christ's blood obtains for us.

1. The blood of Christ gives us access.

Access means that we are able to enter into a place that is otherwise inaccessible. We have access to the most holy place in the universe because of the blood of Jesus, and we can go there with confidence.

Having therefore, brethren, boldness to enter into the holiest by the blood of Jesus, By a new and living way, which he hath consecrated for us, through the veil, that is to say, his flesh; And having an high priest over the house of God; Let us draw near with a true heart in full assurance of faith, having our hearts sprinkled from an evil conscience, and our bodies washed with pure water. Let us hold fast the profession of our faith without wavering; (for he is faithful that promised;)
Hebrews 10:19–23

Twice we are told, "let us," meaning that we need to take continuous action to maintain our faith. This refers to the fact that there is turbulence ahead in the Christian life. We need to continually come to Jesus with open hearts and to hold on tight while speaking out our declaration of faith because the promises that are waiting for us are worth the struggle.

2. The blood of Christ redeems.

Redemption is an action (a legal process) for gaining something in exchange for payment. The payment is Christ's blood, the action taken is the sacrifice of Christ on the cross, and the legal process to obtain the judgment of not guilty is the covering of the blood over our lives by confession of our mouths and belief in our hearts that Jesus Christ is Lord and Savior.

> *Forasmuch as ye know that ye were not redeemed with corruptible things, as silver and gold, from your vain conversation received by tradition from your fathers; But with the precious blood of Christ, as of a lamb without blemish and without spot.*
>
> **1 Peter 1:18–19**

Who are the redeemed? We are. Who is the enemy? Satan is. What is the incorruptible payment given? Christ's blood. Through the blood of Jesus, we have been redeemed out of the hand of the enemy! "Let the redeemed of the Lord say so, whom he hath redeemed from the hand of the enemy" (Psalm 107:2).

3. The blood of Christ cleanses.

Cleansing is the removal of something unwanted or defiling. Cleansing is also a form of preservation. When we wash every day, we reduce our risk of disease, and when we keep our car clean, it is less likely to rust. Christ's blood does all these things and more for us.

> *But if we walk in the light, as he is in the light, we have*
> *fellowship one with another, and the blood of Jesus Christ*
> *his Son cleanseth us from all sin.*
>
> **1 John 1:7**

If we are living in the light, then we will have a relationship and fellowship with God. This verse also implies that if we live in the dark, we cannot have fellowship with God, and the blood of Jesus does not cleanse us. Satan would have everyone believe that there is no sin because, without sin, there is no need for Christ's redeeming blood. This is why moral relativism is Satan's gospel; it tries to diminish Christ's blood. But the truth is that sin exists and that God's morals are firm. We are but filthy rags in need of cleansing, and Christ has washed us clean with His blood. "Purge me with hyssop, and I shall be clean: wash me, and I shall be whiter than snow" (Psalm 51:7).

When David was seeking forgiveness from God for committing adultery with Bathsheba, his prayers for forgiveness referred back to the hyssop for sprinkling the blood at Passover. Jesus' blood is potent enough to wash us once and for all, and it cleanses whiter than snow.

4. The blood of Christ gives us justification.

When we are justified, we are made righteous. We are declared righteous by God for a legitimate reason. The power of the blood comes from the legal legitimacy it has in the courtroom of God. It is the legal action taken to make us righteous before God. "Much more then, being now justified by his blood, we shall be saved from wrath through him" (Romans 5:9).

Because we are justified by the blood of Christ, we are not appointed unto God's wrath. What comfort there is in that! Can you imagine the wrath that would come from one who is just and has seen every act of evil ever done? This does not mean that God won't bring us correction when we need it; in fact, He promises to because He loves us. But praise God that the wrath of God will never fall upon us!

I will greatly rejoice in the Lord, my soul shall be joyful in my God; for he hath clothed me with the garments of salvation, he hath covered me with the robe of righteousness, as a bridegroom decketh himself with ornaments, and as a bride adorneth herself with her jewels.

Isaiah 61:10

Our righteousness is but filthy rags (Isaiah 64:6), but the blood of Jesus covers us with the righteousness of Christ and frees us from a guilty verdict in the courtroom of Almighty God.

5. The blood of Christ gives us sanctification.

Sanctification is God's process of setting us apart for the purpose of being made holy. Through the blood of Jesus, we are sanctified, set apart to God, and made holy with God's holiness. God will mold us to be more like Christ. What a blessing it is that we are His and that all of the sinful nature in us, connected to this world, is being removed from us so that God may prepare us for the world to come!

For they verily for a few days chastened us after their own pleasure; but he for our profit, that we might be partakers of his holiness.

Hebrews 12:10

"Wherefore Jesus also, that he might sanctify the people with his own blood, suffered without the gate" (Hebrews 13:12).

There is nothing we can do to sanctify ourselves. Only God can do that through the blood of Jesus Christ. Walk in peace, knowing that Christ has paid the price for us.

6. The blood of Christ gives us everlasting life.

We are given a chance to live forever after escaping death and damnation. As Christians covered by Christ's blood, eternity with Him is exclusively made possible by His blood.

> *Then Jesus said unto them, Verily, verily, I say unto you, Except ye eat the flesh of the Son of man, and drink his blood, ye have no life in you. Whoso eateth my flesh, and drinketh my blood, hath eternal life; and I will raise him up at the last day.*
>
> **John 6:53–54**

When we receive the blood of Jesus, we receive the divine eternal life of God. There is life in the blood of our mortal bodies, but how much more life is there in the supernatural blood of Christ? Are you walking in eternal life? Are your decisions and actions reflecting this fact? This is part of the renewing of our minds: it is the understanding that we no longer live life making decisions based on the lifespans of our mortal bodies, but we start making decisions based on the fact that we have everlasting life.

7. The blood of Christ provides us with intercession.

Intercession is an action of intervening on behalf of another, and Christ's blood intervenes on behalf of us. There is no power that can usurp this intercession.

> *And to Jesus the mediator of the new covenant, and to the blood of sprinkling, that speaketh better things than that of Abel.*
>
> **Hebrews 12:24**

When we are covered by the blood of Christ, the blessing of intercession is at work in our lives, and there is no force that can stop it. So the question is, "Are you covered?"

Christ's Blood versus Man's Blood

The blood of man has a built-in expiration date, but Christ's blood contains the DNA of God. The affliction of death due to sin is absent, giving it eternal properties. The blood of Christ speaks for you and for me! Abel's blood said, "I didn't want to die!" but Jesus' blood said, "I am willing to die for you." Abel's blood soaked into the ground, but Jesus' blood covered the altar. Abel's blood cried out for vengeance, but Jesus' blood cries out for mercy. The blood of this world speaks worldly things, but the blood of Christ speaks the will of God. As Christians, regardless of where we are, what we are going through, or how we are feeling, the blood of Jesus Christ is always speaking out for us. Even when we are stuck in paralysis, the blood of Jesus is crying out on our behalf.

Christians have been given the blessings of the blood of Jesus Christ. Christ has purchased us in a one-time transaction with that blood, giving us eternal life. But even after this, there are still some Christians who are living life robbed. The robber cannot steal from Christ His blood or His ownership over us, but he will steal the knowledge of its continual applications, power, and purpose if we let him. Ignorance, rebellion, and laziness may keep us from using this superweapon in our lives. We don't merely overcome death because of the blood, but we can also overcome Satan and his plans because of the blood. We do this by applying the blood, praying the blood, and living covered in the blood. While God's Word is "a lamp unto our feet" lighting our path (Psalm 119:105), it is God who holds that lamp, not us. His Word is unchanging and fixed in truth, and when we walk off the path, His light doesn't come with us. The blood of Christ stays under His covering; it can't be found anywhere else. To walk fully covered is to walk following Christ, and there is no better place to be.

We have the privilege of the blood of Christ, but there are billions of people who are guilty, tormented, and going to hell because of their sin, and they have no idea where to go. Do you carry a burden for them? Will you share the power of Christ's blood with them? Are you compelled to show them that Jesus is the only one to turn to for help?

A Testimony of The Blood

Here is a story about how I witnessed the blood working in power in someone's life. One Sunday morning, after church service, a married couple in their fifties approached me. The wife explained that her husband hadn't accepted Jesus Christ as Lord but was willing to talk to me about salvation. I took them to a private room where we could talk. The husband was a tall, muscular man, covered with tattoos, and was part of a biker gang. I could tell by looking at him that he had lived a hard life. As I asked him about his life story, I couldn't help but notice the way his wife looked at him with the love of Christ in her eyes. She really wanted him to become a Christian and experience the peace of God that she experienced in her own life.

The more the husband shared, it became apparent to me that his biggest obstacle to accepting Jesus Christ was not that he didn't believe He was real, but that he believed he had done too much evil in his life to be redeemable. I began to share about the transcending power of the blood of Christ and declared that there was no sin so great that it could not be overcome by the blood. But he interrupted me with protests that I didn't understand how bad the things were. He tried to describe what he had done, but it was my turn to interrupt him by explaining that I didn't need to know the details because God already knew all. I told him that the Bible declares that for Christians, "if we confess our sins, He is faithful and just to forgive us our sins, and to cleanse us from all unrighteousness" (1 John 1:9).

Noticing that he was still hesitant to believe in the power of Christ's blood to forgive, I inwardly asked the Holy Spirit for help. The Lord led me to ask him about any unforgiveness he held toward other people in his life. He replied that there were two people that he struggled to forgive: his father and a close friend who had betrayed him. I outlined the many dangers of unforgiveness to him and explained that if we were unwilling to forgive people who had offended us, we could be given over to tormenting spirits mentioned in Matthew 18:33–35. I informed him that we could be held captive by Satan to do his will through our unforgiveness (2 Timothy 2:26). I also explained that Matthew 6:14–15 and Mark 11:25–26 both describe the importance for us as Christians to forgive others, as our Lord forgave us. These things captured his attention, so I asked if he was willing to forgive his father and his friend. He said that he could say he forgave them aloud, but he could not feel like he could mean it in his heart. So I explained to him that forgiveness was a choice, not a feeling, and that forgiveness was about letting ourselves off the hook from the people we forgave. It was about declaring our forgiveness with our mouths and allowing God to come into our hearts to do a healing work inside of us. He finally agreed to forgive them for the first time, and the moment he spoke forgiveness out loud to each of them, he broke down and started to cry. I could see the Holy Spirit bringing the walls around his heart down.

In a moment, he could see that if he could forgive the people who had hurt him, the power of Christ's blood could forgive him. He was ready to accept Jesus Christ as Lord and Savior. As he confessed his sin to God and asked for forgiveness and for God to enter his heart, a great peace came over him, and instantly, he looked very different. This big, tough guy suddenly became a teddy bear! He couldn't stop smiling as he felt washed clean by the blood of Jesus. He said that it was an amazing feeling to have all the heaviness of past bitterness and wrongdoings instantly washed away. This man's salvation experience may be different from some others'. He needed to forgive others first, and God used this action to supernaturally show him that he was also able to be forgiven. There is wonderful power in the blood of the Lamb!

Our Testimony: A Story of Christ

Looking unto Jesus the author and finisher of our faith; who for the joy that was set before him endured the cross, despising the shame, and is set down at the right hand of the throne of God.

Hebrews 12:2

The Christian testimony has an important place in the world today! The personal story of faith in God, truth of His Word, and walk with Jesus is an important part of evangelism. It is the most direct means of declaring God's work in one's life, and every Christian has a testimony to share. Imagine the joy God feels every time He hears us sharing our testimony about Him and the power of His blood with others.

Because I was raised in both the Lutheran and Assemblies of God churches, the importance and sacred nature of the blood of Christ was clearly taught to me, so it is particularly apparent to me now that this emphasis on the blood is often missing from modern-day pulpits. From an early age, I understood that the blood was precious, holy, and never to be disrespected… but my understanding of what our testimonies were to be about was inaccurate. Whenever I heard someone share his or her testimony, it seemed like it was all about him or her and how he or she became a better person by becoming a Christian. The testimony of Jesus Christ was more often than not a period at the end of his self-focused story, rather than the entire point of the story. So, having never been taught biblically what our testimonies were really about, I assumed that what I heard from the stories people told was what a testimony was supposed to be. Since I believed that my testimony was about me, every time I would read Revelation 12:11 about overcoming by our testimony, I would cringe. The idea that my testimony was even mentioned in the same breath as the blood of Jesus Christ and even seemed to have equal overcoming power was sacrilegious to me. How could something that was all about me, a sinner, compare to the precious blood of Christ?

After living through decades of churchgoing and Bible camps without ever being taught that our testimony was not about us, I later wondered if I was an anomaly. I have since realized that a quick look at modern church culture and listening to personal testimonies reveals that this misunderstanding is common and has grown worse with time. With the help of social media and reality television, an entire generation has now been programmed to live lives with an all-about-me attitude. As an example, college students in 2009 scored 58 percent higher on a narcissism scale than college students in 1982.[109] As a result, I believe that even evangelism has been influenced by this narcissist's paradise. With more testimonies from Christians fitting into this worldly model, it's time for a change. It's time to discard the modern, hip personal testimonies that point others to us and bring back testimonies that point to the resurrection of Jesus Christ and the power of His blood to save us from the consequences of sin and death!

I have heard the church encouraging new believers to share their testimonies with the words, "It's easy! You just tell your story." Although this encouragement may be effective enough for baby Christians, as we mature, we need to be aware that our testimonies are God-centered. I was encouraged to share my own story growing up, and it was this partially true encouragement that prevented me from grasping the purpose of my testimony until much later in my life. Don't make the mistake of replacing the gospel of Jesus Christ with a man-centered testimony of a changed life. Keeping the gospel of Jesus Christ and the power of His blood at the center of our testimony requires us to read the Word of God.

Testimony: A Word Study

When we look into what "they overcame him …by the word of their testimony" in Revelation 12:11 really means in the original language, there are three things that come to light. First, the Greek word used here for "word" is *logos*, meaning "communication, preaching, utterance of a word concerning doctrine."[110] It is the recorded Word of God, set in stone, the divine expression of Christ. This word emphasizes that Jesus Christ, the Word made flesh, sacrificed Himself for us so that we could be redeemed by the power of His blood, and this is the focus of our testimony. The Greek word *logos* comes from the word *lego*, meaning "to lay forth, to build, describe, give out, put forth."[111] The Word of God lays forth the truth. It builds a foundation for life and describes God's plans, will, and purpose. It gives hope, and it puts forth the offer of eternal life through Jesus Christ. These are the building blocks of Christianity.

Second, the Greek word used here for "testimony" is *marturia*, meaning "evidence given judicially or generally, a record, report, testimony, witness."[112] In Hebrew, this same word is *ed*, meaning "a recorder, witness."[113] These words emphasize that our testimony is our own witness account of the Word of God, the redeeming blood of Jesus Christ, and our relationship with Him in our lives.

The third thing to notice is that the Hebrew word for "testimony" comes from the word *uwd*, meaning "to duplicate or repeat, to encompass, restore, earnestly lift up, call (take) to record, relive, give warning."[114] This emphasizes the need to passionately and diligently share our testimonies for the purposes of sharing God's plan of restoring man to Him and of giving warning to those who reject the offer of restoration with God. Let's look at the physical aspects of this.

In the chapter "Our Identity In Christ," we talked about how we are taught in school that time is linear, a straight line starting at point A (the Big Bang) and ending at point B (the heat death of the universe), and we are all heading in one direction. This view teaches that there is a beginning and an end. It was the Greek view of time during Christ's life, called "chronos," but the Hebrew perspective of time was much different.[115] According to this perspective, time was circular with no beginning and no end, just like God. This is where we get the sayings "If we don't learn from history, we are doomed to repeat it" and "Time has come full circle."[116] When you look down on time from above, two-dimensionally, it looks like a circle, but I see it more like a corkscrew. As Christians, there are circular seasons and patterns in life on earth, but for us, time keeps progressing upwards toward the appointed time when we will be with God in the new heavens and the new earth.

In the Christian life and in a spiritual sense, when things come full circle, we don't stay on the same plane. We are elevated and move closer to God, from glory to glory, as we are refined to be more like Him. So as we share our testimonies of the promises of God's Word and the power of Christ's blood, our words become building blocks connecting to the examples of His faithfulness in the past to be done again in the present and the future. The purpose of knowing biblical history from Scripture isn't for our intellectual benefit; it's for the purpose of drawing on the power of God's eternal promises made throughout history. We are not called to remember the stories of people in Scripture so we can memorialize or idolize them. We are meant to recognize God's glory and power and realize that the same God Who did the wonders of yesterday can and will do the same wonders today!

When we testify to the promises of God, we are building a connection with our words to the supernatural source of power because we are agreeing with God. It is not our opinion or feelings that are involved, but "the Way, the Truth, and the Life" (John 14:6)! This is giving God all the glory. This is also an invitation for God to move in the moment, and the invitation requires us to give our testimonies. What are you building with your words when you share your testimony? Are you building bridges that connect to the promises of God, or are you carelessly tossing out ambiguous spiritual words like scattered Lego building blocks for others to step on and get hurt?

David's Testimony

In 1 Samuel, we find an example of the overcoming power in the words of our testimonies when we use our words to build bridges to God's faithfulness and promises. David, a young shepherd boy, was summoned to King Saul at a time when the king was coming face to face with a giant problem. Goliath the Giant and the Philistine army had marched to Israel's door, ready for battle. David, confident in God and the only one from Israel who was willing to step up and face the giant, volunteered himself. But the king was reluctant to send him until he heard David's testimony.

> *And Saul said to David, Thou art not able to go against this Philistine to fight with him: for thou art but a youth, and he a man of war from his youth. And David said unto Saul, Thy servant kept his father's sheep, and there came a lion, and a bear, and took a lamb out of the flock: And I went out after him, and smote him, and delivered it out of his mouth: and when he arose against me, I caught him by his beard, and smote him, and slew him. Thy servant slew both the lion and the bear: and this uncircumcised Philistine shall be as one of them, seeing he hath defied the armies of the living God. David said moreover, The Lord that delivered me out of the paw of the lion, and out of the paw of the bear, he will deliver me out of the hand of this Philistine. And Saul said unto David, Go, and the Lord be with thee.*
>
> **1 Samuel 17:33–37**

Have you ever thought about the political and moral risks the king faced by sending an underage shepherd boy out onto the battlefield to take on a literal giant born to fight? It would have been assumed that whomever the king sent out to face Goliath would have been Israel's finest soldier, and to send out a boy who would only be squished like a bug would have devastating repercussions. Despite the many ways this confrontation could go horribly wrong, the king changed his mind after David shared his testimony. David's testimony built bridges to God's faithfulness in delivering him, and it built bridges to the promises of God concerning Israel. These truths convinced the king to make an otherwise illogical decision. So the story continued:

> *And he took his staff in his hand, and chose him five smooth stones out of the brook, and put them in a shepherd's bag which he had, even in a scrip; and his sling was in his hand: and he drew near to the Philistine.*
>
> **1 Samuel 17:40**

When David walked onto the battlefield, he took with him the testimony and promises of God, the tools with which God had equipped him, and the identity God had given him. The tools God gave David were the tools of a shepherd: a sling and stones for protection against the thief. God's calling for David at the time was that of a shepherd, not of a soldier. Aware of this, David didn't walk into battle wearing another man's armor but carrying the bag of a shepherd. Whose testimony are you living out now, God's specific story for you, or someone else's?

True Testimony

I have seen a disturbing trend in testimonies over the years that has become especially evident since the testimonies of my grandparents' generation. This trend has gone from being rooted in biblical truth and promises to being based on opinions and personal feelings about God. The two main reasons for this, I think, are the increase of Bible illiteracy and the societal shift toward a more narcissistic culture. One problematic concern is the elimination of any mention of sin and what God thinks of sin.

When giving their testimonies, Christians will often skip over their early salvation years because they continued to sin. Instead, they choose to share their later experiences, as if their first dedication to Christ didn't count. If we do this, we paint an incomplete picture, which negates God's work of sanctification in our lives, especially if our journey is like that of the prodigal son. The glory in such testimony is the promise that Jesus will leave the ninety-nine to go after the one who goes astray!

The reality is that we all have to deal with sin until the day our carnal bodies die. None of us are perfect, and we all face challenges and temptations that may knock us down for a time. But Christ is always there to lift us back up. The same goes for Christians who are struggling with habitual sin. Though God makes it clear in Hebrews that "there remaineth no more sacrifice for sins" after "we have received the knowledge of the truth" (10:26), sin still remains a part of many Christians' lives. When we struggle with sin, it becomes a valid part of our testimonies. Questioning whether we were saved yet after accepting Christ because we still struggled with sin becomes unnecessary because God receives the glory for helping us to overcome our sin. Be truthful about your life's testimony, even if there is still some brokenness. We are all clay in the Potter's hands!

Today, because of the influence of infomercials, we can easily confuse the word "testimony" with the word "testimonial," in which people offer their personal encounters with a product. Our testimony of Christ is different. The former is described by what a product can do for us, while the latter is defined by what He has already done for us. Our testimonies are not intended to be marketed the way this world markets stories of change. Infomercials will try to sell us products based on before and after testimonies, but the fact is that changed lives are as common as dirt. People can change by going to the gym, dieting, or even joining other religions. As a Christian, a changed life isn't the main selling point; the finished work of Jesus Christ is! When we testify to this world about change in our lives without keeping the reason for the change the focus, we diminish the gospel down to the world's level. We are not called to deliver a watered-down testimony that this world wants to hear, but to share the testimony this world is literally dying to hear the need for and the work of Christ's blood in our lives! That is the difference between a worldly testimony focused on a self-changed life and a Christian testifying about the power of Jesus Christ to save us from certain death.

Our testimonies are not merely about a singular life-changing moment but more about the overall flow of life itself and God's work along the way. They are a valuable way to share the good news about Jesus when we keep it real and keep it about Him. When we share anything other than the truth, we do a disservice to everyone. Challenges and struggles are guaranteed in the Christian walk. Temptations and failures are as real as blessings and miracles. Our testimonies are our real-life stories of faith in God. Don't be obsessed with having a dramatic testimony of a perfect conversion because ups and downs are normal in life. Some of us have grown up in Christian homes and may have less dramatic experiences than others, but when Christ is the center of our testimonies, sensationalism isn't needed for them to be impactful.

Seven Reasons to Share Your Testimony

In our call to share the good news of Jesus Christ, we are given tools and directions in Scripture on how to do so. We are called to share our testimony of Jesus Christ first and primarily in evangelism, but the thief is on the move to replace the blood of the Lamb and the word of our testimony with a focus on praying for signs and miracles first to evangelize. I have witnessed this type of evangelism many times before, and seldom, if ever, is a testimony told. The robber can use signs and wonders to lead people astray as long as the testimony of Jesus Christ isn't the emphasis. In the book of Revelation, the Antichrist and False Prophet will use signs and wonders to deceive the entire world into believing a false Christ, so why do Christians use his template by allowing signs to replace the testimony of the true Christ? A study of Scripture reveals that signs and wonders always followed the preaching of the good news as confirmation of the Word. We must put God first before any miracle, and we do that by sharing our testimony of Him, partnering with the Holy Spirit's work in the lives of unbelievers. There are many good reasons to share our testimonies, but here are seven upon which to reflect.

1. God's Word tells us to.

But sanctify the Lord God in your hearts: and be ready always to give an answer to every man that asketh you a reason of the hope that is in you with meekness and fear: Having a good conscience; that, whereas they speak evil of you, as of evildoers, they may be ashamed that falsely accuse your good conversation in Christ.

1 Peter 3:15–16

If Jesus Christ is truly living in our hearts, then our desire will be to follow Him and obey His Word. When we walk in a place of worshiping Him with our lives, we will be ready to share our testimony of Him whenever anyone asks or when we are prompted by the Holy Spirit to share. This also means we need to know Scripture so that we can give a defense of God's Word whenever we are questioned about the truth of God. Our preparation ahead of time to know the truth and to be able to share it is an act of obedience to God.

2. Our testimonies are unique.

But ye are a chosen generation, a royal priesthood, an holy nation, a peculiar people; that ye should shew forth the praises of him who hath called you out of darkness into his marvellous light.

1 Peter 2:9

Each of us is one-of-a-kind, living unique experiences with other unique people in a single moment of time and space. Where we were, where we are, and where we're going is all part of the testimony of who God is in our lives. We have all "sinned and come short of the glory of God" (Romans 3:23), but the story of how God uniquely reached out to each of us is a part of our testimonies. It is all a display of His love for us and how well He knows us.

3. Unbelievers cannot argue with our testimonies.

The law of the Lord is perfect, converting the soul: the testimony of the Lord is sure, making wise the simple.

Psalm 19:7

Unbelievers sometimes argue over the facts of Scripture, and not every Christian is equipped to deeply discuss apologetics and hermeneutics at a moment's notice. This is why sharing our testimonies is always beneficial with our more argumentative nonbelieving friends. They cannot argue with our personal stories of Jesus Christ. Your testimony is yours alone. Either the unbelievers will believe it, or they won't, but they can't argue with it. When your testimony glorifies God and reveals His loving nature, you can be confident in knowing the Holy Spirit will minister to them.

4. Our testimonies help build relationships in the church.

But ye shall receive power, after that the Holy Ghost is come upon you: and ye shall be witnesses unto me both in Jerusalem, and in all Judaea, and in Samaria, and unto the uttermost part of the earth.

Acts 1:8

We are called to share our testimonies throughout the earth, not only to sow seeds in unbelievers but also to build new relationships in the body of Christ. Unfortunately, pride is a deterrent to this work. This pride desires to be as perfect as possible in others' eyes. When the flesh takes over, we may look good on the outside, but we keep our mistakes hidden inside. Walking in pride is living the lie that we somehow can make ourselves clean instead of facing the fact that only Christ can make us clean. Living a lie will keep people from being able to relate to us, but being honest about our mistakes will have the opposite effect. Honesty about our testimonies brings people closer to intimate conversations and gives God all the glory.

5. Our testimonies become resources for others.

That in every thing ye are enriched by him, in all utterance, and in all knowledge; Even as the testimony of Christ was confirmed in you.

1 Corinthians 1:5–6

Our testimonies about how God has worked in our past help to encourage others who may be walking through the same battlefields where we once were. The work of Christ in us is an example of God's faithfulness to others because if He has done a new work in our lives, then He will surely do the same for others. And because in sharing our testimonies we make ourselves more relatable to others, we can more easily help them through battlefields we once traversed and which we now have victory over in Christ.

6. Our testimonies grow as God continues His work in us.

But I would ye should understand, brethren, that the things which happened unto me have fallen out rather unto the

311

furtherance of the gospel.

Philippians 1:12

Our testimonies will never end until our race is won. From now until then, we are clay in the Potter's hands, being molded, refined, and purified. From the works He did before we were born to the point of our salvation and beyond, as we apply God's truth to our lives and are led by Him, our testimonies will undergo continuous change. Will you continue to have a desire to share your testimony?

7. Our testimonies glorify God.

For God sent not his Son into the world to condemn the world; but that the world through him might be saved.

John 3:17

Our testimonies are paired with Christ's blood because they are not really about us but about what He did for us and what He is doing in us. Sharing our testimonies is sharing the gospel because it is Christ's finished work on the cross that gives us hope. This hope means that our lives have changed for the better with the kind of transformation that can only be accomplished through Christ's blood. God interrupts our selfish rebellion and shines a light to help us see our sinful ways, calling us to repentance after we have recognized our need for a Savior. These are the testimonies that glorify God.

Building Blocks for Your Testimony

Our testimonies point to the story of Jesus Christ and the power of His precious blood at work in our lives. Whenever we tell the story of His finished work and its impact on our lives, we are giving honor and glory to God. Regardless of how miraculous or mundane you think your testimony is, it is as miraculous as any other testimony because of the great lengths that God has gone through to give you eternal life and a relationship with Him. Your testimony is your personal account of how God rescued you from sin and death through Jesus Christ and the results that follow. Sharing your personal testimony with others is the equivalent of taking their hands and walking them over to personally introduce them to Jesus Christ.

It can be easy to assume that we do not need any preparation to share our testimonies because we already know our own stories, but the reality is that many of us struggle to put those stories into words, or we may even say that we don't have a testimony. We need to be ready at all times to share our testimonies, yet distractions in life, fear of speaking publicly, absent-mindedness, or laziness can sabotage us. Every Christian needs to be diligent in preparing his or her testimony before the time comes to share.

Start by taking time to pray and ask the Holy Spirit to help you put your testimony into words. Be honest about your feelings and struggles, even toward God. People respond to the stories of those who are real about their relationships, and there is no relationship that is more important than the one with the creator of the universe. Don't feel like you need to sell people on Jesus like a car dealer. Just be positive and let the Holy Spirit do His work in drawing them to Him. Think about the people you are speaking to, and communicate in a way that they can understand and relate to. Try to keep it short, under three minutes, to ensure that you don't lose their attention. If the people you are witnessing to are interested to know more, that is when you can unpack it further for them. It is always good to practice sharing your testimony too. Personally, I like to record myself and listen to it later. I have even been encouraged by hearing my own testimony. I recommend that you do whatever works for you!

We need to be effective in communicating our testimonies, and one way we can do that is by laying a good structure. Let me share with you the five keys to effective storytelling my mentors in the movie industry shared with me as a film producer. These will help you build your testimony to be efficient and effective. The five keys are the characters, the setting, the plot, the conflict, and the resolution. Let's look at each as it applies to sharing our testimony.

1. The characters

The primary character of your testimony is God, and you are secondary. This is why our testimonies are mentioned with the power of the blood of Christ in Revelation 12:11—the testimony has the power of the blood at its core. If you can keep God primary and yourself secondary when sharing your testimony, then God will receive all the glory He deserves. Every good story starts by introducing the main characters.

2 . The setting

What was your life like before Jesus Christ was your Lord and Savior? How did you identify with God at the time, what was your spiritual condition, what were your relationships like, and what was your occupation? Only share the details that are central to describing your life before you were born again. Don't spend too much time on past sins or struggles, but share enough so that people can see the contrast between your life then and now to give them an idea of your need for Jesus Christ.

3. The plot

The main plot of your testimony is how and why you came to Jesus Christ. Your description of why, at its core, is the gospel of Jesus Christ, and the how is that you repented of your sins, believed in your heart, and confessed with your mouth that He is Lord and Savior, in general as well as personally. When communicating this, make sure that whoever your audience may be will understand how they can accept Jesus Christ too. Even if they are not ready, God will use your testimony to plant seeds that will continue to draw them closer to Himself.

4. The conflict

Our lives after coming to Jesus Christ change because we are born again and that we are now soldiers for Him. Being born again means that we are no longer of this world but are still in it, and being called as a soldier for Christ means that we are at war with the sinful nature that is in the world. The conflict between light and dark becomes more evident to us as our spiritual eyes open. Share the changes that Christ has made in your life and the victory that you now have over sin because of the blood of Jesus Christ. Talk about the changes in your attitude, perspective, and relationship with God. Be truthful about the fact that you, along with all Christians, still struggle, but that life now is full of purpose and meaning with your new identity.

5. The resolution

This is the closing of your testimony. Summarize your testimony by connecting everything back to what Jesus Christ did for all of us before we were born, that the forgiveness of sins is a gift freely given that cannot be earned by works. You may even want to share a Bible verse that speaks to your testimony. Close by telling them who Jesus Christ is to you and asking them if they would like to know Him.

A Testimony of Impact

Recently, I received an invitation to help with prison ministry. I had friends who were already involved in this particular ministry, but I had never before volunteered there. My first thought was that this particular type of ministry was not my calling because I could not relate to the prison culture. After taking time to pray, I quickly realized that this was something God wanted me to do anyway, which led me to accept the opportunity.

When I arrived, I was asked to share my testimony. My initial thought was that people would have no interest in my testimony because there was no way it could be nearly as exciting as theirs—after all, they were in prison, so they must have led much more eventful lives than I had. I had to remind myself that it was not about me but about Jesus. Sharing my testimony wasn't about being in competition with anyone else; it was about being real about myself and my witness to God's faithfulness!

Once I was given the opportunity to speak, I began to share my testimony using the five keys to effective storytelling. To my surprise, everyone was giving me their full attention. I had not expected everyone to be as respectful as they were, and as I continued to describe the importance of Christ and His blood, I felt the Holy Spirit moving in the room. After I finished, many of the audience members had very thought-provoking questions for me. Several of them had already had spiritual encounters in their pasts, either with God or with Satan, so the spiritual realm was already real to them. Most wanted prayer, and some asked for counseling, which I was able to give to them.

My day volunteering with the prison ministry was an amazing opportunity for me to minister, and the outcome far exceeded my expectations. A comment I heard over and over again from the inmates was that they appreciated how real and sincere I was with them. I was also told several times that people had visited from churches to speak, but the inmates could tell that those speakers were not genuine. All credit belongs to God for a genuine testimony. A story about me may be interesting to some, but a story about Him speaks to everyone. And a story about Him will be more than interesting; it will be life-changing!

Closing Prayer

Almighty God, Creator of heaven and earth, thank You for sending Your Son Jesus Christ to stand in our place. Thank You for the overcoming power of the blood of Christ and for the words of our testimonies, which speak of Your sacrifice on the cross for the purpose of redemption. Help us to understand and apply the blood of Christ and to effectively share our many testimonies of Your faithfulness and promises. To You be all the honor and the glory and the power forever! Amen.

In Closing

Jesus saith unto him, I am the way, the truth, and the life: no man cometh unto the Father, but by me.

John 14:6

In this book, we have looked at eight biblical keys to living a purposeful and blessed life, free from thievery. But the most important thing we can take away is the greatest key of all: making Jesus Christ our Lord and Savior. There is no truth or hope without Jesus Christ. We all have built-in desires that no experiences of this world will ever fully satisfy—that is how we know that we were created to live in another world, a world of eternal life with God! This is only made possible through Jesus Christ.

The most dangerous place to live is in a life without Jesus Christ. With Him, this life will be the closest we will ever get to hell. Without Him, we will die in our sin and be eternally separated from God. God will not force us to live in eternity with Him; that is our choice to make. We are not saved because we go to church, we are not saved because we call ourselves Christians, and we are not saved because we may live a good and moral life—we are saved because of the grace of God through Jesus Christ! Jesus already paid the price to make it a free gift for us, but we need to take action in order to come under its protection. If we want a full, prosperous, and purposeful life, then we need to be covered by the blood of Christ and be freed from the bondage of sin.

The first step to freedom is recognizing that we are sinners who have fallen short of the glory and perfection of God (Romans 3:23). First John 1:8–10 declares that,

If we say that we have no sin, we deceive ourselves, and

the truth is not in us. If we confess our sins, he is faithful and just to forgive us our sins, and to cleanse us from all unrighteousness. If we say that we have not sinned, we make him a liar, and his word is not in us.

Though Christ has already paid the price, there are active steps we need to take to be able to walk in the freedom He has given us. In recognition of our sin, we need to take steps for deliverance by:

1. Confessing all sin to God.
2. Forgiving everyone who has offended us.
3. Denouncing Satan and his kingdom.
4. Confessing with our mouths and believing in our hearts that Jesus Christ is Lord and Savior.
5. Calling on the name of Jesus Christ to fill us with His Holy Spirit and wash us clean with His blood.
6. Receiving deliverance and walking in salvation through grace, in relationship with Him, and in obedience to His Word.
7. Being baptized by water as a public confession of Jesus Christ and as a testimony of being born again.

I pray that you have already accepted Jesus Christ as your Lord and Savior. Even if we have been Christians for many years, it is always beneficial for us to reflect on our relationships with Him. So let's look at some things to remember about living out the Christian life.

Things to Remember

As Christians, we are always living in three tenses of being saved. Understanding this can bring much understanding to the Christian life. First, we have been saved from the penalty of sin. Ephesians 2:8–9 clarifies: "For by grace are ye saved through faith; and that not of yourselves: it is the gift of God: Not of works, lest any man should boast." Once we have accepted Jesus Christ, His finished work on the cross has saved us from eternal separation from God.

Second, we are being saved from the power of sin. The book of Romans chapter 6 speaks directly to this. We are no longer slaves to sin but servants to God. Though we live on Earth under a period of grace as our mortal bodies are still subjected to sin, sin doesn't have dominion over us.

> *Let not sin therefore reign in your mortal body, that ye should obey it in the lusts thereof …For sin shall not have dominion over you: for ye are not under the law, but under grace.*
>
> **Romans 6:12, 14**

Grace is not an excuse for compromise but a gift for overcoming. God's grace is not for us to flounder around in, but it is to raise us up to His purposes and blessings for our lives. Remember that God's grace told Noah about the flood, but his obedience to God kept him above the waters.

Third, we will be saved from the presence of sin.

> *For we know that the whole creation groaneth and travaileth in pain together until now. And not only they, but ourselves also, which have the firstfruits of the Spirit, even we ourselves groan within ourselves, waiting for the adoption, to wit, the redemption of our body.*
>
> **Romans 8:22–23**

There is a promised day in our future when we will receive new glorified bodies that will be completely free from sin in every way! Not only us, but all of creation will be free from sin as well when sin and death are cast into the lake of fire and will be eternally bound forever. What a day that will be!

Until then, walk in your identity in Jesus Christ with the confidence that your walk will put the robber out of business. Walk in spiritual power of who God called you to be; however He made you operate in the five callings. Bless others with your spiritual gifts and talents. Know the Shepherd and build a foundation on the rock of Christ who gives you stability while being mindful that any compromise will make the pursuit of purpose more difficult. Know the will of God, and in His perfect will, He will always be Lord in your situation. Hear the voice of God, and have an intimate relationship with Him, being aware that if you don't open your mouth in communion with Him, then things stay stagnant. Do not be deceived into rejecting the authentic in favor of the synthetic, which will leave you vulnerable to the robber's deceptions. Let the Holy Spirit occupy the spaces in your life that are currently occupied by things that have no business being there. Under the blood of the Lamb and with the word of your testimony, be an overcomer by applying the power of the blood and sharing with others its wonder-working power.

As Ecclesiastes says, "To every thing there is a season, and a time to every purpose under the heaven" (3:1). Now is the time and the season to build like Noah, lead like Moses, fight like David, pray like Nehemiah, obey like Daniel, serve like Martha, believe like Mary, educate like Paul, warn like John, and love like Jesus.

You are purposeful, you are intentional, you have a purpose, you have a destiny, you are called, you will always be loved, you are valuable enough to die for, you are one-of-a-kind, and I am thankful you are a family member of the body of Christ. God bless!

Closing Prayer

Dear Lord, help us to dedicate our hearts to You, to choose to always remain faithful, and to rely on Your protection and divine direction. May our eyes always be open to see the opportunities around us and be receptive to divine confirmation or correction from You. May we flourish in our areas of weakness as a testimony to Your goodness. May we follow Your heart in giving all that You have given us to give. Fill us with strength to walk in humility and recognize our need for You to be our strength. Let us always avoid the pursuit of foolish things and lay hold of the promises and blessings You have made available to us. All glory and power are Yours forever. Amen.

Endnotes

1 Antonio Regalado. (February 11, 2019). More than 26 million people have taken an at-home ancestry test. Retrieved from https://www.technologyreview.com/s/612880/more-than-26-million-people-have-taken-an-at-home-ancestry-test/

2 Michelle Castillo. (September 18, 2013). Report: 2008 financial crisis increased suicide rates in U.S., Europe. Retrieved from https://www.cbsnews.com/news/report-2008-financial-crisis-increased-suicide-rates-in-us-europe/

3 "The Author" (November 20th 2013). The Impact of Television Viewing on Brain Structures. Retrieved from https://academic.oup.com/cercor/article/25/5/1188/311796.

4 Wikipedia. (February 11, 2020). The War of the Worlds (1938 radio drama). Retrieved from https://en.m.wikipedia.org/wiki/The_

War_of_the_Worlds_(1938_radio_drama)

5 Joseph Trevithick. (January 24, 2017) How The Military Conducts PSYOPS. Retrieved from https://taskandpurpose.com/ gear-tech/military-conducts-psyops

6 Deborah Hardoon. (January 2015). Wealth: Having it All and Wanting More. Retrieved from https://www-cdn.oxfam.org/s3fs-public/file_attachments/ib-wealth-having-all-wanting-more-190115-en.pdf

7 Deborah Hardoon. (January 2015). Wealth: Having it All and Wanting More. Retrieved from https://www-cdn.oxfam.org/s3fs-public/file_attachments/ib-wealth-having-all-wanting-more-190115-en.pdf

8 Ashley Lutz. (Jun 14 2014). These 6 Corporations Control 90% Of The Media In America. Retrieved from https://www. businessinsider. com/these-6-corporations-control-90-of-the-media-in-america-2012-6

9 Simon Tabor. (August 16, 2013). Highlighting Our Reliance on Google. Retrieved from https://engineering.gosquared. com/ googles-downtime-40-drop-in-traffic

10 Nielsen Report. (Q2 2015). Comparable Metrics. Retrieved from https://www.nielsen.com/wp-content/uploads/sites/3/2019/04/compara-ble-metrics-report-q2-2015.pdf

11 Chuck Missler. (August 1, 1997). Mischievous Angels or Sethites?. Retrieved from https://www.khouse.org/articles/1997/ 110/

12 James Strong. (1822–1894). Strong's number Hebrew 120. King James Version New Strong's Exhaustive Concordance of the Bible. Thomas Nelson, Inc.

13 James Strong. (1822–1894). Strong's number Hebrew 990. King James Version New Strong's Exhaustive Concordance of the Bible. Thomas Nelson, Inc.

14 James Strong. (1822–1894). Strong's number Hebrew 5038.King James Version New Strong's Exhaustive Concordance of the Bible. Thomas Nelson, Inc.

15 James Strong. (1822–1894). Strong's number Greek 4983. King James Version New Strong's Exhaustive Concordance of the Bible. Thomas Nelson, Inc.

16 James Strong. (1822–1894). Strong's number Hebrew 7307. King James Version New Strong's Exhaustive Concordance of the Bible. Thomas Nelson, Inc.

17 James Strong. (1822–1894). Strong's number Greek 4151. King James Version New Strong's Exhaustive Concordance of the Bible. Thomas Nelson, Inc.

18 James Strong. (1822–1894). Strong's number Hebrew 5315. King James Version New Strong's Exhaustive Concordance of the Bible. Thomas Nelson, Inc.

19 James Strong. (1822–1894). Strong's number Greek 5590. King James Version New Strong's Exhaustive Concordance of the Bible. Thomas Nelson, Inc.

20 James Strong. (1822–1894). Strong's number Greek 1097. King James Version New Strong's Exhaustive Concordance of the Bible. Thomas Nelson, Inc.

21 James Strong. (1822–1894). Strong's number Greek 4309. King James Version New Strong's Exhaustive Concordance of the Bible. Thomas Nelson, Inc.

22 James Strong. (1822–1894). Strong's number Greek 2644. King James Version New Strong's Exhaustive Concordance of the Bible. Thomas Nelson, Inc.

23 James Strong. (1822–1894). Strong's number Greek 487. King James Version New Strong's Exhaustive Concordance of the Bible. Thomas Nelson, Inc.

24 James Strong. (1822–1894). Strong's number Greek 859. King James Version New Strong's Exhaustive Concordance of the Bible. Thomas Nelson, Inc.

25 James Strong. (1822–1894). Strong's number Greek 3084. King James Version New Strong's Exhaustive Concordance of the Bible. Thomas Nelson, Inc

26 James Strong. (1822–1894). Strong's number Greek 1344. King James Version New Strong's Exhaustive Concordance of the Bible. Thomas Nelson, Inc.

27 James Strong. (1822–1894). Strong's number Greek 59, & 5092. King James Version New Strong's Exhaustive Concordance of the Bible. Thomas Nelson, Inc.

28 James Strong. (1822–1894). Strong's number Greek 4972. King James Version New Strong's Exhaustive Concordance of the Bible. Thomas Nelson, Inc.

29 James Strong. (1822–1894). Strong's number Greek 4355. King James Version New Strong's Exhaustive Concordance of the Bible. Thomas Nelson, Inc.

30 James Strong. (1822–1894). Strong's number Greek 4982. King James Version New Strong's Exhaustive Concordance of the Bible. Thomas Nelson, Inc.

31 James Strong. (1822–1894). Strong's number Greek 4286. King James Version New Strong's Exhaustive Concordance of the Bible. Thomas Nelson, Inc.

32 James Strong. (1822–1894). Strong's number Greek 2822. King James Version New Strong's Exhaustive Concordance of the Bible. Thomas Nelson, Inc.

33 James Strong. (1822–1894). Strong's number Greek 25. King James Version New Strong's Exhaustive Concordance of the Bible. Thomas Nelson, Inc.

34 James Strong. (1822–1894). Strong's number Greek 1659. King James Version New Strong's Exhaustive Concordance of the Bible. Thomas Nelson, Inc.

35 James Strong. (1822–1894). Strong's number Greek 2198. King James Version New Strong's Exhaustive Concordance of the Bible. Thomas Nelson, Inc.

36 Research Release in Culture and Media. (October 21, 2003). Americans Describe Their Views About Life After Death. The Barna Group Ltd.

37 Research Release in Culture and Media. (October 21, 2003). Americans Describe Their Views About Life After Death. The Barna Group Ltd.

38 Joseph Thayer. (August 1st, 1995). Strongs NT #622. Thayer's Greek-English Lexicon Hardcover.

39 Ecology. (2011). World Birth and Death Rates chart. Retrieved from ecology.com

40 Pew Research Center. (2015). The Changing Global Religious Landscape. Retrieved from pewresearch.org

41 The Barna Group. (October 21, 2003). Americans Describe Their Views About Life After Death. Retrieved from https://www.barna.com/research/americans-describe-their-views-about-life-after-death/

42 The Barna Group. (October 21, 2003). Americans Describe Their Views About Life After Death. Retrieved from https://www.barna.com/research/americans-describe-their-views-about-life-after-death/

43 Caryle Murphy. (November 10, 2015). Most Americans Believe in Heaven and Hell. Retrieved from https://www.pewresearch.org/fact-tank/2015/11/10/most-americans-believe-in-heaven-and-hell/

44 Isaac Asimov Memorial Debate. (Apr. 8, 2016). Is the Universe a Simulation?, and (February 15, 2018). Artificial Intelligence. Museum of Natural History.

45 "Because that which may be known of God is manifest in them; for God hath shewed it unto them. For the invisible things of him from the creation of the world are clearly seen, being understood by the things that are made, even his eternal power and Godhead; so that they are without excuse" (Romans 1:19–20, KJV).

46 David Pratt. (June 1996). The infinite Divisibility of Matter. Sunrise magazine.

47 Editor, Angus Stevenson & Christine A. Lindberg. (August 2010). Third Edition. New Oxford American Dictionary.

48 James Strong. (1822–1894). Strong's number Greek 2564. King James Version New Strong's Exhaustive Concordance of the Bible. Thomas Nelson, Inc.

49 Jim Lucas. (September 27, 2017). Newton's Law of Motion. Retrieved from https://www.livescience.com/46558-laws-of-motion.html

50 James Strong. (1822–1894). Strong's number Hebrew 4496. King James Version New Strong's Exhaustive Concordance of the Bible. Thomas Nelson, Inc

51 James Strong. (1822–1894). Strong's number Greek 165. King James Version New Strong's Exhaustive Concordance of the Bible. Thomas Nelson, Inc.

52 James Strong. (1822–1894). Strong's number Greek 18. King James Version New Strong's Exhaustive Concordance of the Bible. Thomas Nelson, Inc.

53 James Strong. (1822–1894). Strong's number Greek 2101. King James Version New Strong's Exhaustive Concordance of the Bible. Thomas Nelson, Inc.

54 James Strong. (1822–1894). Strong's number Greek 5046. King James Version New Strong's Exhaustive Concordance of the Bible. Thomas Nelson, Inc.

55 James Strong. (1822–1894). Strong's number Greek 4487. King James Version New Strong's Exhaustive Concordance of the Bible. Thomas Nelson, Inc.

56 James Strong. (1822–1894). Strong's number Hebrew 4483. King James Version New Strong's Exhaustive Concordance of the Bible. Thomas Nelson, Inc.

57 Susan Tomas Springer. (March 29, 2017). Best practices for fighting counterfeit. Retrieved from https://independentbanker. org/2017/03/best-practices-for-fighting-counterfeit/

58 James Strong. (1822–1894). Strong's number Hebrew 3701. King James Version New Strong's Exhaustive Concordance of the Bible. Thomas Nelson, Inc.

59 Bob Smietana. (April 25th 2017). Americans Are Fond of the Bible Don't Actually Read It. Retrieved from https://lifewayresearch. com/2017/04/25/lifeway-research-americans-are-fond-of-the-bible-dont-actually-read-it/

60 Pew Research Center. (October 17, 2019). In U.S.; Decline of Christianity Continues at Rapid Pace. Retrieved from https://pewforum. org/2019/10/17/in-u-s-decline-of-christianity-continues-at-rapid-pace/

61 James Strong. (1822–1894). Strong's number Greek 4114. King James Version New Strong's Exhaustive Concordance of the Bible. Thomas Nelson, Inc.

62 James Strong. (1822–1894). Strong's number Greek 3372. King James Version New Strong's Exhaustive Concordance of the Bible. Thomas Nelson, Inc.

63 James Strong. (1822–1894). Strong's number Greek 899. King James Version New Strong's Exhaustive Concordance of the Bible. Thomas Nelson, Inc.

64 James Strong. (1822–1894). Strong's number Greek 5311. King James Version New Strong's Exhaustive Concordance of the Bible. Thomas Nelson, Inc.

65 Matt Williams. (December 10, 2014). A universe of 10 dimensions. Retrieved from https://phys.org/news/2014-12-universe-dimensions.html

66 J. de Rosnay. (July 3, 1998). Entropy and the Laws of Thermodynamics. Retrieved from, pespmc1.vub.ac.be/ENTRTHER.html

67 Matt Strassler. (October 12, 2011). Most Particles Decay-Yet Some Don't!. Retrieved from, https://profmattstrassler.com/ articles-and-posts/ particle-physics-basics/why-do-particles-decay/most-particles-decay-yet-some-dont/

68 James Strong. (1822–1894). Strong's number Hebrew 120. King James Version New Strong's Exhaustive Concordance of the Bible. Thomas Nelson, Inc.

69 James Strong. (1822–1894). Strong's number Hebrew 8352. King James Version New Strong's Exhaustive Concordance of the Bible. Thomas Nelson, Inc.

70 "And Adam knew his wife again; and she bare a son, and called his name Seth: For God, said she, hath appointed me another seed instead of Abel, whom Cain slew" (Genesis 4:25). (Seth: Heb. Sheth: that is, Appointed, or Put)

71 James Strong. (1822–1894). Strong's number Hebrew 605. King James Version New Strong's Exhaustive Concordance of the Bible. Thomas Nelson, Inc.

72 James Strong. (1822–1894). Strong's number Hebrew 7015. King James Version New Strong's Exhaustive Concordance of the Bible. Thomas Nelson, Inc.

73 James Strong. (1822–1894). Strong's number Hebrew 4110. King James Version New Strong's Exhaustive Concordance of the Bible. Thomas Nelson, Inc.

74 James Strong. (1822–1894). Strong's number Hebrew 410. King James Version New Strong's Exhaustive Concordance of the Bible. Thomas Nelson, Inc.

75 James Strong. (1822–1894). Strong's number Hebrew 3381. King James Version New Strong's Exhaustive Concordance of the Bible. Thomas Nelson, Inc.

76 James Strong. (1822–1894). Strong's number Hebrew 2596. King James Version New Strong's Exhaustive Concordance of the Bible. Thomas Nelson, Inc.

77 James Strong. (1822–1894). Strong's number Hebrew 4191. King James Version New Strong's Exhaustive Concordance of the Bible. Thomas Nelson, Inc.

78 James Strong. (1822–1894). Strong's number Hebrew 7971. King James Version New Strong's Exhaustive Concordance of the Bible. Thomas Nelson, Inc.

79 James Strong. (1822–1894). Strong's number Hebrew 3929. King James Version New Strong's Exhaustive Concordance of the Bible. Thomas Nelson, Inc.

80 James Strong. (1822–1894). Strong's number Hebrew 5091. King James Version New Strong's Exhaustive Concordance of the Bible. Thomas Nelson, Inc.

81 James Strong. (1822–1894). Strong's number Hebrew 5162. King James Version New Strong's Exhaustive Concordance of the Bible. Thomas Nelson, Inc.

82 James Strong. (1822–1894). Strong's number Greek 4183. King James Version New Strong's Exhaustive Concordance of the Bible. Thomas Nelson, Inc.

83 James Strong. (1822–1894). Strong's number Greek 5039. King James Version New Strong's Exhaustive Concordance of the Bible. Thomas Nelson, Inc.

84 James Strong. (1822–1894). Strong's number Greek 1722. King James Version New Strong's Exhaustive Concordance of the Bible. Thomas Nelson, Inc.

85 James Strong. (1822–1894). Strong's number Greek 40. King James Version New Strong's Exhaustive Concordance of the Bible. Thomas Nelson, Inc.

86 James Strong. (1822–1894). Strong's number Greek 4151. King James Version New Strong's Exhaustive Concordance of the Bible. Thomas Nelson, Inc.

87 Logan Craft, Walt Ruloff, John, Nathan Frankowski. (2008). Expelled No Intelligence Allowed. United States. Premise Media Corporation

88 Maryann Mott. (January 25, 2005). Animal-Human Hybrids Spark Controversy. National Geographic News.

89 Sarwant Singh. (November 20, 2017). Transhumanism And The Future Of Humanity: 7 Ways The World Will Change By 2030. Forbes.

90 Dennis Overbye. (October 22, 2019). Quantum Computing Is Coming, Bit by Qubit. The New York Times.

91 Niall Firth. (January 16, 2019). CERN wants to build a particle collider that's four times bigger than the LHC. MIT Technology Review.

92 James Strong. (1822–1894). Strong's number Greek 728. King James Version New Strong's Exhaustive Concordance of the Bible. Thomas Nelson, Inc.

93 James Strong. (1822–1894). Strong's number Greek 907. King James Version New Strong's Exhaustive Concordance of the Bible. Thomas Nelson, Inc.

94 James Strong. (1822–1894.) Strong's number Greek 4137. King James Version New Strong's Exhaustive Concordance of the Bible. Thomas Nelson, Inc.

95 James Strong. (1822–1894). Strong's number Greek 1651. King James Version New Strong's Exhaustive Concordance of the Bible. Thomas Nelson, Inc.

96 James Strong. (1822–1894). Strong's number Greek 26. King James Version New Strong's Exhaustive Concordance of the Bible. Thomas Nelson, Inc.

97 Joseph Thayer. (August 1st, 1995). Strongs NT #26. Thayer's Greek-English Lexicon Hardcover.

98 James Strong. (1822–1894). Strong's number Greek 5479. King James Version New Strong's Exhaustive Concordance of the Bible. Thomas Nelson, Inc.

99 James Strong. (1822–1894). Strong's number Greek 1515. King James Version New Strong's Exhaustive Concordance of the Bible. Thomas Nelson, Inc.

100 GreekMythology.com. (February 14,2020). Atlas. Retrieved from https://www.greekmythology.com/Titans/Atlas/atlas.html

101 James Strong. (1822–1894). Strong's number Greek 3115. King James Version New Strong's Exhaustive Concordance of the Bible. Thomas Nelson, Inc.

102 James Strong. (1822–1894). Strong's number Greek 5544. King James Version New Strong's Exhaustive Concordance of the Bible. **Thomas Nelson, Inc.**

103 James Strong. (1822–1894). Strong's number Greek 19. King James Version New Strong's Exhaustive Concordance of the Bible. Thomas Nelson, Inc.

104 James Strong. (1822–1894). Strong's number Greek 4102. King James Version New Strong's Exhaustive Concordance of the Bible. Thomas Nelson, Inc.

105 James Strong. (1822–1894). Strong's number Greek 4236. King James Version New Strong's Exhaustive Concordance of the Bible. Thomas Nelson, Inc.

106 James Strong. (1822–1894). Strong's number Greek 1466. King James Version New Strong's Exhaustive Concordance of the Bible. Thomas Nelson, Inc.

107 The Biology Project. (March 30, 1998). Blood Types Tutorial. Retrieved from www.biology.arizona.edu/human_bio/ problem_sets/ blood_types/inherited.html

108 Editor, Angus Stevenson & Christine A. Lindberg. (August 2010). Third Edition. New Oxford American Dictionary.

109 Joel Stein. (May 20, 2013). Me Me Me Generation.Time magazine.

110 James Strong. (1822–1894). Strong's number Greek 3056. King James Version New Strong's Exhaustive Concordance of the Bible. Thomas Nelson, Inc.

111 James Strong. (1822–1894). Strong's number Greek 3004. King James Version New Strong's Exhaustive Concordance of the Bible. Thomas Nelson, Inc.

112 James Strong. (1822–1894). Strong's number Greek 3141. King James Version New Strong's Exhaustive Concordance of the Bible. Thomas Nelson, Inc.

113 James Strong. (1822–1894). Strong's number Hebrew 5707. King James Version New Strong's Exhaustive Concordance of the Bible. Thomas Nelson, Inc.

114 James Strong. (1822–1894). Strong's number Hebrew 5749. King James Version New Strong's Exhaustive Concordance of the Bible. Thomas Nelson, Inc.

115 James Strong. (1822–1894). Strong's number Greek 5550. King James Version New Strong's Exhaustive Concordance of the Bible. Thomas Nelson, Inc.

116 Jeff A. Benner. (December 1, 2019). Concepts in Time: a Hebrew Perspective of Time. Retrieved from https://www.ancient-hebrew.org/ philosophy/concepts-in-time.htm)

CPSIA information can be obtained
at www.ICGtesting.com
Printed in the USA
FSHW022250191221
87036FS

9 781685 561673